DOUBLE BLESSING

DOUBLE BLESSING

Clergy Marriage since the
Ordination of Women as Priests

Sue Walrond-Skinner

MOWBRAY

Mowbray
A Cassell imprint
Wellington House
125 Strand
London WC2R 0BB

370 Lexington Avenue
New York
NY 10017-6550

www.cassell.co.uk

© Sue Walrond-Skinner 1998

British Library Cataloguing-in-Publication Data
A catalogue record for this book is available from the British Library.

ISBN 0-264-67340-9

The prayer on p. 27 is taken from *A Wee Workshop Book*, copyright 1989 WGRG, Iona Community, 840 Govan Road, Glasgow G51 3UU, Scotland.

Typeset by Janice Baiton Editorial Services
Printed and bound in Great Britain by Biddles Ltd, Guildford and King's Lynn

CONTENTS

Preface   ix

1   Setting the scene   1
2   Stories   8
3   Preparing for ordination   27
4   Marriage   39
5   What makes marriages happy?   61
6   The clergy as individuals   71
7   Clergy marriage   86
8   Joint clergy couples   105
9   The couples and the questions   116
10 Experience of marriage and ministry   129
11 Twelve couples tell their story   161
12 Role changes and relationships with others   186
13 Clergy couple differences   202
14 Towards the future   217

Appendix A: Methodology   233
Appendix B: The interview study   236
Appendix C: The psychometric tests   245

Bibliography   248
Index   255

For Graeme,
my dearest partner
in marriage
and ministry

PREFACE

Several years have elapsed since the General Synod of the Church of England made its historic decision to admit women to the priesthood for the first time. Much has been written and spoken about the effects of this decision upon the Church, but little work has been done on trying to understand how this sea change has affected the personal lives of the women themselves, especially in relation to their marriages.

This book describes a piece of original research into the effects of the ordination of women to the priesthood on the marriages of a group of dual-career clergy couples. As such, it is a contribution to that substantial body of psychological and sociological literature which has investigated the effects upon marriage of the dual-career lifestyle. It is also one of the first investigations into the effects on family life of the ordination of women as priests.

Whilst its focus is upon one small group of professional couples – the clergy – and it is therefore of particular interest to those who are engaged in the management, deployment, pastoral care and counselling of clergy, and to the clergy themselves, its relevance is of wider importance. The research has its roots in clinical work undertaken with a wide range of clergy couples, and the study therefore raises questions and offers pointers that should be of particular relevance and interest to those working within the fields of marriage and family counselling.

The dual-career life style has become increasingly normative; yet there have been few studies of those couples where both partners share the same career. A small amount of work has been done on the marriages of couples where both partners are lawyers, physicians, farmers and psychologists and, in terms of American couples, the clergy. But there has been no research investigation of couples who are both ordained in England. This book therefore fills a gap in the literature, for it provides a detailed picture of one example of this type of dual-career couple and of the vulnerabilities and strengths of their marriages.

Because of its particular focus, it also represents a contribution to the growing body of feminist literature on marriage. Ambert *et al.* (1995), referring to Haraway (1988) and other feminist researchers, remark in their comprehensive discussion of qualitative research that 'the researcher's social position influences his or her approach and interpretation, and that knowledge is socially situated and does not take place in a cultural vacuum' (p. 882). They further state that researchers should 'identify their own ethnic, class and gendered perspectives and abandon the illusion that researchers, their informants and the research setting do not influence each other reciprocally' (p. 882).

It is important therefore that I, as the author, begin by acknowledging my own particular interests, connections and involvement in the subject area of this book, particularly since this study has made use of a mixture of qualitative and quantitative methods, and since much of the richest material and information emerges from the qualitative data. My professional interest is straightforward – it is that of a professional family therapist who has, for nearly thirty years, been engaged in working with and writing about couples and families in various kinds of difficulty. For the last fifteen years, this work has been undertaken for the Church. During this period, I have therefore specialized almost exclusively in work with clergy couples and their families. The original questions and hypotheses for the research described in this book have therefore arisen out of clinical work done with these couples, particularly during the time leading up to and immediately after the ordination of women to the priesthood.

But I have not simply been a disinterested, observing clinician to these families during this uniquely interesting moment of history. As a priest myself, as a feminist and as part of a joint clergy couple, my own 'story' connects closely with the couples and families with whom I have worked and the interaction between their story and my own has in large part determined the choice of topic and subject matter for this study. I come to the material with some passion and with much personal involvement and, as the research progressed, I have found many aspects of the stories of the couples and individuals that have been the subjects of this study connecting closely with my own.

Thus the questions that I have wanted to ask other clergy couples stem centrally from my own experience as a priest, as the wife of a priest, as being a priest in relation to whom my husband has become a 'clergy husband' and as part of that small minority of clergy couples who, because both partners are ordained, are dual-career or 'joint clergy couples'. The questions have also arisen from my professional curiosity as a family therapist, and my perceptions as a woman and as a feminist. These personal/professional concerns may and probably have introduced bias into this study. They are issues about which I have tried to be continuously aware and to use as useful drivers, giving authenticity, vitality and subjective meaning to the work, without, hopefully, being unaware of the need to inspect the underside of every potential conclusion.

The lenses of age and ethnic origin are least obvious to me, but since my recent acquaintance with my research assistant during the last two years, they have become a new arena for curiosity. Nicola Rollock's presence as a young black woman nearly thirty years younger than myself, and someone who stands outside the faith community of which I am a part, reminds me of the very limited perspectives I bring to bear on any aspect of human experience and of my own profound and unavoidable limitations both as a clinician and as a researcher. For this I want to thank her, as well as for the expertise and enthusiasm with which she has helped me in this endeavour. She has been largely responsible for undertaking much of the statistical analysis of the data in this study and her assistance has therefore been invaluable.

My thanks are due first and foremost to the couples who were the participants in this study and gave so generously of their time. Then to a number of colleagues at the Tavistock Clinic and Birkbeck College, London with whom this work was discussed but especially Dr David Jones, Senior Lecturer at Birkbeck College, for his expertise, humour, patience and encouragement all the way along the line and to Professor Renos Papadopoulos who helped me make the necessary linkages between the research and clinical bases of this work. To the Iona Community for permission to include the prayer on p. 27. Finally my thanks are due to Ms Jane Wallworth, who helped with the final preparation of the typescript.

1 SETTING THE SCENE

For the first time in my adult life, I am who I am meant to be.
Revd Dr Una Kroll, *Christmas letter after being ordained as a priest*

A week after the Church of England's General Synod vote removing the barrier to the ordination of women as priests, a woman deacon 'phoned, asking to come and talk urgently. She had worked hard for this moment for some years, but now it had arrived she was thrown into crisis. It was all so unexpected. Deep down, she now realized, she had never believed it would really happen. Not only she herself, but her priest husband too – perhaps more than anyone – had longed and prayed for this moment to come, but now that it had, *did she really want it?* That was the question she suddenly found herself pondering. Yet how could she admit such doubts even to herself, much less to her husband who would feel utterly confused, and even betrayed by her apparent 'volte-face'?

This woman was far away from being able to anticipate the feelings expressed by the woman whose words are quoted at the head of this chapter, for whom ordination, when it came, represented the climax of a long and varied career of service, and a delight and joy to her whole family. For others again, the moment of decision and the months leading up to and after their ordinations faced them with many difficult, joyful and unexpected experiences within their closest personal relationships.

This book is about trying to understand some of these different experiences. Its main focus is on that small group of clergy couples where, as a result of the admission of women to the priesthood, *both* partners are now ordained as priests. But since the ordination of women in the English Church is so recent, we know little about its effect on the marriages of *any* of the women involved, whether they were married to a priest or to a layman at the time. This study is a preliminary attempt to repair this gap and to discover whether there has been any effect on their marriages. It is also an attempt to discern what, if any patterns, trends or directions can be found in the way this effect has occurred.

The profound experience of being amongst the first women to be ordained priest in the Church of England may or may not have had a significant effect upon the marital relationships of those who were married at the time. But looked at from the perspective of the magnitude of the event itself, we might reasonably ask, how could it not have had? For years in some cases, for almost a lifetime for a few, this small group of women – perhaps around 1,400, of which about half were married – had been struggling, striving, labouring, begging, praying for what they believed to be the right to be fully included in the Church. The struggle was about claiming those qualities of acceptance, collaboration, equality, co-operation, inclusivity and welcome, not only for themselves but for *all* women and for the Church as a whole. They have believed that, in so doing, the Church's own credibility as a symbol and hope of justice for all people would be vindicated.

On the other hand, those who have opposed the ordination of women to the priesthood have seen the moment when it first happened as bringing about an equally profound change. They also have viewed it as having ramifications beyond the life of the Church, not least within family relationships and in the intimate relationships between women and men. The 'equal but different' argument has been advanced by opponents in many different ways, from different theological positions and wings of the Church, and the power of the event in its potential for damage and hurt cannot but raise the same set of questions – how could the ordination of women not have had a powerful effect upon the marital relationships of those who have been caught up in the experience of opposition, and, because of the depth of the anger and disappointment experienced by many women and men, their own marriages must surely have acted as containers for these deeply negative feelings? Moreover, those who were couples in ministry in the sense that the husband was a priest and the wife a deacon at the time of the vote, may, as they lived through that experience and the next two or three years afterwards, have found themselves affected in double measure by all that has occurred.

For some women, their ordination to the priesthood was inextricably linked with their status as a wife and a marriage partner. For some, their priest-husbands had taken a long and active part in the movement, perhaps as members of the group, begun in 1984, called 'Priests for Women's Ordination'. Some husbands took part in the ordination ceremony itself, placing hands on their wife's head to assist in the conferring of the special grace of priesthood. There were husbands, whether priests or not, who stood on and wept as they saw the results of a struggle in which they had played an equal part, come to fruition. There were others who, deeply opposed to the principle of the ordination of women, stayed far away, not knowing how to reconcile their gladness for their own wife, with the pain of seeing their worst fears realized. Some women likened the ceremony to their marriage. Others experienced it as an even more powerful moment of decision and change than that of their own wedding day. And many outsiders who were not so personally involved as the central participants and their families, still described those first ordinations of 1994 as being 'nuptial' in some strange but real way.

Many questions suggest themselves. The parallel imagery, the association of emotions, the intense involvement of women's marriage partners in the ordination event (still intense, even in those painful, though less numerous situations where the woman's husband was opposed). It is the contention of this book that some relationship between these two powerful experiences of life – the spiritual/vocational and the intimate relational/sexual – will exist. Whether and how this might be understood and discerned will be discussed in later chapters. Moreover both institutions, of marriage and of priesthood, have undergone a prolonged period of crisis during this latter part of the twentieth century. We may wonder whether those who inhabit both worlds experience the stresses of each in double measure, or, alternatively, whether being married makes the living out of priesthood more luminous and vibrant and whether being a priest gives added support to the structure and framework of marriage. Similarly, does the advent of women priests create new stresses or new lifeblood both for the priesthood as a whole and for the marriages of those women who are both married and ordained?

On the wider social and ecclesial levels, the ordination of women as priests has indeed been a profound movement of change, the effects of which have yet to be fully understood. In his review of the events of 1992, the editor of the 1993 edition of the *Church of England Year Book* comments that 'November 11th 1992 will rank as one of those occasions in the Church of England when its history turned on a hinge' (p. xxii). It has been one of the greatest historic moments in Anglican Church history and, for those in favour, it has been seen by many as 'a symbolic victory for all women' (Dowell and Williams, 1994, p. viii). It has been for them essentially a struggle for justice. How then could such a struggle not have affected the most intimate relationships of those who took such a central part? How could their family life not have been touched by the changes that were taking place in the women themselves as they lived through the struggle to create a more just and equal and inclusive Church? This must surely, at the very least, have been matched by the hope and expectancy that the same claims on justice, equality and inclusivity might be delivered in even fuller measure within their personal relationships.

It is likely too that the very struggle to become more just and inclusive and equal in oneself and the experience of at last being recognized as such by the Church, would have beneficial consequences for those with whom one is most personally connected. Equally, the long haul of the struggle and the wounds that had perhaps been incurred, may have left many of these 'first wave' women priests arrested in combative mode and consequently less able perhaps than before, to exercise those other relational qualities that build and sustain one's closest intimate partnerships. If so, their marital relationships may have suffered accordingly.

On the other hand, perhaps our lives are so compartmentalized that none of these effects for either those in favour or those against the ordination of women may necessarily have occurred in this way. Or, perhaps other more significant changes, such as the progressively greater participation of women in the Church that had gone on steadily since the latter part of the nineteenth century, culminating in the highly symbolic moment in 1987 when women were admitted to the diaconate (and thus to Holy Orders) for the first time, had had a more profound effect earlier than the great watershed moments of 1992 and 1994. Or perhaps again, such shifts and changes are too subtle to measure; or perhaps they take place over a longer period of time, with their antecedents buried deep in the individual's personal and collective past, with tips of growth reaching out into a future whose harvesting is yet to be fully achieved.

The purpose of this book is to examine the effects of the ordination of women to the priesthood on the marriage relationships of clergy. There are a number of ways in which the priesthood can be exercised today by men and women, and several different contexts in which priests may work. These differences are likely, in themselves, to have an effect upon people's marriages and family worlds and need therefore to be taken account of, not to mention the many demographic differences that exist within the families and marriages of clergy as they do amongst any other professional group. All of these make a nonsense of the idea that the term 'clergy marriage' describes either a discrete or a homogeneous concept or pattern of marriage today, if indeed it ever did so.

Although, as we will see in Chapter 7, many writers have been able to discern some particular characteristics and parameters that are useful descriptors of the marriages of clergy, arising from what are perhaps some of its unique features, general descriptions of clergy marriage only allow a broad comparison to be made between the marriages of clergy and those who are not ordained and not the more subtle and interesting comparison between different types of clergy marriage. In trying therefore to examine the dynamics of clergy marriage and the way in which some of its characteristics may be more problematic than others, the question arises as *how* best to define areas of potential difference amongst clergy marriages, which can then enable a range of variables to be usefully compared? This may then allow a more sophisticated analysis to be attempted – comparing not simply clergy and non-clergy marriages with one another (though this comparison will always be implicit) but enabling some intra-group comparisons to be made which may yield a more fine-grained and detailed picture of the relationship between ministry and marriage.

It was therefore decided that, for the purposes of this study, three main types of clergy marriage would be compared, two of which have emerged since the admission of women to the priesthood: marriages where both partners are priests (joint clergy couples);

marriages where the woman but not the man is a priest (women only ordained) and marriages where the man but not the woman is a priest (traditional clergy marriages). The study involved comparing these three types of clergy couples by testing them on two different occasions – once immediately before the ordination of women to the priesthood and again two years later.

It needs to be said immediately that these shorthand terms are not very felicitous. Some will take issue with the inference that the term 'joint clergy couple' is being limited to couples who are clergy, as though, by definition, other couples do not have some form of 'joint' ministry. However, the use of this term in this context is not meant to imply that other marriages between Christians, whether lay or ordained, may not be predicated upon a model of 'joint ministry'. In following the convention adopted by the first documents on the subject published by the Church's Advisory Board for Ministry, the term is being used in preference to the more cumbersome expressions 'partners in ministry' or 'couples in ministry', neither of which in any case avoids the same criticism. Other readers will object to the term 'traditional' being used to describe those couples where a clergyman is married to a non-ordained wife. It is however the *model* of clergy marriage that is being, correctly, described as traditional. The term does not imply any comment upon the *attitudes* of those couples described by this term.

As will be discussed later, some considerable concern has been expressed about the possible negative effects of the ordination of women on the marriages of those involved. In other words, the two new forms of clergy marriage that have emerged since the ordination of women to the priesthood – those of 'joint couples' and 'women only ordained' – have caused anxiety, over and above the wider concern about clergy marriages in general, that has been expressed over the last ten or so years. In studying a small sample of each of these three kinds of clergy marriage, it will hopefully be possible to either confirm or dispel these anxieties. It will do so by offering some useful discussion of the many issues involved and by drawing some tentative conclusions from the data that have emerged from this study.

But first, some personal stories will be described. These emerged during the period leading up to and immediately following the first ordinations of women as priests in 1994. They arise out of several different contexts and include some examples of difficulties presented to the author clinically for help, as well as from three problem-solving groups, who struggled as the women prepared themselves to be ordained. Because the material is personal, its anonymity and confidentiality have been carefully protected. This has been done by disguising and altering the details of the cases and by selecting clinical material from a wide geographical area. In one or two instances, where a more detailed description has been required, the individual or couples have given their express permission and they have agreed to the text as printed. All names are of course fictitious.

2 STORIES

Each Morn a thousand Roses brings, you say;
Yes, but where leaves the Rose of Yesterday?
The Rubaiyat of Omar Khayyam

The ordination of women to the priesthood in the Church of England for the first time was an event of far-reaching historical significance for the Church, the nation, the women themselves and for their families. Afterwards, those most closely involved spoke repeatedly of their surprise in realizing just how important an event it turned out to be, even for those with little or no connection with the Church. Before it could occur however, there was a journey to be travelled – by those to be ordained, by those who opposed them, by the partners and the families of both – without any clear idea as to what course the journey would take or where it would end. This journey often brought to the surface painful experiences from the past as well as exposing hidden vulnerabilities in people's closest personal relationships.

In this chapter we will take a step back from the research material, the main focus of this book, and examine instead some broader personal experiences, out of which the research questions and hypotheses for this study were developed. What meaning did the ordination event have for the individuals most closely involved? How were people preparing for it? How were they already affected by the difficulties and dissensions that preceded the decision taken in November 1992 to ordain women to the priesthood and how were these effects being expressed within people's closest of personal relationships, their marriages?

Therapeutic work undertaken with about a dozen couples is described, all of which relates in a specific way to difficulties

around the ordination of women for which they had sought therapeutic help. Some of this work was undertaken during the period
that this research has been in progress; some describes more general clinical situations undertaken in different settings by the
author with clergy and their families over a longer period. The situations described are highly disguised in order to protect the
anonymity of those concerned and in some cases, a composite picture of strands of work from several different clinical situations is
presented, in order to ensure the protection of privileged material.
The work illustrates some important themes of marital interaction
that routinely occur within dysfunctional clergy marriages, and
which interconnect very specifically with the ordination of women
to the priesthood.

Chapter 3 is closely connected, for it describes work done with
three different kinds of problem-solving groups, all of which met
for nearly two years during the time that this research was being
undertaken. Both chapters have a close connection with Chapters
11 and 12 which report the results of an interview study of twelve
non-clinical joint clergy couples. Although these latter couples
were not in treatment nor, as far as is known, had sought professional help for their marriages, nevertheless the difficulties and
challenges faced by both the clinical couples, the non-clinical couples and members of the problem-solving groups were very similar
and the issues arising from all of these qualitative data are clearly interrelated. These chapters reveal some consistent themes
which helped in the formulation and development of the emergent
research questions and hypotheses for this study.

Individuals, couples and change

The problems that individuals present 'on behalf of' their relationships always have elegant systemic connections with the dynamics
of the relationship itself, as well as with the wider context, and it
is in discovering those connections that the therapist is able to help
the couple to understand and change the dysfunctional patterns
that are troubling them. Likewise, individuals can be attracted to
certain occupations, as indeed to particular marital partners, as a

means of creating, on an unconscious level, a milieu for healing the faults, splits and unintegrated parts of their psyches. Clergy may 'choose' to become clergy because they perceive at some level that this calling holds out to them the possibility of enabling them to exercise parts of their personality that are partially repressed, thus offering them the potential for finding those parts that have been 'lost'. They hope, on some level, for healing and wholeness, through a greater integration within their personality makeup. This has been true for women entering the priesthood for the first time as much as for men.

But because entry into the full ministry of priesthood has been delayed for many women, some different pressures have also been exerted upon their marriages and some different needs have been experienced, over and above some of those that are likely to affect clergy marriages of all kinds. The long build-up of frustration and pain for the woman has often been in contrast with the career development of her husband. In some cases this may have produced no greater imbalance in their relationship than that which is common to many marriages where the wife takes time out from her career to care for children. However, for many women who are now in the last phase of their working lives, they have had to manage a continuous sense of disappointment and hopelessness as they have lived through their working lives in the belief that nothing would change in time for them to be able to express and experience their deepest vocational longings.

For women who had worked within the Church for many years, the use of their gifts and skills has often been overlooked, because of the way in which more responsible and more senior appointments have been inextricably linked with being a priest. The difficulty for some women in retaining their sense of self-esteem over this prolonged period in these circumstances has often been intense. For some, their continuous treatment as 'junior partner' in the Church's ministry had the effect of overloading their marriages with the need to compensate for this unsatisfactory situation. Envy and guilt have undergirded the marital experiences of women and men respectively in many clergy marriages where the vocation of one partner has been so continuously thwarted.

The abusive past and the abusive Church

These developmental difficulties of marriage and ministry may have been compounded by their interaction with aspects of the individual's personal psychological history and by the broader movements of change taking place in the Church. For example, the sudden psychic shift that took place in the organism of the Church on 11 November 1992 seemed to release for many women suppressed experiences of abuse, encountered both in their personal lives and, for many, in their long ministry as deacons in the Church. The frequency with which these experiences have been described over the last few years is quite striking and suggests that there may be something in the image of priesthood that is profoundly attractive (and also profoundly problematic) for those who have experienced physical or sexual abuse. At the point when the Church was perceived as becoming structurally less abusive to their identity as women, these women were able to acknowledge the awful backlog of pain that they carried from the complex intertwining of various kinds of emotional and sometimes physical or sexual abuse.

Experiences in the 'family' of the Church had, until then, compounded for many of them the abusive experiences they had encountered in their own original families. Charlotte for example telephoned two days after the ordination, urgently requesting some help. She said that the moment she was ordained, memories of early sexual abuse by a member of her family had come flooding back. The partial resolution of this early trauma achieved through previous therapy had been thrown into disequilibrium by the psychic shock of the ordination. She felt that this might have occurred, in part, because of the unexpected experience of 'all the men (i.e. the Church) suddenly being so nice!' The 'laying on of hands' at ordination had, paradoxically, evoked for her that other, abusive, 'laying on of hands' in her childhood years.

Although the opening up of the priesthood for women who had been abused as children and more recently, as they experienced it, within the structures of the Church, was often seen as an important reversal of the past and a real affirmation of their personhood and gifts, accepting ordination posed many problems. The degree to which they could welcome and receive this new moment seemed to be highly dependent on the extent to which they had worked through their experiences of abuse. The need to do so, and the shortage of time, created complex needs for several couples. As the wife's need to work through the effects of her past increased, her struggle to do so inevitably involved a therapeutic regression, which in turn imposed new pressures upon the marriage. Some husbands were able to accommodate their wife's needs because at that time their own psychic needs were manageable and their emotional resources strong. Tony and Freda's relationship for example moved into a phase whereby Tony surrounded Freda with a strong containing presence, for a prolonged period of some months, lending her his own ego strengths while she relived some of the trauma of her past and worked through the resulting ambivalence she was experiencing in relation to her present vocation to priesthood.

Pauline on the other hand entered therapy immediately after the vote in favour of women's ordination. The fact that the priesthood to which she felt herself to be strongly called was now open to her threw her into a crisis. It activated all sorts of unresolved feelings inside her in relation to her own feelings of self-loathing. These related to a prolonged experience of sexual abuse around the age of puberty by a male relative, the trauma of which was compounded by her sense of abandonment by her parents and other relations who knew what was going on but who failed to protect her. In common with so many adult survivors, Pauline's consistent defence against acknowledging the abusive behaviour of others was to blame herself for what had happened and this in turn led her to experience severe guilt, and a masochistic need to be punished for 'what she had done'. Thus the prolonged experience of rejection by the Church in general and by her immediate colleagues in particular (several of whom were adamantly opposed to women's ordination) was experienced by her as syntonic with her self-punitive needs.

The sudden lifting of the prohibition on her ordination threatened to release, in an uncontrollable way, the long repressed psychic material around her abuse. During the period between November 1992 and the beginning of 1994, Pauline worked on this material in weekly or bi-weekly therapeutic sessions. At the height of the experience she wrote long detailed letters in which she wrestled with how to let go and move beyond the many blocks she experienced in herself. The period between the vote and the ordination was just long enough for the work on her early traumas to be 'good enough' to release her to move on. She became sufficiently freed from her past to accept the gift of ordination despite some residual guilt and a continuing sense of having, long ago, been made 'unclean'.

New challenges of course immediately faced her which needed ongoing work in the subsequent months. For example, Pauline who was drawn to reject her femininity because of all that it had 'caused', was now suddenly faced, as a result of becoming a priest, with becoming in a more profound sense 'mother' to her congregation. She commented three weeks after the ordination 'It was odd to begin with ... will I be more mothering? I don't feel like the mothering bit at all.' Yet, for this childless woman, becoming a 'mother' was deeply attractive at a profound level of her psyche, holding out the prospect of being reparative at an unfulfilled level of her being.

She was conscious of the somewhat paradoxical change in her relationship with the congregation, to which she seemed to have become both closer, as their mother and more distant as their priest. 'I've been wondering about loneliness ... I realize that the loneliness is quite profound and doesn't feel as though it can ever be less deep.' As she continued to wrestle with closeness and distance in her personal relationships, this struggle was reflected in her relationship with the congregation. At points, the juxtaposition of the personal/sexual with the priestly/spiritual dimensions of her relationships became very close. 'I've got one woman madly in love with me, sending notes, telephone calls and invitations. What would I do if it was a man ... there's the crunch. I'm worried about the woman, how will it be when it's a man?'

As in Pauline's case, the gateway into a more literal and intense experience of 'motherhood' was opened up for many women when they became priests in charge of their own congregations. For some of these, even the title of 'mother' was claimed and granted, as an equivalent to that of 'father' for a man. But are the two equivalent? The regressive images of dependency, important and healthy as these are, and certainly not to be 'pathologized', are nevertheless different from what is called out of the congregational group by the outwardly directed momentum of the term 'father', and hence different from what the woman herself experiences in assimilating and responding to the transactional, circular feedback of the congregation's perceptions of her role.

The different meanings attributed to the two titles are complex and overlaid with the multifaceted resonances of people's experiences in their own families of origin. The gendered relationship of parenthood is as intricate as that of marriage and each role will attract to itself projections which need to be understood and used for the psychological growth of both the priest and her people. Such understanding requires a continuous effort at self-knowledge and for many of the women, this was gained during this period of rapid and confusing change, within the containing experience of therapy.

Listening to women talk through these experiences suggested how finely poised the ordination experience has been between 'healing' and 'cleansing' the pollution of abuse, and the powerful release of anger for the pain of the past. On the one hand the access to 'holy things', reserved only for the ritually clean, holds powerful resonances for those who have experienced themselves as being unclean. By the same token, the admission at last into the company of those who have symbolically or actually participated in the abuse, may create an ambivalent tension between relief and fear and may act as a powerful invitation to take revenge on others for the individual's own wounds and scars. This has been a very complicated area for women to negotiate who are married to priests, where the husband may have had to hold many conflicting projections as his wife has worked towards being able to receive her own priesthood.

Becoming what one is

Even without the need to work through significant psychopathology from the past, this move towards priesthood involved, for most women, a considerable shift in their sense of personal identity. One of the great benefits of marriage is the opportunity it gives for the couple to re-experience and deal more effectively with what Skynner (1976) calls 'the unsurmounted challenges of childhood'. As well as enabling each to grow into a fuller knowledge of their personal identities as individuals, it also acts as a container for the development of their social identities experienced within and beyond their marital relationship.

For Adrian and Nancy however, these two were in conflict. The ecstatic new fulfilment which Nancy perceived might at last be hers was greeted by Adrian with apprehension and fear. His counter-dependency was severely threatened, and although during the course of therapy he was able to reframe positively some of its fear and threat, Nancy's obvious blossoming created prolonged disequilibrium within their marriage, which was not relieved until some time after her ordination, when Adrian received promotion at work, and a considerable increase in his salary.

This strong centrifugal force which operates between people who have ultimate concerns of overriding importance to them, but who are nevertheless in conflict, can operate cohesively when both partners are pulled closer together through a shared goal. In the following example, the wife was seen on her own in therapy, when she presented for help after participating in a workshop. Participants had been asked to think of all the names by which they were, or had been known during their lives and she had volunteered the term 'illegitimate'. After the workshop, she asked to see me, and during the first session she said that this was the first time she had ever told anyone outside her family that she was 'illegitimate'. Amy was married to Clive and both were clergy. Amy as a deacon was preparing to be ordained as a priest in a few months time but she was encountering a great deal of resistance and ambivalence in herself. Her unexpected revelation of the word 'illegitimate' to the workshop group had made her realize in a very powerful way that she had not come to terms with her early rejection by her birth mother, even though she had experienced a happy childhood in her adoptive family.

Clive and Amy's parish was part of a deanery where, in common with most deaneries in their diocese, some of the parishes and their clergy were strongly opposed to the ordination of women. The matter had been debated very publicly and acrimoniously in the deanery, and this had left Amy feeling exposed and humiliated in a very personal way and then guilty about having these feelings. She had realized that her overriding feeling was that her forthcoming priesthood was, in some sense, 'illegitimate', and that this experience was connecting powerfully with her repressed feelings of rejection, and 'uncleanness' surrounding her birth. Perhaps, she wondered, it was right that the priesthood of an 'illegitimate' person should be automatically deemed to be 'illegitimate'.

Amy felt deeply responsible for and guilty about the pain that her priesting was causing to others and a major part of the therapeutic work that was done with her was targeted at trying to separate out the feelings which appropriately belonged to the different parts of her life, past and present, and the different people caught up in the current painful struggle that was going on in the Church. Gradually Amy felt more able to claim her own vocation to the priesthood and differentiate it out sufficiently to feel sad rather than guilty for the pain that this was causing others.

An important part of Amy's development during those three months, however, was made possible because of the central importance that her priesting held for Clive, her husband. Actively involved in an organization for joint clergy couples, Clive's experience of his own vocation was deeply interconnected with Amy's. They had trained together; they had been ordained to the diaconate together and when Clive, the following year, had been priested without his wife, this had been felt by both of them to be a severe deprivation. They experienced it as being seriously unbalancing to their marriage as well as to their ministry. The fundamental egalitarianism of their relationship, which was an important commitment for them both, had been undermined. Clive was protective of Amy and determined in his efforts to forward the cause of women's ordination. This unequivocal support from Clive served both to affirm Amy's tentative sense of her own vocational and personal identity and to strengthen the solidarity of the marital relationship.

During the retreat before the ordination, the person conducting it offered everyone an opportunity to consider if this might be the moment to lay aside some long-standing pain and move on to the next stage in life freed from this burden. Amy chose to write on her paper 'I do not need to carry the name illegitimate anymore', and she placed her paper along with those of others in the blazing fire provided for this purpose. The following day, the group was reminded that, as at Baptism, ordination was an occasion when a new name could be taken. Later in the day, Amy found the word 'chosen' coming into her mind. She realized that, with the legitimizing of her priesthood, the word 'chosen' could now replace the word 'illegitimate', as a description of herself. She had been chosen by her adoptive parents, chosen by Clive and now chosen by the Church as a priest. As she processed very slowly into the Cathedral, the next morning, at the beginning of the ordination service, she found herself thinking: 'this is the way that people walk to their death'. But she knew that this death was, for her, something freeing and liberating in terms of all that had shackled her in the past, and that this new step she was taking was life-giving and changing for her both in terms of her own identity and in terms of the new freedom and growth in her marriage.

In strong contrast to the unifying experience of this joint clergy couple, some joint couples experienced the wife's call to priestly ordination as an explosive ingredient in their relationship, because of its effect upon relationships with colleagues. The close working relationships between male and female priestly colleagues led in some cases to severe confusion between the sexual intimacy of their marital relationship and the professional/spiritual closeness of their professional relationship. Some of the public 'scandals' that resulted have contributed to the anxious response of Church authorities in their dealings with joint couples.

The challenge to marital roles and stability

The material from some of the couples who came for therapy opened up broader questions. How does the powerful symbolism of the priestly role interact, for those who are married, with the symbolic phantasies within the marital relationship? What differences do the new symbolic roles make, whatever they may be, to the *partner's* experience of his wife and of their marriage?

This is an elusive and difficult area to explore as it involves largely unconscious material. The violence of some of the symptomatology expressed within some couple's relationships suggested that the possibility of the wife being ordained constituted a major assault on the couple's defensive system. Deeply unconscious psychic needs for dependency, sexual pairing and generativity were, for some couples, severely disturbed, because the accommodation of their emotional needs had hitherto been predicated upon the need for the husband to be the 'priestly' person, whether he was ordained or not. This might have been experienced quite straight-forwardly as a need for the husband to have an overtly more dom-inant role within the marriage, which the priesting of his wife now challenged. Or it might have been experienced more elusively, as the need for the husband to be the purveyor of the 'feminine' qual-ities of care, acceptance, forgiveness and compassion which seemed now to have been 'taken over' by the wife in her new priestly role.

Ruth and Joel's marital relationship, for example, could no longer act as a container for such a profoundly disturbing shift between them – for it exploded the myth of Joel's covert dependen-cy. His anger was immense. He left the relationship precipitately, in the most destructive way he knew – by forming a relationship with a young girl from his wife's parish. In a very economical way he was thus able simultaneously to restore his primary relational experience to one with a dependent and vulnerable woman; and to humiliate and punish his wife for becoming her own person. From the wife's perspective, his action was particularly potent in its destructive consequences, as it came at the point when she was actually at her most vulnerable, as she took on her new priestly role for the first time.

Sometimes these experiences of threat and disequilibrium were nearer the surface and were therefore more accessible to thera-peutic change. When couples were able to see the changes in their relationship as being more to do with changes in gender roles, these, although still very difficult to confront and modify, were less likely to be expressed through such violent acting out of unman-ageable pain. Nevertheless, the fact that parts of the Church still subscribe to an ideology of gender relationships which are firmly embedded in the husband's proper place being 'head' of the family, meant that a wife's entry into the priesthood constitutes a more than usually strong challenge to many marital relationships. Although the ordination of women poses a particular challenge for these couples, when successfully negotiated, it often has the power to bring about a healthier transformation in the balance of rela-tional power.

Audrey and Alex for example had lived within conventional gen-der roles in their marriage for over twenty years. Alex had worked hard at his business and Audrey had brought up their four children, staying at home to do so from the moment they had married until the present. Both Audrey and Alex were devoted members of their local village church, and Alex had been churchwarden for the last ten years. Three years earlier, Audrey had begun training on a non-residential training course for ministry in the church. Although the course did train priests and deacons, it also trained people for other non-ordained roles, to which Audrey had initially aspired. Her contact with other students however opened up whole new worlds for her. She swiftly realized that she was being called to be a priest and realized perhaps even more forcibly that a world of work existed outside the home.

Much of the therapeutic work with this couple consisted in helping them to discuss a more equitable sharing of the household chores and the responsibilities that still remained towards their largely independent children. Whilst creating ambivalence in Audrey and threat in Alex at first, both were able to see how such changes could bring real benefit to their relationship by enabling them both to learn new skills, share the experience of both paid employment and domesticity, and the new enjoyment and mutual respect that accrued. The pragmatic need to arrange a more equal sharing of household tasks, brought about by Audrey's studies and aspirations to priesthood, also helped Alex to feel more comfortable about Audrey becoming a priest and vice versa. In this case, Audrey's ordination was experienced as a real help in creating some necessary changes in the distribution of tasks and roles in the marital relationship, which in turn served to strengthen the marriage itself.

The opening of the priesthood to women for the first time confronted some couples with a severe threat to the equilibrium of their relationship. For some women, the choice seemed to be between following through with these new vocational possibilities or continuing in their marriage, although the choice might not have been consciously articulated as starkly as that. Hazel and George's marriage for example was suddenly transformed from an outwardly happy and settled 'traditional' relational pattern, into a new and bewildering series of crises, whereby she ran away from home, began a short-lived affair with a colleague and then attempted suicide.

He sought some brief crisis help in the shock and panic that this produced in him and she sought help, separately, after recognizing that her behaviour had something to do with trying to express the impasse she felt she was in. She felt called to be a priest, yet she knew that to pursue what was now an actual possibility, would have presented her husband with an overwhelming threat to his own perception of their marriage, which required his wife to function within a traditional role of 'vicar's wife'. His own frail ego strengths seemed threatened to the point of collapse at the prospect of his wife both withdrawing from her hidden role as his constant background support, *and* simultaneously adopting the role that gave him unique status in their marriage.

Neither felt able to continue with professional help, and gradually over the months, she perceived herself to have been misguided in her aspirations. She sought advice and support from amongst her Christian friends, with a view to regaining her previous contentment with her role as her husband's helper. As she regained a position which was now in conflict with her own developmental needs but was once more syntonic with the marital 'fit' between them, he adopted the role of a forgiving and loving husband-cum-therapist, concerned to assist in every possible way his wife's 'recovery' from her bizarre and inexplicable behaviour.

On the other hand, the wife's ordination had a powerful stabilizing effect for some marriages. Phoebe and Miles had been married for ten years. Both had moved effortlessly through the early stages of their careers, she as a consultant gynaecologist and he as a priest. Both worked long hours at careers to which they were deeply committed, as well as caring for their three young children with the help of outside carers. They came for help, each complaining that the other was unable to give the love and attention that they needed, nor take an equal share in home duties. Each experienced the other's career and their partner's commitment to it as the cause of the problem.

During a quite prolonged process of therapy, each learned to value the other's work by understanding it better and affirming each other's success. As this new process developed between them, both began to 'let go', of their compulsive need to hold on to work as their primary commitment, and gradually during this process, the wife began to feel a call to ordination. Although this was not wanted by her at first and seemed a frightening prospect, she was gradually able to go forward. As she did so, she experienced the profound care and nurture of her husband for the embryonic vocation within her. His obvious delight strengthened her own sense of calling and as they moved through her training and ordination together, it dawned on them that this new 'career' was going to have quite different relational consequences for their marriage from the old one – it was going to draw them together instead of pulling them apart.

Clergy husbands

When the wife is ordained and the husband is not, he may be cast into the role of some kind of 'consort', but without the traditional appurtenances of the role of clergy wife. However distasteful it is to many women, the role of clergy wife nevertheless provides a framework within which to function, and a model to accept or reject or make her own in new and different ways. A man on the other hand must now try to find his own level in a role which has been gender specific to women until extremely recently. Thus there are as few role models for male partners of clergywomen as there are for women priests themselves.

For some couples, a painful juxtaposition arose between the new potential fulfilment opening out for the wife and the retrenchment or loss being experienced in a variety of forms by the husband. Sometimes the husband was facing a job loss; sometimes the loss or absence of a physical function, such as fertility. Sometimes it was the grief attendant upon the loss of an important relationship through separation or death. None of these experiences sat easily alongside the contrasting joyful, if anxiety-laden, experience of the wife. Some of these couples, therefore, were facing emotional overload, as each partner tried to grapple with the challenges facing them as individuals while simultaneously trying to be open, empathic and responsive to the very different needs of the other. In the following examples, the pain and the difficulties that the couple was experiencing were expressed initially by the husband.

One couple came for help because Paul, who had recently been made redundant from his job in the city, had become clinically depressed, experiencing severe loss of self-esteem and self-confidence. Rachel had just completed her theological training and was, conversely, highly motivated to begin her ministry in the Church. She however was experiencing the general lack of opportunities in terms of employment which continued to be part of the reality for women, after the Church's bar on ordination had been lifted. This insecurity resonated with her early experiences of being part of a fragile and undependable family of origin, which made 'finding her place' and seeking out 'somewhere to belong' recurrent, pressing emotional needs. In many ways however, her adult experience in the family of the Church, far from providing for these needs, echoed the fearful fragility of her childhood family.

It soon became clear that their needs were sharply in conflict. In marrying Paul she had married a man who could provide little of the strong dependable structure that she both longed for and feared. He was the child of successful middle-class professional parents, whose strongly expressed hopes for their children's choices of career and future life pattern had created a rebellious response in several of his brothers and sisters. Paul however vacillated between his desire to articulate his own identity and his compulsive need to conform and win his parents' approval. For this couple, Rachel's ordination presented a severe crisis. As the date for the ordination approached, Paul sank more deeply into depression, until he finally had to be hospitalized. For Rachel, the most important moment of her life was approaching, which would demonstrate that she now belonged irrevocably to this new 'family' of the church and was wholly acceptable to it. Even more powerfully, she knew that she would now belong to the Church as one of its primary symbolic figures – as a priest – having from now on a more interior, less replaceable, less dispensable position. Her unmet needs of childhood had therefore emerged to produce an enormously powerful centrifugal pull, away from the marriage and towards her 'mother' the Church.

Both partners had sustained the same kind of psychic damage in their childhood years, but such was the extent of their individual need that they could not offer each other or the relationship any sustenance in their crisis. Paul was deeply jealous of the reparative affect of the ordination for Rachel to the point that, for some time, he had an increasing need to attack the Church and Rachel for the diminishment that he now experienced. The sharp contrast between his own sense of futility, lack of affirmation and rejection compared with all that he saw happening to Rachel was too great.

But although Rachel's ordination carried with it no actual change in either the volume or the status of her work commitments, the power of its symbolism revealed the profound threat to the couple's marital equilibrium in relation to anything which might enhance the power and status of one in relation to the other. This fragile 'Doll's House' marriage was in fact predicated upon the need to ensure the joint and equal diminishment of them both.

And yet as they confronted these issues in a new and more realistic way after the ordination had taken place, both were able to recognize that the dreadful crisis that had erupted between them had also been survived. Paul, as he sobbed his way through subsequent sessions, recognized very clearly how he had, in that process, broken through to some new-found ability to express his feelings of anger and pain and to articulate these to Rachel, instead of withdrawing from the field. Rachel's compulsive overactivity, which had previously served to prevent Paul from expressing his pain to her, and defend her from the inadequacies of the marriage, was reduced by her new sense of her own acceptance and worth, so that she began to be able to listen and hear Paul for the first time.

For some couples, particular factors made it difficult for the wife's ordination to be assimilated into their perceptions of each other as marriage partners. Tim, for example, was a member of the Orthodox Church which provided him with very clear imagery of the nature of priesthood. For him, priesthood symbolized a very special, mysterious and exalted vocation, someone set apart and to be revered. He held the priesthood in high esteem and having contemplated the idea for himself, had not pursued it because of his own sense of unworthiness. Yet he retained a deep sense of disappointment in relation to this unfulfilled vocation. He was therefore confronted with the complicated emotional task of relating to Moira – a wife whom, now she had become a priest, he must simultaneously regard as someone with whom he was intimate, someone who was set apart and someone who was inherently unworthy for something so sacred.

As he compared her with the images of priesthood derived from his childhood, he could only feel the incongruity between the two. His frail masculine ego desperately needed the reassurance of a Church which had retained a secure masculine model of priesthood with which he could identify. As he tried to hold together the two contrasting images, of a masculine Church and a feminine priestly wife, it was the image of his wife that he felt compelled to reject. For Tim, the idea of his wife becoming a priest was grotesque. Whilst consciously, he had always wanted to offer Moira strong support for her vocation, when confronted with the immediate prospect of her ordination, his defences crumbled. He was overwhelmed by this eruption of emotion, which coalesced around the sharp contrasts between his own sense of futility, lack of affirmation and rejection compared with all that he saw happening to Moira. His jealousy was immense and it frightened him. The imbalances of their new statuses had finally been tipped beyond what he was able to tolerate. He feared the power of her new priestly potency, which he experienced in stark contrast to his own disappointed priestly vocation. He angrily rejected the privileged role that he saw his wife attaining, and he resorted to denigrating her priestly identity and her 'worthiness' for it.

For similar reasons, Jack's and Helen's marriage ran into difficulties when the way was opened for Helen to become a priest. Helen entered therapy about a year before the first ordinations took place, but Jack refused the invitation to accompany her. Jack's model of priesthood had been formed since childhood within the Anglo-Catholic tradition of the Anglican Church. It was predicated upon an extreme rejection of the possibility of women being priests and he currently worshipped in a church where women were not allowed to sing in the choir or to enter the sanctuary. Deep-seated taboos about female impurity were stated quite openly in literature at the back of Church, and these combined with consistent teaching by the clergy team to create a powerful defensive structure which Jack in turn transferred to his marriage. His obviously competent wife had consciously chosen to try not to disrupt their marital equilibrium any further than it had already been disrupted by her ordination as a deacon. She had half decided therefore not to be ordained a priest. But as the ordination drew near, Helen struggled to come to terms with the conflict between what she wanted for herself and her desire to preserve her marriage. Helen would weep silently as she reported the escalating rows at home and Jack's unpredictable outbursts of rage.

Shortly before the ordination, Helen made the final decision not to go ahead. The conflict lessened for her, although she knew that she had achieved this lessening of tension at the cost of losing something that was deeply precious to her own sense of herself and of how she experienced her vocation. Nor did she feel that her withdrawal had greatly helped Jack who remained alternately filled with rage or despair. Gradually however she began to feel calmer and stronger and able to view the future in such a way that it held a variety of options. One of those might be ordination at a later date, as a still risky choice in terms of her marriage. Another might be some further encouragement to Jack to enter marital therapy with her and try and deal with some of the long-standing difficulties in their relationship for which the ordination issue had only been a trigger.

In a later chapter, some of the dynamics of clergy marriages will be discussed from a theoretical position. At this point we might simply note how the issues raised for the couples described here around the ordination of women to the priesthood often relate to the way in which the couple handles emotional closeness and distance between them; how they manage the boundary around their relationship and how far they are able to give sufficient energy and time to the consolidation and development of each partner as an individual *and* to their relationship as a couple.

All three types of clergy marriage have to struggle with difficulties and challenges which are peculiar to being clergy, but these may be experienced in different ways and produce different vulnerabilities. For the traditional couple, where the husband is ordained but not the wife, it may continue to be difficult for her to exert an equal claim on her husband's attention comparable with that of the parish or for her to fully establish her own vocational identity apart from his. Joint clergy couples, where both partners are ordained priest, may find that the natural empathy between their parallel vocations and the greater equality now made possible between them since the ordination of women, helps them as a couple but hinders their separate development as individuals.

Couples where the woman but not the man is ordained may find the reverse to be the case. For them, the critical change brought about by the ordination of women to the priesthood may be experienced as destabilizing in its impact upon the marital relationship, even though growth-promoting for the woman as an individual. It is to these preliminary questions that we will return later, for they provide the basic ideas out of which the formal research hypotheses were constructed.

3 PREPARING FOR ORDINATION

You keep us waiting.
You, the God of all time,
want us to wait
for the right time in which to discover
who we are, where we must go,
who will be with us, and what we must do.
So thank you ... for the waiting time.
Iona Community, *A Wee Worship Book*

The material described in this chapter comes from work done with two groups for women deacons and a mixed group for male and female clergy. They are described as 'problem-solving groups', this being as near to what seems the most accurate description. They were not therapy groups, yet they all met to try to tackle the personal issues arising for members, first as the time drew near for the voting to take place by the Church of England's General Synod on the ordination of women to the priesthood; and then during the interval between the decision being made and the first ordinations taking place. The period spanned about eighteen months. It was a time of anticipation and preparation; a time when some very difficult and quite complex issues needed to be faced and explored, including the way in which the marriages of those women who were married might be affected.

Women deacons groups

Two groups of women deacons met at approximately three-weekly intervals during the period between the vote in November 1992 and the ordination ceremonies in the summer of 1994. About eight women belonged to each group although membership fluctuated somewhat over the period. Some of the women were married, some were single and there was great variety in terms of age, length of service in the Church, prior occupations and types of ministry being currently pursued. The task of the two groups was outlined as follows:

> The task and purpose of the group will be to explore our feelings within this wholly new situation and the way that they are emerging, changing and to be discovered differently by each of us. Members will be encouraged to examine the meaning of the priesthood for them and the way in which we can locate the truly feminine within the truly human and how both may be brought to a new vision of the priesthood. More importantly perhaps, the group will enable members to explore their own sexuality in relation to their ministry. Some questions we might want to ponder include how to manage the more primitive feelings that the changing role and status of women may engender in both women and men.

Members were asked to commit themselves to attending the group regularly other than for exceptional reasons and gradually, as trust increased, both groups became safe places for important questions to be raised and answered. Although there were obviously differences in the way that these two groups developed, which partly reflected the membership differences (one group having a larger proportion of older women who carried particular experiences of sadness and anger at the wasted opportunities in their lives, as well as fears as to whether it would all be 'too late' for them), there were many themes in common and much overlap between the groups in terms of material. As the purpose of this chapter is to draw out some of the feelings and experiences of women approaching their ordination as priests, as pointers to the way in which ordination might affect their marriages, the material that emerged from these groups will be discussed as a whole.

An early theme was ambivalence. Some members had been campaigning for the ordination of women to the priesthood for many years, but now that it was on offer, did they really want it? Such a question seemed shocking but very real. Priesthood might mean having to do all the 'chores' in the Church which no one else except the vicar had to do and this seemed too like the way in which all the 'chores' fell upon the woman at home. Or it might mean having to be 'too responsible' or it might mean having to 'be mother'. The theme of how a female priesthood might differ from a male one and whether a woman priest would hold the role and maybe the title of 'mother' in a way that was analogous to that of 'father' was explored and revisited many times. One woman described the way in which at present she was often left holding the fort as the woman deacon, while her two male colleagues were away. When they were away she assumed a new status along with many extra duties, but when they returned, they were welcomed with open arms and she was relegated once more to her background position. It was 'just like being a mother in the home, with all its taken-for-grantedness'. Would it be different when she was a priest, or would the fact of her being female always mean this 'taken for granted-ness' about her function and being?

Some of the women's ambivalence stemmed from the feeling that they were 'a priest already'. Many women had coped with the unmanageable pain of repeated rejection by denial. They had argued that they were 'to all intents and purposes priests', able to do almost everything already. These women were left therefore with the dilemma of how to make sense of what was happening now that the Church had officially opened the barrier. Should they welcome 'the welcome', and if so, how was this to be done without denying their denials? For others there was a sense of whether, now that the priesthood was on offer, was it really worth it? This was sometimes expressed as being 'the Church's problem', of how to recognize or regularize the position of women within it. The Church had created the difficulties and it was now trying to resolve them for the sake of its own good name, or its own credibility or, even more basically, as a means of solving its own shortage of priests. For the individual woman then, perhaps there was no gift being offered at all. The question then became 'What more will *I* become if anything, if I accept the Church's offer of ordination?'

The anger at what the institution 'should have done centuries ago' produced powerful interior conflicts for some members, who nevertheless longed for the external recognition and validation of the priesthood that they felt was already theirs, alongside feeling sometimes all but overwhelmed by the pain and hurt of the rejection they experienced at the hands of the Church. Ambivalence also arose because of the pain that their vocation was obviously causing others. To feel, or to be made to feel 'responsible' for the major splits which were threatened within the Church was a heavy burden. The paradox of *causing* pain when one was there to *relieve* pain was keenly felt. This led to discussion as to how to respond to the defensiveness, opposition or patronization that was often experienced from opponents, in such a way that one did not do an injustice to one's own desire to conform to the ethics of treating one's opponents with love and respect.

For these individuals as women, and particularly as women in the Church, this was experienced as a continual double bind – how to do justice to the self and the other simultaneously. Understandably too, there was a strong sense of inadequacy experienced at now at last receiving the gift that had been longed for for so long. Was one up to it, worthy of it, ready for it? And did these feelings of inadequacy come from within, arising from early familial experiences of abuse or rejection; or had they been put there by the long years of rejection, marginalization and denial of one's personhood, by the Church as a whole over the centuries and perhaps by particular individuals in the person's ongoing experience? Often both had been true, making it more difficult to sort out what might be *real* deficits in knowledge, skill or experience which needed addressing in order to prepare as well as possible for this new role.

Belonging to these all-women groups and participating in other conferences and seminars provided by the Church for women deacons, during the interval between the vote and the first ordinations, brought women deacons into a closer awareness of some latent issues relating to being women together. The years leading up to the vote in 1992 had been experienced as a time of great solidarity and common purpose by many women in ministry. The vote had marked the successful accomplishment of this campaign but it marked too the moment when new difficulties had to be faced. Solidarity would soon change to rivalry and competitiveness, to envy and disappointment, when it began to be evident that not every woman deacon would be recommended for ordination as a priest and not every new priest would easily find the area of ministry that was commensurate with her long years of responsibility and experience in other walks of life.

The 'sameness' of being female and all being in the 'same boat' together had to give way to exploring the 'differences' of views and beliefs, talents and gifts, which would inevitably set women one against another. In addition, the 'hierarchy' which had hitherto always been male would now begin to become more mixed, with some senior appointments beginning to be open to women. This would confront women (as well of course as men) with the need to deal with the many unresolved conflicts contingent upon relating to powerful 'mother-like' figures and all the ambivalence that such relationships inevitably reactivate from the past. Some women were able to grieve quite consciously and openly for the loss of the secondary gains derived from being the 'only woman' in a staff group or other kind of Church structure. The 'specialness' of this position had often conferred latent power even when depriving the occupant of any real authority. On the other hand, some women were able to feel strongly positive about 'becoming ordinary' at last – just one priest amongst others – no longer having continually to explain the difference between what one was and what one was not.

But the difficulty of trying *to work out* who one was and who one was not was an important struggle during this period. It became an important exploration of identity. All the models of priesthood were inevitably male; they were, as one woman expressed it 'not full and not empty'. Yet many women felt strongly that being a woman priest ought to be different in some way. Again the paradox was strongly felt – the desire had been to enter into the one same historic priesthood that had for nearly 2,000 years been barred to women; yet the purpose in entering it was in some sense to make it new. Women were claiming the priesthood by virtue of their common humanity, yet they were experiencing their call as women, and not as requiring of them that they become surrogate men. Thus the question of identity – confronting women as it did with the most fundamental question of all – was a very powerful theme for these groups.

The question of identity connected strongly for a considerable number of women with early childhood confusions, stemming from abuse and deprivation. The offer of priesthood threw many back onto reviewing painful early experiences which had resulted in experiences of uncertainty, unworthiness and a deep sense of personal rejection. This newly revealed material was often difficult to deal with in the marriage, giving rise to new and unexpected demands upon the women's husbands for reassurance and support. Some women found that they needed to take this journey of rediscovery and inner healing onto a much deeper level. They needed to engage with those issues through a more formal experience of therapy before it became possible for them to receive the gift of their new identity as priest, and before being able to be comfortable at the prospect of being both priest and woman. For some, the disequilibrium created within the marriage led the couple to seek help together.

The identity of becoming a woman priest developed gradually over the months leading up to the ordination, and the degree and pace of this development was greatly influenced by the response of others. Just as a child needs, in Lacan's terminology, the presence of a 'mirror' to help him or her 'become what s/he is', so the women who were to become this new thing needed the response and recognition of others to help them discover who it was they were. This recognition and response was needed both from the woman's closest significant others, as well as from her wider circle of contacts, colleagues, parishioners and friends.

But of the two, those whose new identity was repudiated by their husbands and immediate family felt the most critically disconfirmed by the experience, and this will be discussed in more detail shortly. However, women who encountered hostility, or simply non-recognition of their imminent priestly role by their congregations and colleagues, also felt disqualified and de-personalized, even when they were receiving strong support from their partner. The husbands of these women found great difficulty in finding ways of responding to their wife's pain in such a way that her self-esteem was enhanced sufficient for her to risk functioning within her new identity. However supportive and empathic husbands were to their wives, the extent of the damage to women who had experienced these responses from their congregations was not easily mitigated. This sometimes led to frustration and tensions within the couple's relationship, as the husband strove to do the impossible for his wife, with apparently no result.

Several women described these kinds of experiences and the complicated feelings of guilt and responsibility they were then left holding, for the unhappiness engendered in their husbands. Although the material being described in this chapter comes only from the women's viewpoint, it was obvious from the responses to a letter sent to husbands immediately after the ordinations how difficult it had been for them to give all the support that they had wanted to give. They were also struggling with their own feelings of anxiety about what might be changing for them and their own lives as a result of their wife's ordination, all of which complicated their ability to empathize fully with their wife's experience.

But the experiences of hostility and opposition were even more powerfully damaging when they came from the women's husbands themselves. The reactions of some of the women's husbands ranged from indifference through ambivalence to strong hostility, and even when these reactions were, for the most part, softened by an overt desire not to hurt their wife, they were very difficult to receive and manage. These situations represented the end point of a continuum. For one woman whose husband had been hostile to the Church throughout their marriage, the experience was one of loneliness. She talked of whether or not she could 'bear the load' of what priesthood might mean, when it meant doing so, as she saw it, on her own. It seemed to be a different kind of aloneness to be married to a hostile partner from being alone in the sense of being unpartnered. Being alone in the sense of being a single person carried none of the disconfirming resonances of the married women's experience.

The repudiation of their priesthood by their marriage partners was experienced by these women as a profound assault on their own sense of identity and well-being and on the quality of the marriage. When judged against the parameters of cohesion, mutual empathy, similarity, androgyny and egalitarianism, some of the determinants of marital satisfaction described in Chapter 5, the inability of a couple to incorporate into the relationship this huge aspect of one of the partner's deeply experienced aspiration and need, created a major crisis. Some of the women who found themselves in this situation described themselves as being faced with a choice between their priesthood and their marriage. Each of these particular women in fact opted to forgo ordination, at least for the immediate future.

Mixed group of male and female clergy

The group for male and female clergy was equally important in providing pointers to research areas in relation to some of the effects of ordaining women to the priesthood. This group met monthly from April 1992 and committed itself to continuing until the summer of 1994 when the women members of the group would be ordained. The group was made up of four priests opposed to women's ordination and five women deacons who felt called to the priesthood. It was therefore a very specialized and potentially challenging experience for those who participated. All four men were active in organizations that had taken a major part in spearheading the opposition to women's ordination and similarly, the women were either active in the Movement for the Ordination of Women or in other women's groups.

The task of the group was simply to meet, to share experiences, to listen to the opposing view and, above all, to continue to meet together regularly before and after the vote, whichever way the decision went. Members of the group committed themselves to pray for each other, to learn from each other and to create and maintain a bond of charity between them which would supersede the passionately held differences amongst them.

Several purposes undergirded this group. It had a 'therapeutic' intention in that, amongst all the bitterness and loudly expressed megaphone opposition from each 'side' of the debate to the other, it was felt that the opportunity to meet face-to-face might allow people from opposing sides to better understand the beliefs, hopes and longings of their opponents, and encounter the human beings behind the views. It was also hoped that members might be able to understand better and in some depth, each other's views and the meaning and importance that these views held for them, in the safe environment of this quite tightly structured group. Hopefully this in turn would enable members to relate more constructively with others with whom they were in disagreement, including in some cases their own families and marriage partners.

The agenda explicitly excluded any effort to change each other's views or even enlighten each other in any explicit way regarding misunderstandings or misperceptions of the other's position. For the first half of its life, the group was tightly structured, to avoid it becoming a discussion group or entering the arena of polemics or persuasion. Silence and creative listening were important ingredients. Members sometimes felt weighed down by the impasse of what was felt to be a useless exercise – living out the experience of being together, and bearing the pain and anger of each person's own rejection, seen mirrored in the face of those who seemed to be its cause. There was perhaps a dawning realization at times that this was how things were going to remain, whatever the Church finally decided – an experience of prolonged immovability, with no light at all at the end of the tunnel.

Undoubtedly however, as the group developed a trusting life of its own, and the quality and depth of sharing between its members increased, each person also found that he or she was growing and changing in relation to the others. In some ways this doubled the pain and the complexity of the situation, because each member found it more difficult to project and displace emotions onto the 'other' or to distort his or her beliefs or motivation now that the 'other' had moved from being a faceless stranger to someone who had become quite well known. There was, too, a growing realization at some level that the movements for and against the ordination of women were opposite sides of the same coin, carrying meaning for the Church as a whole and catalysing a new emotional working through of issues of gender, sexuality, power and personhood at both individual and institutional levels.

As the Synod vote grew closer, group members expressed considerable anxiety, and strong feelings that perhaps the group should now discontinue because the pain was becoming too great. One of the men said that he did not want the vote to take place because 'either way the result will be awful'. The group had now been meeting for nearly six months and members had grown much more strongly aware of the experiences of other members and had developed an empathic bond across the divide. There had been, for some of the women in the group, a discernible movement from the position of 'victim' to a growing sense of empowerment and rootedness in their own achievements and self-worth and an increased understanding of how to hear the anger and pain of others without taking personal responsibility for its cause. One member described this as a shift to a place where she was able to say: 'I hear you, I have some understanding, but I do not accept personal responsibility for the stance you are taking.' However, as the moment for the vote passed and the women's position was radically changed, more complicated feelings on both sides had to be handled. The need to rejoice was severely impaired by the knowledge of the pain being experienced by the men. Yet the men's pain was also deeply changed by the gladness they felt for these and other women who had become friends and colleagues over the months and years.

As all but one of the women deacons prepared for their ordination, the four men moved gradually towards their own resolution of what was for them an appallingly painful crisis. Their position could be summed up in Greenacre's (1993) comment: 'To stay in the Church of England and to leave the Church of England both seemed almost equally impossible choices' (p. 366). One of the four came to feel that, partly because of his close experience of women deacons in the group, he was now able to reflect upon the Church's situation in a new way and to feel that God was now opening new possibilities for his own ministry alongside women priests. A second felt that he should stay in the Church of England and continue to act as a focus for those who opposed the decision. From a new senior appointment in the diocese, he would play an important part in pastoring those who continued within the Anglican Church as well as trying to build bridges across the divide. The third priest remained troubled and uncertain as to what he should do. He described his position as one of feeling immobilized – sometimes feeling he should leave, sometimes feeling he should stay.

Two members of the group, a woman and a man, both faced the additionally painful situation of finding themselves taking different positions from their marriage partners. These two members of the group, although representing the two different views, were able to share with one another something of their own painful journeys and to give and gain from one another considerable mutual support. They were much more strongly united by the fact that their marriages were affected by the opposing views of their partner, than they were divided by the issue itself. They were also able to gain in understanding and personal experience of how to work the issues through in their marriages, by expressing and sharing their painful feelings in the group.

The fourth priest member of the group decided he should leave the Church of England and asked to be received as a Roman

Catholic. As well as risking the loss of his priesthood, he and his wife faced losing their home and all that had contributed to their security over the years. Moreover, because he and his wife held different theological positions on this issue, they had now to face, at least for the time being, the fractured unity of their previously shared spiritual experience. He wrote to his parish announcing his decision, saying 'I have had to take what may well turn out to be the most painful and difficult decision of my life'. He went on to say: 'those women who will be ordained ... have a right, now that a decision has been taken, to expect their ministry to be accepted ... I have respect for those who feel passionately that this is right; it is partly because of that respect that I feel the time is right for a loving and caring parting of friends.'

For some male priests, membership of an all-male priesthood had enabled them to function creatively and maturely in a secure environment and this fact could be acknowledged in this group. It was one of the major losses with which the four male members were grappling, as the Church moved towards making its decision. Several of them were cognizant of the fact that an all-male priesthood had allowed them to exercise their compassionate, intuitive gifts amongst their largely female flocks whilst at the same time maintaining their male identity within their colleague group. It was clear that part of the experience for the four men was a profound sense of invasion and attack at the prospect of so radical an alteration in the symbolism of priesthood. For them, the presence of priestly women was felt to dilute the powerful reparative need which, for some of them, lay deeply within their motivation in becoming priests. Their vocation had enabled them to 'make reparation' on behalf of their gender for the ills that are perpetrated by men against women. This reparative possibility had also allowed them as men to sublimate their own 'violence' and channel it instead through the 'violence' of the Eucharist. Acknowledging some of these issues was made particularly difficult by the presence of the very women who were the 'cause' of their problems, but, by the same token, their acknowledgement in the women's presence had the reciprocal effect of engaging the women's understanding of the other side of the dilemma.

In the same way, it was painful, and in some cases deeply distressing for the men to hear the way in which the women's experience of marginalization and rejection had been sustained in some cases for many years, and that they were in some senses its 'cause'. One of the women likened the experience of attending the group to being asked, as a black person, to sit down in the same room with the Ku Klux Klan. Another often felt anxious about the fact that the group reduced her to tears, since this might confirm the prejudices of the male members against her as being 'merely an emotional woman'. In fact it led one of the men to comment increasingly on the difference he was beginning to perceive between the way in which the women and the men handled their emotions in the group. He said that he had begun to realize how 'cerebral' he was, not only within the group but in other situations too, including personal ones, and he became much more aware of his experience of wanting to but often feeling unable to express his emotions.

Perhaps the major experience of the members of this group was that of confronting and attempting to work through the deep differences which, although acted out *between* them, were also experienced *within* them. During the life of the group, divided up as it was in a particularly sharp and memorable way into the period before and after the vote, members experienced many changes in their own internal world of emotional experience as well as in their external worlds of professional and personal relationships. The two interacted one with the other, and both found a container within the monthly meetings of the group. Only three of the nine members were married and of those, two of them were married to partners who took an opposite view on the issue to their own. Other than for these two members for whom the group gave an important opportunity to consider the effects of the issue on their marriages, the group did not impinge directly on the marital relationships of women who were about to be ordained. However, it raised in a powerful way the many interacting aspects of gender relationships and drew attention at first hand to the enormously powerful issues which the ordination of women represented on the emotional, relational and psychological levels.

4 MARRIAGE

> When you make the two one and when you make the inside like the out-
> side, and the outside like the inside, and the above like the below, and
> when you make the male and the female one and the same, so that the
> male not be male nor the female ... then you will enter the Kingdom.
> *Gospel of Thomas*

Part of the underlying rationale for this study of joint clergy couples is to try to understand more fully their vulnerabilities and
strengths. But in order to understand the specifics of their situation, it is important first for us to consider the current climate in
relation to marriage and the wider context in which clergy,
whether male or female, are living out their own marriages.

The contemporary context of marriage

The fact of being married and the quality of people's marriages continue to be consistently associated with being healthier, happier,
more fulfilled and more productive. Likewise, when a person's marriage is in difficulties, each partner is likely to suffer considerably
from the emotional, physical and psychological consequences.
Clearly, marriage has undergone considerable change over the last
few decades and these changes have been well documented. The
inherent contradiction between the desire for intimacy and the
goals of personal fulfilment and autonomy for example, creates a
fundamental tension for many couples. The fact that we live in
what Lasch (1979) described as 'a culture of narcissism' makes the

giving of the self to another in the way that a fulfilling marriage demands, an extraordinarily difficult concept.

Similarly, the expectation and hope that both partners will be able to pursue fulfilling careers *and* manage the vast number of activities involved in what has come to be described as 'family work' *and* create a warm, emotionally fulfilling family environment for one's partner, one's children and oneself may lead to stress, role strain and role overload for one or both partners. Moreover, as long ago as 1972, Bernard identified the fact that in every marriage there are in fact two marriages, 'his' and 'hers' and that they are very different experiences. This relates to the central fact that marriage is the primary institution which contains and mediates all the dilemmas and difficulties of the gender debate. In other words, it is within marriage more than in any other institution that men and women are confronted with how to bring about a 'good enough' resolution of the inequalities, sexism and oppression that continue to exist in the relationship between women and men in society today.

Likewise, it is within the institution of marriage that men and women have to confront the perennial challenge of how to be 'one flesh yet separate persons'; how to be intimate and in connection with another without becoming fused; how to be fully differentiated as a separate self, without losing connection. There is a continuing need to balance both poles of what becomes the 'couple system' as well as maintaining the system itself. In marriage, there are, as Solomon (1989) points out, three systems in interaction – the self system, the couple system and the social system. 'At one end is the need for inclusion, the lack of which leaves a sense of cosmic psychic isolation. At the other extreme is the experience of absolute enmeshment, total transparency, in which no single corner of potentially shareable experience can be kept private' (Solomon, 1989, p. 28). Put another way, the problem that confronts women and men in marriage is how to cherish sufficiently both their individual personhoods *and* their profound connectedness in such a way that both the individuals and the relationship between them flourishes and grows throughout what may be a lifetime? Clergy have to struggle with these issues alongside everyone else, and in order to understand those issues that relate to clergy marriage and, in particular, to those marriages where both partners are now ordained as priests, these more general factors must not be neglected.

One way of examining this question is to reflect upon the different challenges and opportunities that confront the couple at different stages of the marriage's life course. The marriage partnership has a developmental life of its own, different from though related to the individual partners themselves. Like individuals and families, marriages experience difficulties particularly at times of change. In thinking about clergy couples, it is helpful to understand the way in which their partnership will move and change developmentally, partly because of the individual choices they make in their marriage and partly because of the particular context in which they live out their marriage as clergy. Moreover the developmental experiences of men and women are somewhat different and this also needs to be borne in mind, when considering the couple as a unit, moving through their marital life cycle together.

1. Partnership choice: isolation versus intimacy*

As early as 1964, the sociologists Berger and Kellner (1964) wrote their extremely influential paper in which they viewed marriage as a search for identity and, to a lesser extent, stability. Earlier still, Jung (1925) described marriage as an emotional 'container' allowing the partners safety and space to regress and move progressively forward towards individuation or full selfhood. These ideas as to 'what marriage is *for*' guide everyone, including clergy, on some primitive level, in seeking out and finding a marriage partner. The image of emotional container may carry particular importance for clergy, for whom both the practice and meaning of their vocation may often make it difficult for them to cherish appropriately a healthy sense of self-esteem.

The work of Dicks (1967) and his colleagues, and more recently of Clulow (1990), and others from the Tavistock Marital Studies Institute, has been extremely influential in examining the

*In adding sub-titles to each of the following stages to emphasize the critical developmental task of each stage, I have followed E. H. Erikson's (1968) original idea when he described the life-cycle of the individual, but I have used different descriptors.

unconscious bases of partner choice. These may include an effort to recreate a relationship with the parent who represented an ideal early relationship or it may be based upon an unconscious attempt to connect with parts of the self that are as yet undiscovered or which have been actively rejected.

The long-running debate in the field, as to whether similarity or complementarity is the more significant factor in partner choice, will not be discussed at this point. Suffice it to draw attention to Hulson and Russell's (1991) comment: that 'the conclusion to be drawn from the evidence is clear; relationships are based on similarity not on complementarity' (p. 38), and they continue: 'From all the evidence it is fair to conclude that a good long-term relationship is founded upon compatibility based on similarity on a wide range of personal qualities' (p. 39). Because these conclusions relate to the factors associated with marital satisfaction, they will be discussed further in the next chapter.

So far, the discussion has related to the partnership choices of all couples. For clergy, the same fundamental dynamics will operate in their choice of a marital partner. In addition however, Kirk and Leary (1994) have suggested, from a qualitative study based on thirty-seven clergy couples, that other factors can also be observed in relation to the way in which clergy make their marital choice, some of which may create difficulties later. For example, clergymen show parallels in their choice of ordination as a calling and in their choice of a wife, Kirk and Leary give as examples of this similarity: the need to find security from both the partner and the Church; the influence of parents on both vocation and marriage; and the desire to find a partner who will be helpful to the individual's ministry.

Obviously these factors are likely to operate more strongly where the juxtaposition of the couple's marriage and the ministerial partner's ordination is close in time. For joint clergy couples, this intertwining of marriage and ministry in their partnership choice may be particularly complex. In addition, the juxtaposition of developmental crises may increase the intensity with which each is experienced. Thus, when the entry into marriage occurs almost simultaneously with the entry into a new career or vocation (as it often does for joint clergy couples) the emotional overload for one or both partners may be considerable.

2. Honeymoon period: idealization versus reality

The second phase consists largely in letting go the original projections onto the partner, sufficient for the 'real' partners to encounter one another. Each partner has to disengage from the transference figure to whom s/he was originally attracted. Each partner has to confront some of the covert issues which drew him or her into marriage in the first place – the desire to escape from unresolved issues in the family of origin for example, or to prove to the self and to others that one is adult, and able therefore to manage in the adult world of intimate and procreative relationships. For those for whom there has been a close interweaving of personal and work-related issues in the choice of the partner, as is often the case for clergy, the honeymoon period will also involve the gradual disentanglement of the two. But there will often have been a heightened sense of idealism and unreality in the early phase of a clergy marriage, because of the way in which the clergy role attracts to itself strong projections of unwavering care, protectiveness, purity and self-sacrificial love.

This will often make even worse the concomitant disillusionment which accompanies the realization that must occur around this point in *every* marriage – that the ideal mate is more than a composite of one's own personal and professional needs, projected onto the face of the other, but a person in his or her own right, with perhaps their own professional aspirations in addition to their personal needs, both of which may be in conflict with those of the self. Thus, difference, conflict and rupture have to be incorporated into a revised view of what constitutes this new partnership at a fundamental level.

3. Growth in connection: separation versus mutuality

Forming a couple involves some loss of individuality, yet part of negotiating this early stage of a marriage will involve balancing the needs of the individual persons with the need to develop the couple's relationship. How to become 'one flesh, separate persons' is the primary task of this stage but, as with the 'work' of each of the stages, it will remain an ongoing task that needs continual renegotiation throughout the lifetime of the marriage. The desire for union with the other and merging into the other is clearly a powerful magnet attracting the partners into the relationship, and it is a desire which is most clearly realized in sexual intercourse. But the need to achieve intimacy without fusion remains an important and difficult imperative in all aspects of the couple's life together.

The couple have to confront the sometimes uncomfortable and always paradoxical truth that it is only possible to be in intimate relationship with someone from whom one is separate. The primary task for the couple is to enable each of the two selves, the other *and* the relationship to flourish and grow so that increasingly, the development of the separate selves will also enhance the development of the relationship.

As Gilligan (1982) and the Stone school of feminist researchers amongst others have pointed out, there are, however, gender differences around the way in which intimacy is construed. 'For boys, the emphasis on early emotional separation and the forming of an identity through the assertion of difference fosters a basic relational stance of disconnection and disidentification. Girls [however] develop the expectation that they can facilitate the growth of a sense of self through psychological connection and expect that the mutual sharing of experience will lead to psychological growth' (Surrey, 1984, p. 5).

Thus the partners, at this still early stage of their development as a couple, will often be moving from different positions and trying to overcome diametrically opposite emotional pulls. This may make empathy and comprehension of the other difficult and challenging, but it also means that, *ipso facto*, the partners *between them* possess the relational dynamics necessary to interact productively, intimately and differently, if these can only be identified and placed at the service of the relationship.

4. Partnership to parenthood: stagnation versus creativity

Part of the creative function of marriage for many couples during this phase will be the procreation of children. This is not of course the only way in which marriages are creative and generative. Work and shared leisure time will offer many opportunities for couples to be mutually creative – or not. In particular, the ways in which the marital relationship enhances or obstructs career development for one or both partners, and the two-way spillover effects between home and work will all determine the extent to which a marriage is able to become creative and outwardly directed.

Some couples will choose to remain childless in order to devote themselves more fully to their chosen career or vocation and this may well be a choice which some clergy couples make. For those couples who have children (and for those couples where the ministry or calling of one or both partners assumes a central place in their concerns), the marriage becomes more complex as the twosome becomes a threesome and as spouses add the roles of parenting to their marital relationship.

The parenting phase of a marriage often involves a reduction in intimacy between the couple, both sexual and emotional; an interruption in the career aspirations of one partner, usually the woman; a rise in conflict between the partners and a reduction in the equitable sharing of household and child care tasks. On the other hand, the presence of young children may, temporarily at least, stabilize a marriage and reduce the immediate likelihood of marriage breakdown.

Various researchers have reported a curvilinear pattern, where marital satisfaction decreases sharply after the birth of the first child and rises again after the children leave home (Belsky *et al.*, 1983), and although this pattern has been challenged by others, Mackey and O'Brian (1995) conclude that 'there is a "U" type pattern to some aspects of relationships during the second phase [i.e. the parental phase] of marriage' (p. 127). Thus the two parenting phases which are likely to produce the highest levels of stress for the couple are the early parenting phase when the children are below the age of five and the adolescent phase, when parents are confronted with the need for high levels of adaptation, as their children move from dependency to adulthood.

On the other hand there may often be growth in much more fundamental relationship qualities such as trust and mutual respect during this stage and continuing over the whole life course of the marriage which, when viewed retrospectively, will seem more important to the couple than the difficulties they have endured.

All through this stage, one or both partners may have been working in the outside world of employment. For those who minister within the Church, the image of marriage as a container for self-worth and self-esteem may be particularly needful, not only because ministry is often stressful, but also because there is a complex challenge at the heart of the vocation to 'lose the self in order to find it' (Matthew 10.39). This may be a well understood or a much misunderstood imperative. In either case, the marriage will be called upon to provide fundamental resources of stability and self-esteem if the individual partners are to thrive. By the same token however, the demands made on the marriage itself may also be significant.

5. Career realignments and teenage years: independence versus interdependence

At this stage in the life-cycle of the marriage, there may be several different kinds of challenge to the marital system coming from the outside world of work. The primary child carer in those marriages that have not shared equally in the child rearing tasks, will, if keen to continue his or her career, need to take steps to re-establish it. This is likely to involve some form of retraining or additional education, and will almost certainly need some help in confidence building to cope with feelings of anxiety and lack of self-worth on re-entering perhaps a very competitive working environment, or, in the case of the Church, one which is largely unaccustomed to providing opportunities for women. Many of the women amongst those couples where the woman only was ordained, were facing re-entry into employment after some years devoted to full-time work in the home.

Usually the primary child carer is still the wife, who is thus confronted with these particular challenges. She may have become depressed at her perceived 'loss of self' and the erosion of individuality that has taken place during the child rearing years. The other partner who has remained the primary worker may be confronted with the very different challenges of disillusionment, redundancy, or early retirement which, even if taken by choice, will inevitably involve a radical change in life-style. Or, alternatively he or she may be reaching the pinnacle of a career which is making even greater demands upon emotional and physical resources of energy and commitment. Those couples described in Chapter 2 were often struggling with these issues.

The needs of the partners at this point may well be in collision, with both of them, for different reasons, requiring extra injections of emotional support from the other, just at the point when the other has little to give. Because of the delay in career development for women clergy currently in post, this may be a particular issue for them and their husbands. But it may also be a time when *both* clergy partners have to decide how to gather new energy and enthusiasm to make the later stages of ministry creative and productive after perhaps (unlike most professional occupations) many years of doing the 'same thing'. At the same time, children may be reaching adolescence and offering the particular challenges of power and independence to parents, who as individuals and partners are already under pressure. For children and young people in clergy families it may be especially difficult for them to define their own identity apart from that of their parents. Shaking off the unwanted aura of being 'children of the manse' may require particularly dramatic ventures into unsocial behaviour and unorthodox relationships, making the value and culture clash peculiarly sharp and painful for clergy couples to handle.

6. Reforming the dyad: holding on versus letting go

Children gradually leave home. The curvilinear pattern of marital satisfaction, which in general is supported by both cross-sectional and longitudinal studies, indicates that marital satisfaction increases again once children leave home. Because of changed economic factors, this may be a much more uncertain and protracted process than it used to be. Both children and parents may feel the need to hold on when they need to let go of one another, or, alternatively, push one another away prematurely in an effort to avoid the painful ambivalence of this transitional stage in their relationships. The more protracted process of contemporary growing up for young people today, may enable marital partners to adjust more gradually to a change in the occupation of their primary role from parent back to partner. On the other hand, the anxiety, uncertainties and disappointments often associated with getting their offspring successfully 'launched' into work, relationships and homes of their own, may produce high levels of stress for parents, often in the form of guilt and self-criticism. This may in turn lead to conflict between the partners as they seek to offload the tensions they are experiencing internally, by projecting blame onto each other.

Moreover, the dynamic involved here is not so much changing 'from parent *back* to partner' but from moving from 'parent *on* to partner', for the partner is now a changed and different person, compared with the person to whom they were first attracted. Obvious as this seems, the difficulty at this stage of the marital life-cycle is to be able to value and honour the changes that have occurred, so that the partner can be recognized and 'refound', and the necessary renegotiations take place regarding the final stages of the marriage. Helping couples to 'hold on' and not 'let go' may be the primary need at this crisis point.

7. Consolidation and celebration: disintegration versus integrity

There are two critical points in the marital life-cycle where the threat of its disintegration is strongest – the early years, during stage 2, when the many different projections onto the partner have to be recognized and owned by the self, so that the couple can begin to relate to the 'real' person of the other, and second, towards the end of the life-cycle, after many of the primary tasks of marriage have been completed. Ideally, this final phase is the phase when the fruits of a long partnership can be harvested, its disappointments can be accepted, its failures forgiven and its scars healed. The couple may have shared the greater part of their lives together. Much of their life experience will be held in common so that it can be valued in a way which increases the meaning given to it by each of the individual members alone. Children and grandchildren may be a part of this harvesting experience as well as the sense of fulfilment from having done the work that one has felt called to do. Where this has been, in part at least, shared work as in ministry, it can again be viewed as the work of the couple, over and above the achievements of the individuals themselves.

However, the sense of limitation, the knowledge that time is now running out, the realization that many of the earlier hopes of life have inevitably not been fulfilled may all get projected onto the partner, and a last desperate effort be made to gain what feels as though it has been lost or never realized. This may take the form of an extra-marital affair, a 'running away' to be alone, or a total absorption in other interests to the exclusion of the partner. The death of the marriage may creep slowly up on the couple, or it may come as a sudden and dramatic event. There are particular potential hazards here for clergy, because of the limited career structure in the Church and the difficulty for some clergy in finding the fulfilment for which they yearn, from the exercise of their vocation. Like their children, clergy may sometimes need to express their long-suppressed disappointments by punishing both the partner and the Church through a particularly dramatic and scandalous excursion into unsocial behaviour or alternative partnerships.

Dual-career marriage

Couples where both partners are ordained function to a greater or lesser extent as dual-career marriages. The characteristics of this type of marriage are therefore of particular interest, not because joint clergy couples are the *only* kind of dual-career clergy couples – far from it. But they express the dual-career life-style amongst the clergy in a particularly clear and unambiguous way, and they may therefore attract to themselves whatever anxieties or criticisms that some may have about this form of marriage.

'For dual-career relationships, there is virtually no past.' This comment made in the series editor's introduction to Gilbert's (1993) important recent book, can be applied even more forcefully to the special type of dual-career couple represented by joint clergy. At this point it is important to try to clarify the way in which joint clergy couples are being considered in this study in relation to their career status.

Because, by definition, both partners are committed to holding a vocational identity by virtue of their ordination, they can, as a group, be considered to be dual-career couples. On the other hand, even leaving aside the reasonable objection that a vocation to the ministry should not be described as a career, many further distinctions would have to be made in describing the employment characteristics of the joint clergy couples in this group, which would make their overall description as dual-career couples more ambiguous.

However, leaving aside for the time being these finer distinctions, there are some important general points to be made about dual-career couples. Early studies focusing on the effect of women's employment on the marriage, often start from the implicit assumption that the amount of time spent working by the wife detracts from marital satisfaction (Barling, 1990a). But the findings of these earlier studies have not been replicated in more recent work. Moreover, as Houseknecht and Macke (1981) and Spitze and Waite (1981) point out respectively, when husbands support their wives' decision to work, and hold positive attitudes about wives' employment, there is no decrease in marital satisfaction for either husband or wife. Considerable dissatisfaction for employed women of course relates to the inequitable sharing of household chores. Nevertheless, as Barling (1990b) points out, 'even though household and child care responsibilities are still not shared equally between spouses, employment helps wives attain greater equity in the marital relationship' (p. 205).

Although there does not seem to be any direct relationship between either the amount of time spent in employment or the irregularity of hours worked with marital satisfaction, there is much more evidence of conflict between work and family when individuals experience job-related stress. There is considerable support for the view that negative work experiences exert a harmful effect on marriages and that the contrary is also true. Negative experiences at work such as discrimination, lack of affirmation or chronic conflict with colleagues are all associated with negative experiences at home. However, positive experiences at work, such as participating in decision-making, opportunities for exercising developing knowledge and skill, and overall job satisfaction have a beneficial effect on the marriage, partly because some of the positive behaviours learnt in the work place can be transferred to the home and partly because of an overall sense of well-being and raised self-esteem that is contingent upon the experience of job satisfaction.

Moreover, various studies have shown that the agreement and collaborative involvement of the spouse by the other's employer positively aids proposed work-related change such as relocation. In other words, involving the partner in decisions about the employee's work is helpful to family life as well as to achieving the organization's aims and goals. In general, if couples experience conflict between the demands of their family roles and their work roles this is a consistent predictor of marital dissatisfaction for both men and women. Thus the best way for an organization, concerned about the well-being of the marriages of its staff, to demonstrate its concern, is to provide them with supportive, participative and affirmative management; equal opportunities for them to exercise their gifts, and jobs which afford appropriate opportunities for them to demonstrate and develop their knowledge and skill over their working lives.

Dual-career couples who work in the same field of employment

Of particular relevance to this study are reports of couples who work together in the same kind of secular employment. The literature on this particular type of dual-career couple is very small. Apart from couples who run a family business together (a somewhat different situation), there have been studies of dual-career farmers (Gasson, 1981), sociologists (Martin et al., 1975), lawyers (Epstein, 1973), physicians (Tesch et al., 1992) and psychologists (Bryson et al., 1978).

Bryson et al. (1978) found that, amongst psychologist couples, the strains of being a dual-career couple 'were more severe for the wife than for the husband, indicating that wives in dual-career couples bear a disproportionate share of the burden of child care'. Nearly fifteen years later, Tesch et al. (1992) compared dual physician relationships with women physicians married to non-physicians and found that in dual physician marriages, the wife undertook significantly more of the child care and household work than women physicians married to non-physician husbands. By way of explanation, they found that physician husbands worked on average fifteen hours more per week than did their non-physician counterparts, suggesting considerable role overload for both partners. However, this also shews how, generally speaking, it is only the husband's overwork, not the wife's, that is given as a reason for low participation in household chores. In handling these two equally demanding careers, the wife is left to either add on to her working day a 'second shift' of housework (as Hochschild, 1989, describes it) or sacrifice her career by going part-time. Does this, perhaps for similar reasons, happen in the directly analogous situation of joint clergy couples?

Barling (1990b) makes the general, though unsubstantiated point that 'employment experiences that are common to both spouses affect their marital satisfaction equally' (p. 212). In fact, there is no particular reason why this should be so. However, the fact that both partners work for the same institution is certainly likely to have a synergistic effect, so that the experiences of one partner will affect and be affected by the experiences of the other, creating a vicious or a virtuous spiral. Thus we might assume that the marital satisfaction of clergy couples where both partners share a common workplace, as do many joint clergy couples, will be affected either positively or negatively to a greater degree as a result of their shared experiences at work.

Gasson's (1981) study of women on farms is also interesting for this present study. She identified three types of women, who might have some parallels with some of the women in the three types of clergy couples being studied. These were farm housewives – traditional couples where it was his farm and her farmhouse; working farmwives – where the couple make a good team, the wife's place being to assist her husband on the farm; and, third, working farmers – where husband and wife were in partnership, with equal responsibility for the running and management of the farm. Of the three groups, she found that the third group 'risked opposition on all sides. As a farmer she will be judged by the yardstick of full time male farmers, regardless of her additional responsibilities in the home. Equally, as a woman she is judged against the full time farm housewife, irrespective of her farm commitments' (p. 469).

What research tells us about dual-career marriage

Rapoport and Rapoport (1971) identified five 'dilemmas' for the dual-career couple: role overload; environmental sanctions militating against the acceptance of the model; personal identity and self-esteem; social network dilemmas and multiple-role cycling, involving the continuous need to mesh the demands of marriage, children and two separate careers. Rice (1979), in another early study, identified some of the particular challenges that can face dual-career couples. These included: the need for achievement on the part of both partners; the need for both to gratify self-esteem needs; the difficulty of making a total commitment to the relationship; creating equity; servicing the needs of others (this includes the emotional and practical needs of children, and maybe other dependants); managing time (including finding quality time for the self and for the relationship); relationships with others (colleagues and friends); handling competition; sharing power; and getting enough outside support to handle all the tasks that have to be done.

Rice's list is very comprehensive and is likely to remain relevant, in that most of these factors are part of the 'givens' of the dual-career life style. On the positive side, a greater understanding of the strategies required to overcome some of the difficulties has emerged as well as a better understanding of the way in which the 'givens' of a dual-career marriage can be transformed into positive drivers. Rice for example found that competition between spouses, although frequently denied, was often synergistic in its effects for both partners, acting as a gentle spur for them to give of their best to their careers, rather than always being disabling or destructive to the marriage.

The literature on dual-career families is wide-ranging and developmental, in the sense that a more complex picture emerges from the later studies. Ray (1990), for example, explored the relationship of interactional patterns with the marital satisfaction of 100 dual-career couples and found that greater marital satisfaction was related to greater equality and reciprocity in relationships. She also pinpointed the difficulties for women who begin their careers after their marriages and found that these women tended to experience less marital satisfaction, less job satisfaction, less support from their husband and greater inequality in decision-making. Ray comments on the need to help women make the transition from homemaker to career woman, an important point which is likely to remain of continuing relevance in enabling women clergy to give of their best.

Attitudes and perceptions of gender role, equity and fairness in relation to task distribution are increasingly viewed as more important than the dual-career marriage structure *per se* in enabling couples to create and maintain a happy marriage. Moreover, mediating factors such as the amount of time a couple spends together have been found to be associated with marital satisfaction and therefore have important implications for dual-career couples. For joint clergy marriages, and others where both partners are practising the same profession, often in closely related areas or even in the same place of work, the couple may be able to spend a great deal of time together, and this may present greater opportunities for creating and building relationship or, alternatively greater possibilities of role blur.

The current research of the 1990s views dual-career couples as the norm and, in the sub-title of Gilbert's (1993) book, as helping actively to bring into being the 'promise of gender equality'. In looking back over the past 20 years, Gilbert (1994) clarifies the fundamental link that exists between this form of relationship and the aspirations to gender equality within and beyond marriage. She comments on the way that at first 'the notion of a two career family was met with both excitement and scepticism. It promised to preserve the best of marriage – intimacy and enduring love – but freed partners from the harness of gender roles. True equality between women and men – social, economic and political equality – seemed highly possible, if not inevitable. Now, some 25 years later, both the excitement and the scepticism appear realistic. Although increasing numbers of couples establish dual-career relationships, the larger promise of true equality has yet to be achieved' (p. 101). Since the dual-career life-style lies at the heart of the joint clergy couple's experience, we need to consider the characteristics of this life-style, in its current form, in some detail.

Gilbert (1993) comments on the implicit assumptions that lie at the heart of current thinking about dual-career marriage – economic equality; compatibility of occupational and family systems;

and gender role attitudes that allow for role sharing, mutuality and interdependency. She identifies some of the harsh realities that lie at the heart of the relationship of women and men, and that although both sexes are restricted by their gender roles, and although these have shifted and loosened to some extent, the complex interaction between the way in which masculinity and power are aligned in our culture makes change both difficult and threatening. It may be easier for a man to want equality and justice for women in the workplace, than 'to embrace in his heart that a woman who is his partner is also his equal – for to do so may require handing over his image of himself as a man' (p. 42). This is particularly difficult to do because of the confusions and contradictions surrounding the construction of masculinity in our contemporary society. Moreover, the ambiguities and losses experienced by men in their social and occupational roles may make it harder for them to give up power over women in their domestic relationships and grasp hold of the potential advantages for men in letting go of gender stereotypes and being enabled to nurture, parent and participate fully in the highly diverse tasks and roles of a dual-career marriage. These occupational ambiguities and losses are also being experienced by men within the Church, so that similar difficulties are as likely to be present for them in their marriages, as they come to terms with the entry of women clergy into positions of collegiality and power.

Gilbert found that 'contrary to what was initially assumed, substantial psychological and physical health benefits occur for women and men' (p. 85) from a dual-career life-style, for it provides each partner with opportunities to develop new parts of themselves and establish a sense of themselves apart from their stereotyped gender role. Amongst dual-career couples she found higher levels of self-esteem and better overall health. She found that there are still three patterns of dual-career marriage: the traditional/conventional model, where the wife remains responsible for the home and the husband 'helps out'; the modern/participant model, where the parenting is shared but the wife manages the domestic scene and is responsible for housework; and the egalitarian role-sharing model where both partners are actively involved in all spheres.

Gilbert believes that this latter model 'best represents the pattern many couples strive for' (p. 87), but marital satisfaction with the pattern adopted depends on 'the degree of congruence and mutuality between partners, partners' perceptions of fairness ... and mutual spousal support and affirmation' (p. 89), as well as the support of external helps such as family-friendly employment policies, high quality child care and a supportive attitudinal environment. The ability of both partners to view dependency as a functional need, from time to time, for either of them, and a potential strength in the relationship is crucial. 'To be able to rely on others and have them rely on you is enhancing and empowering to partners and to the relationship' (p. 90).

Silberstein (1992), in another important recent work, studied twenty dual-career couples. Like Gilbert she views gender as a central issue for these couples and comments: 'Today dual-career marriages occupy centre stage in the drama of changing gender roles' (p. 2) for 'the dual-career marriage is, at its core, an attempt to redefine the relationship between work and family, the two primary spheres of modern life' (p. 3). She sees part of the task of dual-career marriages as undermining the 'myth of separate worlds' which has prevailed in thinking and theorizing about work and the family.

Silberstein was able to study these twenty couples in considerable depth. She found that 'the dual-career family structure represented a significant and profound departure from the families within which the women and men in the study grew up' (p. 17). Husbands and wives were both negatively influenced by the roles they had seen their parents adopt and they also experienced the ongoing effect of, in the case of the wives, their mothers living out *their* frustrated careers vicariously through them. Part of the process for these couples, in living out their dual-career marriage, was through the women identifying with the cross-gender parent, as well as accepting the discontinuities with the same-gender parent. Of the two spouses, the wife defies tradition more blatantly for what she is doing and goes against 'deeply ingrained beliefs and traditions' (p. 35). Silberstein found that a woman would revert to gender-stereotypical behaviour under pressure in order to reaffirm her sense of gender to herself and to others.

In terms of careers, the man's continued to be salient, so that on the whole, the wives were more junior in their occupations than the men. Nearly half the men but none of the women had highly specific goals for their work career that they would like to achieve. Both partners felt that the other helped them in the pursuance of their careers, although there was asymmetry between husbands and wives, with husbands finding they got more help than vice versa. Nevertheless, 'common interests and professional passions provide a bond between spouses and a way to integrate work and family' (p. 59). The need to manage home and work demands meant that neither could be as immersed in their career than if they had not had family demands. They also experienced difficulties over playing the supportive role to each other on public occasions because these often conflicted with the demands of the other spouse's job, but neither husbands nor wives felt that this had hindered their own career. Difficulties over job moves were felt keenly and it was in this area that the husband's automatic right to have his career put first came most under pressure.

Couples estimated that they spent half their talking time talking about work, and found that this was a means of staying connected with each other. It also allowed them to unwind and put a closure on the working day. There were differences in the *ways* in which each wanted to talk about work: the wives wanted to talk about interpersonal and emotional dimensions and the husbands about how to solve problems and offer advice.

Like Rice (1979), Silberstein found that competitive feelings were often denied. She comments on the difficulty that couples have in this area and suggests that whilst competition is acceptable in the work place it is apparently not acceptable in the family; that competition is more acceptable for men than for women and that neither has a model of cross-gender competition to draw on easily as a model. Particular difficulties were experienced when one partner's career was going better than the other's or when one was encountering particular difficulties in their work place. Factors which mitigated the effects of competition included close synchrony of career development, and conversely, wide differences, as well as a genuine desire for the happiness and well being of the partner. 'Success is desired for each spouse in order to increase the joint level of job satisfaction and hence marital and life satisfaction' (p. 78). However, 'If the woman is also successful, that is fine; but if she is successful *instead* of the man, that threatens a basic, deeply ingrained assumption' (p. 79).

Of particular interest for this study of joint clergy couples, Silberstein found that a third of the couples were in the same occupation. She found that 'dual-career couples who shared a field described many more benefits than the dual-career couples in different fields imagined. Spouses in the same field spoke frequently of the tremendous support and understanding that a fellow insider can provide.' Silberstein continues: 'Rather than viewing it primarily as a disadvantage to be in the same field, almost all spouses perceived their shared field to be an advantage. Some found it hard to imagine being married to someone in a different field' (p. 82). However, it may also be the case that these couples experience more comparison and competition with one another because of operating within the same career structure.

Many of the tensions for these couples were around the desire to be giving more to both home and career demands – there seemed to be a constant tug-of-war between the two. But a lot of tension also remained around the whole area of shared household work and 'whether husbands felt it was properly their sphere of activity and whether wives felt there was fairness in the division. Women usually remained "chief executives" in the domestic sphere which made true parity difficult.' There was also some ambivalence about making use of outside help. Couples almost always pointed to the need for 'more time and more slack in the system' (p. 126). Spillover from work to home was common, and this was variously experienced as cathartic, contaminating, influential (on methods of doing things at home) or intrusive. Less spillover was reported from home to work.

The arrival of children marked a significant turning point for the couple. Good child care was crucial, but even so it left half the couples feeling anxious and guilty as to whether the care of their children was adequate. Guilt was found still to be mainly a woman's issue. About half the couples felt that there were benefits for the children in having both parents contributing actively to the running of the home, setting the children a good example in terms of shared responsibilities and expanding, through child care arrangements, adult models for the children.

Couples felt that the effect of their dual-career life style on their marriage was mixed. The costs included there being too much to do, with always a tug-of-war between the world of work and the world of family. Lack of time together as a couple was cited as a cost by over half the group. Couples would tend to put their energy into not neglecting the children, but that left 'marital neglect as an unanticipated, even unnoticed result' (p. 146). Over three-quarters of both husbands and wives reported that their sex lives were impeded by work. Most commonly cited reasons were the way in which work precipitated fatigue, depression, emotional withdrawal, anxiety, hyperactivity, chronic stress, tiredness and staggered bedtimes. 'We need a wife' seemed a striking shorthand way of describing the sense of abandonment both partners feel as a result of moving away from the woman's traditional role and a sense of helplessness in finding satisfactory alternatives. However, there were many benefits too, especially the way in which each partner had an independent source of self-esteem. 'The spouses perceived that they benefited as a couple from the combined stimulation of each partner's work life' (p. 143) and the way in which each gained through the exchange of intellectual ideas, varied experiences and new people which both partners met through their work. The dual careers gave balance and equality to the relationship.

Silberstein viewed these marriages as representing a 'system in transition'. Even in the 1990s there is a 'striking lack of change in societal structures that might facilitate dual-career marriage' (p. 156). And she continues: 'As a result, the current generation of dual-career couples continues to feel it is blazing new trails rather than treading established new ones' (p. 157). On the other hand there had been some significant changes. Many couples now perceived the possibility of creating an egalitarian, role sharing relationship; dual-career couples feel less need to justify themselves and their life-style; and issues of comparison and competition are more openly acknowledged and discussed, reflecting a more equal acknowledgement of the status of the woman's career.

In many ways, the dual-career marriage encapsulates the problems and potential for creating workable solutions to the many social, relational, economic and ethical problems with which human beings are confronted at the end of this millennium. How to honour difference; how to share; how to integrate our inner self along its masculine and feminine dimensions; how to do justice to the demands of family and occupational need simultaneously; how to create a quality environment for one's own most intimate network but also for others and for the next generation as well. These are some of the primary questions which confront every dual-career couple. We should not therefore be surprised to find that these are also the issues with which the joint clergy couples in this study are struggling. They are confronted with all of these challenges in microcosm, in their day-to-day existence, for the joint clergy couple's life style brings together the private world of family and the public world of work in an exceptionally challenging way. It is to all of these essential matters that the joint clergy couple's life style is addressed.

5 WHAT MAKES MARRIAGES HAPPY?

Alice never could quite make out, in thinking it over afterwards, how it was that they began: all she remembers is, that they were running hand in hand.
Lewis Carroll, *Through the Looking Glass*

In trying to understand whether the ordination of women has affected clergy marriage for better or worse, research into marital satisfaction *per se* is clearly of interest and importance. It is from the pool of the many variables identified by researchers into this topic that the selection was made of five to use as yardsticks for comparing the three groups of clergy couples before and after the women's ordination. This chapter will therefore be devoted to establishing the credentials of the five variables selected, and discussing their usefulness for comparing the three different kinds of clergy marriage being investigated.

For the purposes of this study, five variables were selected for use in comparing the three clergy couple groups. Each has its own body of support in linking it with marital satisfaction. Religious affiliation, belief and practice have, in their own right, been associated for many years with higher levels of marital satisfaction, but because these are likely to be shared characteristics of the greater majority of *all* clergy marriages (and by definition of every joint clergy couple's relationship), this could obviously not be used as a measure with which to discriminate *between* the three clergy couple groups. However, since religious affiliation and practice have been shown to correlate so consistently with marital satisfaction, it is very likely to be one explanatory factor in the perceptions of marital satisfaction amongst these couples, and it may also help to account for the much lower incidence of marital breakdown amongst clergy couples.

One variable – similarity – was selected because of the enormous amount of interest it has attracted amongst quantitative researchers and because a substantial body of opinion has found that it correlates highly with marital satisfaction. Three variables, androgyny, mutuality and equity, were selected from the feminist approaches. Cohesion was selected as a central variable, routinely investigated in quantitative research into family functioning, and used as a fundamental criterion of family functioning.

Similarity

Similarity between marriage partners is viewed by most researchers as an extremely important variable in understanding the dimensions of marital satisfaction. Perceptions of 'being like' one's partner, or being 'homogamous', is an important factor in drawing couples together in the first place and it remains an important aid in the well-being of their relationship. Although many facets of being similar are important – including early family experience, educational attainment, occupation and leisure interests – similarity in attitudes, values and goals are most important of all.

Richard et al. (1989) comments that 'the concept of homogamy as opposed to complementarity has been supported by the majority of the literature' (p. 40). In other words the commonly held 'Jack Sprat' view of what makes marriages work is entirely erroneous! Recent research into similarity between marriage partners and its relationship with marital satisfaction has generally confirmed a high association between the two. Weisfeld et al. (1992) studied correlates of satisfaction in over 1,000 British marriages to see how far American research findings on marital satisfaction were upheld. Although several predictions from the American research were not confirmed, the data did support the homogamy principle. Moreover, the authors felt that their findings were suggestive of the continuing influence of homogamy during the whole course of the marriage relationship.

Three kinds of assessment are typically used in evaluating attitude similarity between marriage partners: *actual* interpersonal agreement independent of the spouses' perceptions of agreement; *perceived* agreement; and *degree of understanding* of each spouse of the other. *Perceptions* of similarity between marriage partners have consistently been found to be stronger predictors of marital well-being than *actual* similarity. The distinction between perceived and actual similarities in couple relationships is clearly an important one and most current research is strongly supportive of the relationship between perceived similarity and marital satisfaction.

Heaton and Pratt (1990) examined the effect of similarity of religious belief and commitment between partners on marital satisfaction and stability and found that similarity in denominational affiliation was highly correlated with marital satisfaction and, to a lesser degree, church attendance, whilst similarity of beliefs on doctrinal issues showed no statistical association. Craddock (1991) also used religious orientation along with marital roles in examining the relationship between attitudinal similarity and marital satisfaction and also found that similar religious orientation was associated with higher levels of satisfaction.

Craddock compared the relationship between attitudinal similarity (in terms of religious orientation and marital sex role attitudes) with the couple's relationship structure (in terms of cohesion and adaptability) and found that as well as a high correlation between similarity of religious orientation and marital satisfaction, similar attitudes towards marital sex roles were also related to higher levels of marital satisfaction. Craddock's study is of particular interest as he compares three of the key variables selected for this present study – similarity, equity and cohesion – and finds that they are all correlated with high levels of marital satisfaction.

Equity

Equity can be defined as the perception by both partners of an overall sense of justice and fairness within the marital relationship. It involves the belief and perception by each spouse that both partners have the same value as persons and should give and receive equivalent levels of emotional and practical input into the relationship. 'Equality' and 'egalitarian' are related terms and in practice they are often used interchangeably.

Scanzoni *et al.* (1989) describe two marital paradigms, based on different assumptions and value bases: the conventional and the equal partner marriage. The essential characteristics that differentiate the equal partner marriage is that everything is negotiable except the principle that everything is negotiable; decision-making is shared on the basis of achieving justice and care for both, and each partner is enabled to function effectively in the spheres of paid work outside the home and family work inside it.

The relationship of equity between partners to marital satisfaction has been the subject of a number of recent studies and the results support a correlation between the two. Pahl (1989) by inference showed a relationship between equity and marital satisfaction, by finding that male dominance over the control of money and decision-making is related to lower levels of marital satisfaction for both partners. Gottman and Levenson (1988) and Millar and Rogers (1988) both showed that in marriages where the wife dominates the verbal communication, marital satisfaction decreases for both partners. Pollock *et al.* (1990) found that egalitarian couples had better communication and Altrocchi and Crosby (1989) found that they invested more in trying to improve their relationship.

The increase in numbers of dual-career couples over the last decade has acted as a spur to examining the ideology and practice of equality. Nicola and Hawkes (1985) in their study of dual-career couples found that the husband's egalitarian attitudes and the wife's self-concept are related to one another and to the satisfaction of both partners in the marriage. Ray (1990) found that greater marital satisfaction was related to greater equality and reciprocity in relationships. Moreover, couples experiencing greater marital satisfaction were likely to both give and receive support from one another; to be involved in one another's careers and to practise equal decision-making.

An important contribution from the clinical literature in understanding the function of equality in the marital relationship has been made by Rabin (1996). The findings of her cross-cultural research into the belief and practice of equity within the marital relationship of a sample of American, British and Israeli couples confirms much of the previously cited work, as well as confirming the discrepancies between ideology and practice reported by many researchers. She comments: 'Many couples believe in equality while playing out sexist interactional patterns at home' (p. 7). The couple may have idealized and vague notions of equal partnership, but these often remain without a 'game plan' to bring them into effect. She makes the important distinction between 'being equal' and 'being the same', and comments: 'It is actually by understanding and honouring gendered differences that the drive to equality can become a beneficial force for couples' (p. 8).

As equity theorists have noted, it is the perception of fairness and justice in the relationship that is of paramount importance. From Rabin's research into this sample, three themes emerged from the couples' definitions of the way they understood equality to relate to marital satisfaction. The first was *equality* as *subjective appraisal* – each person is perceived as both contributing and securing their fair share. This does not have to mean a 50/50 split of doing the work and receiving the benefit: 'sharing is more embedded in a system of mutual trust that each partner will do their fair share' (p. 40).

Rabin uses the construct of friendship as that which best sums up a truly egalitarian marriage. She cites Brehm's (1985) description of three 'justice rules' that are commonly employed by couples to maintain fairness within the relationship: a half-and-half division; a proportional division (on the basis of whoever gives more gets more); and a division according to need, so that the changing needs of each partner for rest, recreation, affection etc. are accommodated within an overall understanding of equity. The second theme that emerged was *equality as equal power* whereby each partner feels equally able to influence decisions and make changes in the relationship. The third theme was that of *equality as sharing household and parenting tasks*. Couples who perceived their relationships as characterized by these three levels of sharing, perceived their marriage to be more equal and experienced high levels of marital satisfaction compared with couples who did not.

Mutuality

The term mutuality, or mutual empathy, as used in this study, is a term that has been adopted by the Stone school of feminist psychologists to describe a central construct of close interpersonal relationships. Genero *et al.* (1992) define mutuality as 'the bi-directional movement of feelings, thoughts, and activity between persons in relationships' (p. 36) and they go on to comment that 'mutuality involves a shared sense of relationship that transcends the immediate and reciprocal exchange of benefits' (p. 37). Empathy makes the development of mutuality possible and is an ingredient of it; the term mutuality, however, also encompasses other aspects of relationship – those which they call engagement, authenticity, empowerment, zest and diversity.

Genero *et al.* (1992) summarize the literature on the relationship of mutuality to the mental health and psychological well-being of individuals, including the way in which it facilitates intimacy; aids self-disclosure; contributes to emotional resilience and to the development of coping strategies. Genero *et al.* (1992) expected that mutuality would be associated with relationship satisfaction, cohesion and the giving and receiving of social support in a range of different relationships, including marital relationships since they view mutuality 'as encompassing diverse modes of social interaction that facilitate participation in and growth through relationships' (p. 37). Specifically, clinical observations suggested 'that participants are enhanced by mutual exchanges in at least five ways. Both participants experience an increased sense of *vitality* by virtue of feeling connected to one another; feel more able to take *action*; acquire an increased *knowledge of self* and the other; gain a greater sense of *self-worth* and validation; and desire more *connection with others* beyond the immediate interaction ... In relationships characterized by mutuality, both people experience growth through the relationship' (p. 37, italics added).

Androgyny

Androgyny can be defined as the combining of high and balanced levels of what have been labelled traditional masculine and traditional feminine qualities in one person. Following Bem (1974), the term is used to describe a sex type which demonstrates *high levels of masculinity and femininity*, as compared with *traditionally sex-typed persons* who demonstrate either high masculinity and low femininity or high femininity and low masculinity or *an undifferentiated person* of either sex who is low in both masculinity and femininity. The term has aroused considerable controversy within feminist circles, chiefly because it seems to suggest that certain personality or behavioural characteristics *are* either masculine or feminine. The descriptions are however used by Bem, and are used in this research, to describe the *generally accepted ways* in which American and British culture attributes masculine and feminine meaning to a range of behaviours. The fact of acknowledging the cultural validity of these attributions does not imply an acceptance of them, or of their desirability or of their factual validity. (For a discussion of these issues, see Bem (1993) and, more succinctly, Graham (1995).)

Notwithstanding the political and ideological reservations that have been expressed almost from the moment it was introduced by Bem, the concept of androgyny appears to be a very promising one in the discussion of marital satisfaction. Although as Baucom *et al.* (1990) point out, 'the investigation of sex-role identity and marital functioning is in its infancy' (p. 160), a number of studies show that sex role identity is correlated with high levels of marital satisfaction.

For example, Antill (1983) found that couples were happier if at least one partner was androgynous or feminine sex-typed. Peterson *et al.* (1990) tested 282 couples and found that 'among the nondistressed community sample, androgynous–androgynous was the most frequent type of couple pair and undifferentiated –undifferentiated couples were the least frequent. Conversely, among the couples seeking marital therapy, undifferentiated–undifferentiated was the most frequent couple type, whereas androgynous–androgynous was the least frequent' (p. 161). They found that higher levels of masculinity and femininity (i.e. androgyny), were consistently related for both genders to higher levels of marital functioning.

The gender identities of both partners have been found to be critical in determining the ability of spouses to sustain a marriage when the wife's attainments are greater. When both had androgynous gender identities, they were more likely to be comfortable about the disparity. Marsh and Byrne (1991) found that androgyny predicts increased mental health and marital satisfaction in both men and women. Rabin (1996) found that the 'happy equal relationships' amongst her sample of couples had 'managed to find a life style that allows them to combine the feminine and the masculine traits in a unique combination suitable to their personalities' (p. 81). And she goes on to suggest that 'both sexes require having both [masculinity and femininity], each being the "shadow" of the other. Neither is better' (p. 96).

In fact some studies suggest that femininity *is* better, in the sense that it is more highly correlated with behaviours that contribute to marital satisfaction for both partners, and may be the more powerful ingredient in the androgyny 'mix'. They suggest that femininity was positively correlated with positive communications and negatively correlated with negative communications. Sayers and Baucom (1989) confirmed the importance of femininity in marital communication. The fact that so-called feminine attributes are linked with behaviours most crucially required to service a relationship may be part of the explanation for this finding.

Baucom *et al.* (1990) comment on the major influence of sex role identity on marital functioning. Preliminary explanations for the consistent link found between androgyny and marital satisfaction to date include the following. Androgynous individuals have access to both masculine and feminine behaviours and therefore have a greater chance of being able to respond to a wider range of situations and challenges than a sex-typed or undifferentiated person. Moreover, the androgynous individual has more to give to the relationship – more masculine attributes and more feminine attributes and if *both* partners have more of both, the sum of available attributes on which the relationship can call is clearly significantly greater.

Baucom *et al.* (1990) suggest a clear link between androgyny and equity/egalitarianism. If both partners are androgynous, they have more equal contributions to offer as well as a greater range of behaviours at their disposal. They therefore have less need to use coercive control in decision-making which is clearly associated with lower ratings of marital quality.

Cohesion

Cohesion is defined by Moos and Moos (1986) as 'the degree of commitment, help and support family members provide for one another' (p. 2). Olson (1993) defines cohesion as 'the emotional bonding that family members have toward one another' as expressed in the keeping of boundaries and the making of time and space for friends, decision-making, interests and recreation (p. 105). Craddock (1991) suggests that it is 'a dimension which involves how close the partners [in a marriage or other relationship] feel to each other and how they balance being together as well as being apart' (p. 11).

A considerable amount of discussion has taken place recently as to whether cohesion should be viewed as defining an absolute family strength – the fundamental unity, warmth, and sense of belongingness that exists within a well-functioning family or between the partners in a marriage – or whether it is curvilinear in its association with health and pathology, representing a mid-point between enmeshment on the one hand and disengagement on the other. In fact both enmeshment (the symbiotic, emotional stuck-togetherness that can occur between couples) and disengagement (the drifting away from any real relationship between them at all) are inimical to establishing a strong cohesive relationship, and both describe very different relational dynamics from that of cohesion. These 'enemies' of a strong, cohesive relationship are particular vulnerabilities of clergy marriages and, as such, will be considered further in Chapter 7.

This is an important clarification in relation to identifying cohesion as a measure of marital satisfaction for this study, since it can only act as one if, like similarity, equity, mutuality and androgyny, it can be assumed that, for the optimal functioning of a marriage, the more of it the better. Several studies clearly reveal this association. Craddock (1991), for example, found that 'high levels of satisfaction were reported by couples who were highly cohesive' (p. 11). Likewise, Cluff, Hicks and Madsen (1994) found that high cohesion scores were associated with better family and marital functioning.

These five parameters of marital satisfaction have, as described in this chapter, been consistently correlated with marital satisfaction.

They have all been the focus of a considerable amount of empirical research, which has been replicated across a variety of different subject groups and in different settings. Taken together they provide a thorough means of evaluating the differences and similarities between the three groups of clergy couples being investigated in this study, in terms of their perceptions and experiences of their marriages.

6 THE CLERGY AS INDIVIDUALS

The entire clerical complement of the Diocese of Lincoln, so the new bishop Edward King was reliably informed, could be divided into three categories: those who had gone out of their minds; those who were about to go out of their minds; and those who had no minds to go out of.

Piers Brendon, *Hawker of Morwenstow*

On the one hand this study must attend to the huge and complex context in which joint clergy marriages are embedded. On the other lies the equally important microsystem of the individual personalities of the clergy themselves. For it is individuals that make up couples, just as it is the experience of being part of a couple that helps create and develop the personalities of its individual members. The male and female clergy who comprised the three groups of couples which were the subjects of this research, were, as individuals, affected by a range of factors, all of which interacted with their experience of marriage and influenced the degree to which they were able to achieve a cohesive, mutually empathic, egalitarian relationship with their partner. Their reasons for entering the ministry; the pattern of their ministerial development; the stresses that they experienced in the ministry; their individual personality characteristics and their gender role characteristics all affected their ability to form satisfying marital relationships. It is these concerns which are the focus of this chapter.

Reasons for entering the ministry

The external factors that contribute to a person's choice of the clerical profession today have probably not altered as radically as might at first appear, from the days when a conscientious student of Jane Austen's novels might quite easily predict which of her characters would become clergy. Clergy are still more likely to come (as was the case with the research samples in this study) from middle-class than from working-class families, be educated to college level, come from families where there is a religious culture and often where a parent or other close relative is themselves a clergyperson and they are still much more likely to be male. They are however likely to be older on entry to the ministry, to have already worked for some years in a secular job and to be eldest or only children in their families of origin.

Unconscious factors in the choice of a clerical identity are also likely to play an important part. Menges and Dittes (1965) suggested that the clergy role affords people the opportunity to be assertive and get close to others without being intimate. The professional persona, together with structured opportunities for relating to people in a stylized way through the pulpit, the confessional and regular pastoral contact all combine to provide a container for shy and introverted individuals. These factors *may* allow clergy to function reasonably or even very satisfactorily in a role which demands high levels of extroversion and contact with people, and which would otherwise be quite unmanageably stressful. This may therefore be an obvious reason why those individuals who are shy and introverted by nature are attracted to the role. However, the defensive potential of the clerical persona may not operate quite like this and may in fact create its own difficulties, as Francis and Rodger (1994) point out:

> Characteristically male clergy seem to possess the personality qualities directly opposite to those generally associated with the public and social profile of their occupation. Such incompatibility between personal preferences and public role expectations may lead to frustration, stress and sense of failure. Coping strategies developed to mediate between the requirements of the role and the personal difficulties in meeting the

expectations may lead to shaping a public persona unhealthily detached from authentic human responses. (p. 29)

If this is indeed the case, high levels of stress may be experienced as a result of this lack of congruence between personality and role, and the development of such a public persona may have a deleterious effect upon the individual's capacity to function well in his or her marriage.

Patterns of ministerial development in the 1990s

The pattern and expression of the clerical ministry have greatly changed over the years. This means that the developmental course of ministry for someone entering the ministry now, may be very different and may require different perspectives and create different pressures. The development of the individual's vocation obviously interacts very intimately with his or her passage through the human life-cycle and therefore with his or her psychological development, so that crises and opportunities that confront the individual in one sphere will have a critical bearing on the other. It also interacts powerfully with the individual's marriage. The way in which his or her entry into the ministry is handled and the stage in the marriage when it occurs may considerably assist or hinder the couple's experience of marital satisfaction.

Of particular importance for this study is the different way in which men and women come into ministry and the different ways in which their ministerial experiences unfold. In relation to the clergy who are the subjects of this study, there has also been a unique experience of entry into the priesthood for those women who were ordained priest in 1994. Because of the barrier to ordination that existed until so recently, the career paths of men and women have been distorted and unbalanced. This means that the lengths, types and contexts in which husbands and wives have exercised their ministries have inevitably been very different. This in turn is likely to have affected the life course of their marriages and impinge upon the way in which they live their family lives. Likewise, the different developmental paths that are taken by women and men towards achieving emotional and psychological maturity will, in turn, have their own inter-relationship with the timing, pace and expression of their ministerial vocations.

A minority of clergy still enter the priesthood in their early adult lives, and it is too early to say whether there will be gender differences in this regard. Those who do are likely to be embarking upon several role transitional experiences simultaneously, ordination, marriage and parenthood within a short time span. Such an experience has been normative for many men and women in a wide range of other jobs and professions, so that the juxtaposition of the stresses involved is well documented even though they may remain hard to handle. What is different for those entering the priesthood in their twenties or early thirties is that they are entering an organizational structure that is very 'flat bottomed' in its career prospects and, for most of its personnel, provides a working environment – that of parochial ministry – that may offer insufficient variety over perhaps a thirty to forty-year period of service.

Here we come up against the dilemma of whether the priesthood can or should be discussed in terms of a career. To avoid doing so however risks disillusionment and 'burn out' later. However deeply spiritual a person's sense of vocation to the priesthood, individuals will have aspirations to use all of their talents and to exercise their gifts in a variety of settings, and for some this will include the desire to use their talents for management and leadership on a wider stage, perhaps beyond the parish. Yet, in structural terms the openings and opportunities are few. And for women, they are likely to remain even fewer. Thus for many who enter the ministry in early adulthood, it will be important that they avoid denying or repressing these personal hopes and ambitions.

Many priests today enter the ministry during their mid-life. The reasons and motivation may be very mixed. The person may have felt the call into ministry at an earlier stage in their life, but felt unable to respond. On the other hand, the priesthood may offer a way out from an intolerable secular job, or as a means of coping with unemployment or redundancy. Such reasons can be extremely productive and growth promoting for the individual and for his or her personal and new ministerial relationships, but they need to be understood as part of what has formed his or her vocation.

For women entering the priesthood in their forties or fifties, there will have been those who have waited to do so for many years, having been employed as deacons in full-time ministerial jobs. Their entry into the priesthood may well have been experienced as a fulfilment of perhaps long years of ministry, but because it came at mid-life or later, may also have been accompanied by overwhelming feelings of loss and regret at 'what might have been' if this particular door had opened for them sooner. There may be the feeling that much needs to be crammed into the few remaining years, and this in turn will require negotiation, adjustments or even considerable re-organization within other aspects of their lives, including their personal relationships. Ray (1990) has drawn attention to some of the difficulties which may accompany the change from full-time family work to full-time work in the outside world, even when the latter is the fulfilment of a long cherished hope.

For those for whom ordination precedes marriage there is the clear expectation for both partners that their marriage will be lived out within the context of priesthood. For those where one or both discern their calling to the priesthood later, after perhaps many years of marriage, a major new variable is introduced into their relationship, creating change in the perception of the other at some deep level, as well as many practical differences in the way that their married life must now be lived. Some of these differences are likely to revolve around the novel experience of having one's partner around the house during the day, and coming and going from the home in an unfamiliar and unpredictable way so that familiar boundaries of time and territory are fractured. Some of the contributors to Brown's (1983) essays from clergy wives comment on their sense of invasion of territory and space – a space that became 'hers' each day in a different way while her husband was out at work in his secular job. Even when the wife was herself occupied in a full-time career, this major difference in their work patterns often created initial tension. A similar readjustment will have been required of the male partners of women priests. Women's entry into the priesthood has been, for the majority of those ordained in 1994, preceded by their marriage so that these major changes of perception and adjustment have, in almost every case, been required of their husbands.

For both men and women, the milestones in the development of their ministry will be experienced differently if they coincide with major changes in the life-cycle of their marriage. Some women for example, who have happened to be pregnant or given birth near the time of their priesting, may have found that the juxtaposition of ordination and pregnancy imbued both with added meaning, but it may have also created an emotional overload, diminishing both events by the level of stress incurred. There was of course a novelty about this particular juxtaposition of events during the ordination of the 'first wave' of women priests in 1994 – the idea of a priest 'giving birth' seemed to have (and does have) a potent symbolism. Some were able to mediate the two experiences in a way that facilitated their emotional integration and deepened the meaning of both. As its novelty subsides, this particular juxtaposition of events in the ministerial and family life-cycles may become increasingly fruitful in their inter-connectedness, and as Hebblethwaite (1984) suggests, bring new insights into the meaning of the priestly vocation.

A complex and unusual issue that has had to be faced by some male priests (and in some cases their wives as well) since the entry of women into the priesthood, has been how to handle their own strong opposition to this new development. At whatever stage this has come for them in their own priestly ministry, the issue has been extraordinarily painful, often releasing feelings of anger, outrage, depression and grief. For those who were moving towards retirement, it may have been possible to avail themselves of the Church's compensatory financial provisions. For some this may even have provided a welcome release from a long period of service.

For clergy at the beginning of their priestly ministries, however, it may have faced them with very hard choices between compromising their beliefs or continuing in their priesthood. This has been a particularly complicated decision for young married clergy or those in their thirties or forties who may have had children to support and many years of their priestly ministry still to exercise. The complete stepping out into the unknown, and in some cases leaving the Church of England with no certainty that their priesthoods would be accepted by other communions, has been the risky and uncertain path trodden by a small minority of priests.

Job satisfaction and job stress

In Chapter 4, we noted the well-documented relationship between satisfaction and fulfilment at work and satisfaction and fulfilment in marriage. Job stress inevitably has a negative effect upon a person's marital relationship and will seriously hamper a couple's ability to achieve a satisfying marriage. Stress levels amongst clergy at work and their causes are therefore important to consider. This has been a well researched area of study (Sanford, 1982; Coate, 1989; Horseman, 1990; Fletcher, 1990), and there are indeed particular pressures and stresses inherent in a clergy person's way of life that are to do with some of the practical aspects of how this life is organized. They will be discussed in more detail in the next chapter in relation to the literature on clergy marriage.

More important however are the more elusive and unconscious areas of a clergyperson's experience which relate to the symbolic meaning of the Church and to the clergy's role within it, a point that is supported by the research of Kirk and Leary (1994) into thirty-seven clergy couples, where the clergy person was in each case the husband. As their study points out, the Church appears to act as a symbol, drawing the projections and identifications, the hopes and fears of society in mysterious and irrational ways. The clergyperson becomes therefore the focus of these perceptions, projections and identifications. He or she is expected to hold, on behalf of others, their ideals of purity, goodness, care and concern, compassion and selflessness for a society which often experiences itself, as well as appearing actually to be, fearfully trapped in its own individualism, materialism, depression and despair. The Church, in the persons of its clergy, may then get recruited into 'conducting' these uncomfortable experiences to earth, by acting as a symbol of community in an alienating world. This feeds the attendant expectation that the Church's chief representatives, the clergy, will always be able to act with unwavering compassion, always extend an ever welcoming hand of friendship and acceptance, always offer an ever open door of fellowship, and an ever open purse of succour and relief.

Thus part of the stress experienced, either occasionally or continually by most clergy is the realization that they do not and cannot live up to these expectations. Coate (1989) identifies four sources of strain – the strain of caring, the strain of relating to God, the strain of proclaiming and the strain of 'being', and she explores these difficulties in some depth from the viewpoint of a psychoanalytic therapist. She describes the way in which the clergy must often painfully experience the gulf between what they know themselves to be and how far their own beliefs, commitment and ability to be either the symbol or the exemplar that others require of them fails to be enacted, or even how they fail to live out in some proximal way the message that they proclaim to others day by day and week by week. Moreover, as Coate points out, many clergy will feel that this inner conflict cannot be shared, even with one's spouse, and that there is an inherent contradiction in the powerful symbolic representative figure, of God and His Church, going himself to someone else for help. However much the Church has made efforts to erode this obstacle and to provide pastoral care and counselling, work consultancy and spiritual direction for its clergy, these phantasies remain powerful determinants in the clergy's experience, and routinely detract from their ability to seek help.

Self-esteem, so crucially important in the formation of a healthy personality, enabling the person to give of him- or herself within both personal and professional relationships, is nevertheless often hard for clergy to nurture, in part for the reasons described in the previous paragraph. Prior to entering the ministry, the clergyperson may, like many other people, have suffered a variety of experiences in childhood or later life which are inimicable to the development of healthy self-esteem. Additionally, it may be hard to distinguish appropriate ways of nurturing and affirming the self that do not lead to narcissism on the one hand or self-deprecation on the other. When a fundamental tenet of the Christian faith, which the clergy represent and teach, is the giving away of the self in costly, sacrificial love, and the following of a Leader whose chief characteristic was humble service, it is crucial that the clergy's own personality is rooted in confident and stable self-respect, and that at a deep level, the individual knows him- or herself to be a loved and accepted person in his or her own right. Blanton (1992) makes the important point that 'because those in the ministry have a tendency to be extremely other-oriented, they find it difficult at times to engage in healthy levels of self-affirmation and are extremely dependent on the affirmations of others' (p. 325).

THE CLERGY AS INDIVIDUALS

Coate (1989) discusses the way in which, without a sufficient and consistent level of self-affirmation, it becomes very difficult for clergy either to withstand the inevitable 'failure' experiences that are provoked by the unrealistic expectations of others, or to find appropriate means of self-reinforcement in a job with few external validators or objective measures of its intrinsic worth. Without it, the clergyperson may find the need to turn too frequently and too inappropriately to others for affirmation and approval, sometimes leading to the manipulation of the pastoral relationship. Even more difficult, the marriage may have to bear too great a burden for supplying the emotional food which builds confidence and self-respect.

Overlaid onto the work stress which exists for male clergy, are the particular difficulties that women clergy have experienced in the years leading up to their ordination and which they inevitably carry with them still, both because they are 'pioneers' in what is still a male occupation and because of what may have been felt to be powerful experiences of rejection. Issues that emerge, particularly for women, from the way in which sexuality and gender have been handled in the Church will be discussed in the next chapter.

If, as noted earlier in this chapter, the typical personality profile of the clergy is that of an introverted and intuitive individual, we may assume that anger will be a particularly difficult emotion to handle and that, when the personality has reached overload in terms of the 'strains of caring' and the 'strains of being', this will typically be turned inwards and be expressed in the form of depression. Neither anger nor depression are very easy emotions for the clergy person to handle and both emotions may get lodged, as a result, within the marriage in a very destructive way. As Coate (1989) points out: 'Christianity ... may have a strangely impeding role in recovery from depression. The genesis of depression often lies in some level of anger that has been denied or has not been able to be expressed ... anger is not an easy emotion for Christianity and the faith itself may actually get in the way of recovery' (p. 197).

Uniquely difficult, perhaps, for clergy both to experience and to express, are the unavoidable crises of faith that inevitably occur during the course of a lifetime, as a necessary part of the person's spiritual growth and development. But how does the professional representative of God and His Church, especially when s/he and the clergyperson's family are housed, paid and pensioned by them, admit to such experiences, let alone see their potential for growth, both personally and ministerially? As Coate (1989) points out, these practical difficulties which may 'put us out of a job and leave us without material security' are 'actually one very good reason why we may, albeit unconsciously, not allow them to rear their heads' (p. 115). But the guilt that they often induce at a deeper level of experience may be even more critically stressful.

Gender difference

An important factor, not taken account of by early studies of gender, is the recent entry of women into the clerical profession. Work has been done in both America and Britain during the last ten years on assessing whether there are significant differences in personality characteristics between male and female clergy. It is of course still the case that the overwhelming majority of clergy are male. (Figures given for the Church of England for 1995 in the *Church of England Year Book*, 1997, state that there were 9,440 male stipendiary clergy compared with 820 women. Many women priests are of course non-stipendiary, which increases the overall figure for women clergy, which was assessed more recently as being around 1,400 (NADAWM, 1996). But even allowing for these additions, the disparity remains, and is likely to remain very large for some time to come.) Even so, the increasing numbers of women now being ordained enables the variable of gender to be studied more systematically, so that some understanding can be gained of its effect upon both the ministry itself and on the personal and family lives of the clergy.

Because the degree to which couples exhibit androgyny – that particular mixture of so-called masculine and feminine characteristics – is so important in aiding marital satisfaction, the work done on the gender characteristics of clergy is of particular interest. Although Towler and Coxon (1979) found little difference between the personality profiles of male clergy and men in general, Ekhardt and Goldsmith (1984) found that male and female candidates for ministry were more similar to one another than were male and female graduate education students. They were also more similar to one another than they were to other college students. There were in fact no significant differences between men and women seminarians on measures of either masculinity or femininity. Male seminarians scored high on the need to give and receive nurturance, and lower on autonomy, whilst female seminarians scored higher on affiliation, dominance, exhibition, understanding and desirability and lower on the need to be aggressive and the need for change. They concluded that seminarians tended to be androgynous and convergent towards each other in personality types, and that there was no evidence from this sample to conclude that there are major differences between male and female clergy, either whilst in training or when they move into positions of church leadership.

A major investigation into the gender differences between male and female clergy and the implications of these for the Church's ministry has been conducted in Britain by Francis and his colleagues (1990, 1991, 1992, 1994) and, in general, they have come to different conclusions. Using the Eysenck Personality Questionnaire (EPQ) with 155 male and 97 female Anglican candidates, Francis (1991) showed that the clear sex differences in personality profiles consistently found in general population samples seem to be not only absent among samples of clergy but actually reversed. The EPQ, whilst not specifically a measure of sex role type, nevertheless measures related dimensions of personality.

Francis (1991) found for example that, in contrast to American studies cited above, male ordinands tend to be introverts. Women entering ministry on the other hand showed personality characteristics nearer to the norm for the male population in general – although Francis makes the important point that this result may reflect the peculiar conditions of conflict and tension experienced by women around the struggle for admission to the priesthood.

However, Francis (1992) describes a study of 92 male and 20 female clergy using the EPQ, and his findings confirm those from his earlier study of male and female ordinands. From his results he concluded that 'the correlations between sex and the three personality variables are totally consistent with the theory that male and female clergy do not reflect the clear sex differences in personality profiles consistently found in general population samples within the UK' (p. 35). He goes on: 'in the present sample there is no correlation between sex and neuroticism, contrary to the general finding that women score higher on neuroticism than men. Second, in the present sample there are significant positive correlations between sex and both extroversion and psychoticism, contrary to the general finding that men score higher on these two scales than women' (p. 35). In other words, he shows that the usual link between gender and both neuroticism, extroversion and psychoticism is not found amongst clergy. Instead, women clergy emerge as no more introverted than male clergy, and, at the same time, a *reverse* link is found between gender and both extroversion and psychoticism, whereby women clergy are found to be more tough-minded, more extroverted and more out-going than their male counterparts.

Thus, the work of Francis and his colleagues points to gender difference, but of a particular kind – male clergy appear to exhibit personality characterictics that are more commonly associated with feminine sexual stereotypes; whilst female clergy exhibit personality characteristics more commonly associated with what is considered to be stereotypically male. These conclusions are compelling as they rely upon empirical research, carried out recently and upon a British clergy population.

However Lehman (1993), in a more detailed American study, examined potential differences between masculine and feminine approaches to the ministry under the headings of interpersonal style, theology, career goals, thought forms, power, authority and ethics. His study is an attempt to test the assumptions of those who argue that women and men 'by nature' approach the ministry in radically different ways and that the arrival of women as full participants in the ordained ministry will have brought a new and different approach. These two different approaches are summarized as being the traditional 'masculine' approach, involving rationality, exclusivity, dominant leadership, status seeking, and an emphasis on legalism in morals and analytic thought. The 'feminine' approach is characterized by intuition, holistic thought, responsible ethics, egalitarianism, collaborative working relationships and inclusiveness.

Lehman examines two empirical questions: whether in fact these two different approaches to ministry, which cohere around two identifiable 'masculine' and 'feminine' types, can be shown to exist; and, second, whether male and female clergy actually differ in the way each type is empirically associated with the two genders. In other words, 'is there a demonstrable feminine style of ministry (in contrast to a masculine approach) among clergy, and do we in fact observe this orientation to ministry more among women than among men?' (p. 19).

Lehman found that only 16 per cent of the questions put to his sample of male and female clergy showed a statistically significant difference between male and female clergy's views of ministry, but they nevertheless reflected important areas associated with cultural feminism's views of gender difference. More men felt that they were essential to the proper administration of Holy Communion; uncomfortable when people shared personal feelings with them; rational and analytical in relation to congregational problems; viewed the appointment to a large church as a symbol of success; insisted that a correct position on ethical issues be preached; preferred programme efficacy over member involvement and rejected democratic decision-making for local church policy. Women ministers on the other hand defined themselves in terms of: dealing with difficult decisions in terms of 'gut' feelings; God working within them to render their work successful; and preferring a collaborative leadership style.

Several of his findings relate to the impact of the minister's family upon his or her ministry. Lehman found that male clergy, whose wives had little economic impact at home, because they were not working outside the home or were working in low prestige jobs, tended to carry their own pattern of 'being in charge' over into their dealings with the congregation and adopt a 'masculine' ministry style. On the other hand, those with wives in high prestige jobs, who had to share power and decision-making at home, tended to do likewise with their congregations. Similarly, women ministers whose husbands had no economic basis for power at home, and over whom they, as wives, tended to be dominant, took a similarly 'masculine' stance towards their ministry with their congregations. Conversely, 'women clergy with working husbands have some competition for power at home, where they then develop habits of consultation and co-operation that are also applied on the job, that is, in a more feminine approach to ministry' (p. 132).

Lehman found that 'the more recently a minister finished theological seminary, the more likely sex is to predict approach to ministry' (p. 137). There was an overall tendency for the ministry styles of male and female clergy to diverge in the more recently ordained. However, the divergence was in the opposite direction from that detected by Francis *et al.* (1990, 1991, 1992, 1994): male clergy were more masculine and female clergy were more feminine in their approach to ministry and thus no different in their sex-role characteristics from the general population.

These findings suggest that whether or not men and women differ in their approach to ministry depends on which aspect of ministry style one is considering; what type of minister one has in mind, when the minister was trained and in what context the ministry is being conducted. All of these variables intervened in such a way as to allow the data to reveal few overall differences, beyond those just noted, either between the ways in which male and female clergy conducted their ministries or between a predominantly 'masculine' or 'feminine' approach to ministry by either gender. However, one of the most significant intervening variables, in relation to the way in which ministry was conducted, was the presence of what Lehman terms a 'co-pastorate' arrangement, especially when the co-pastors were a married couple. The effects of this work pattern will be considered further in Chapter 8.

Studies of the differences in personality profiles between male and female clergy are obviously of great interest to a study of clergy marriages in general, and to this study of joint clergy marriages in particular. Both Francis's and Lehman's studies focus on the implications for the work situation, and they observe different results and come to different conclusions. But it is likely that the different personality profiles exhibited by male and female clergy, if indeed these exist, will have an important effect upon the marital system and will influence the way in which the marriage is experienced. If clergymen as a group and clergywomen as a group tend to exhibit personality characteristics different from the norm for their respective genders (either because they are more similar to the other gender or because both genders are more androgynous), this might be expected to have differential effects upon the three

by Carr (1989). Transitional objects enable the child to negotiate a gradual relationship with primary objects, by acting as an intermediary between the self and the real world, making the real world and relationships with real human beings less frightening and more manageable. Adults often need to regress to earlier, more infantile ways of coping in the face of stress or new external challenge, and often need the help of a transitional object (a cigarette being an obvious example for some people).

For those able to make use of the cognitive belief system of a religious framework and for the vast majority of others too, God seems to function as a transitional object in moments of crisis of varying degrees of extremity. Where family members share some degree of belief in God, they may construct a system of family myths in which God plays an important role in the ongoing development of their family history over time. As with all family myths (Ferreira, 1963; Byng-Hall, 1973, 1995), these may play an important part in sustaining the family through periods of dysequilibrium and be of great help in maintaining cohesion and stability in the face of external threat. Thus, viewed systemically, the couple's relationship with God performs the same function as any other family myth – it provides meaning and structure for understanding life events, promotes a sense of relational identity and defends the couple from being overwhelmed by unmanageable psychic material.

Sexuality, gender and Christianity

The way in which gender relationships have been structured within the Church has both reflected and guided the way in which gender has been understood within the secular world. Thus, issues of equality and power are as complex for those working within the institution of the Church as in every other sphere of social life and they significantly affect the way in which people approach and experience marriage. Male and female clergy are shaped in their understanding of gender relationships within both their personal and professional lives, by the way in which these have been construed by the Church throughout its history as well as by the ongoing effect of the Church's engagement with issues of gender and sexuality on a day-to-day basis. The couples described in Chapters 2, 11 and 12 reflect the importance and difficulty of gender issues for the clergy and the way in which these profoundly affect their experience of marriage and ministry.

For example, women inherit a tradition of ambiguity, disqualification and outright rejection which has been institutionalized in the structures of the Church, and in the way its sacred texts have been interpreted. The degree to which ordained women are able to function effectively within their work settings is highly determined by the way in which those they are working with are influenced by these stereotypes, because, as discussed in Chapter 4, the degree to which the individual gains affirmation in his/her work setting, enhances his/her perceived satisfaction in his/her marital relationship. This interconnectedness clearly has particular potency for all those clergy couples who can be described as dual-career couples, whether both work for the Church or not. It may have particular meaning for joint clergy couples where the interweaving of work and family, lived out within the same institutional framework, may be particularly intense.

The view of women as impure and imperfect undergirds in some fundamental way the two major objections to them being ordained as priests – the arguments of 'representation' and of 'headship'. If impure and imperfect they cannot reasonably represent Christ at the altar or act as leaders in His Church. Although these arguments did not in fact carry the day when the Church of England finally decided to open the priesthood to women, the painful expression of what lay behind them and the complex experiences of rejection, anger and guilt which ensued have needed to be managed by clergy couples in their ongoing life as marriage partners and priests. Again, the couples described in Chapters 2, 11 and 12 give expression to some of the feelings engendered by these experiences.

Profound questions for all clergy couples arise from the close juxtaposition of the sacred and the sexual at these unconscious and preconscious levels. But this is particularly true of clergy couples where the woman holds the priestly role because of the kind of unconscious projections made onto the role of priest which sit in contradiction to the unconscious projections onto femininity. The joint clergy couple, even more than couples where the woman only is ordained, may bring together these projections of the sacred and the sexual in a particularly unambiguous and perhaps shocking way. Many couples have spoken of the quip that was initially made in varying forms after the ordination of women as priests, around the idea of the 'vicar going to bed with the vicar'.

In addition to this unconscious material, clergymen and clergywomen are confronted, like others, by the many broad contemporary questions of what it means to be a man and what it means to be a woman. How are the images of male and female to be understood, experienced and lived out in the light of the many different understandings and views about gender and sexuality that exist and the serious tensions between them? How do those who minister as priests understand both their personal and their professional image of male or female persons and how do they bring these together in their marriage and their ministry?

Alongside the unconscious projections of others and the social imagery of male and female, both of which interconnect with clergy couples' experience of marriage and ministry, another important strand of gendered experience is that of parenthood. For many clergy, whether male or female, the concepts of 'fatherhood' and 'motherhood' as applied to their role as priest have to be reinterpreted in the light of what it means to 'father' and 'mother' in appropriate ways today, both physically and symbolically within the adjoining spheres of family and religious community. Even where the priest does not come from a Christian tradition that articulates the role of the priest in these terms, there are nevertheless underlying parental projections onto the figure of the priest which emerge from the necessary dependency invoked by religious activity and experience. As Carr (1989) has pointed out, part of the role of the priest, whether male or female, is to help others handle and manage this dependency in ways which allow growth to maturity to be achieved.

Since the advent of women priests, the question arises as to whether there are fundamental differences (and different potential psychological functions) between the imagery of 'fatherhood' and 'motherhood' when applied to the priest, arising from the different ways in which these roles are currently understood and constructed. If so, both male and female clergy are challenged by the developing understanding of these differences and they are further confronted by their reciprocal influence upon the functioning of the familial roles from which they are derived.

Sources of stress in clergy marriages

The traditional marriage of a clergyman to a non-ordained woman and some of the pressures upon it have been well described (Rogers, 1991; Mickey *et al.*, 1991; Lee, 1988; Horsman, 1989; Frame and Shehan, 1994; Morris and Blanton, 1994; Winchester, 1997). Writing in the late 1990s, it is possible to discern more clearly the even greater pressures and stresses that affect *all* clergy marriages at the present time. The continuing erosion of shared belief within society; the fact that much advertising material makes use of religious motifs for its own different purposes and the confusing messages that this gives; the severe internal conflicts within the Church over issues of sexuality and the threats of division and secession which they pose; the challenge to modernize the Church's structures without compromising its task to purvey eternal and unchanging truths; fears and uncertainties generated by falling rolls, depleted finances and competing faiths and ideologies – all of these create real challenges to those who are charged with leading and guiding the Church at the end of the millennium and have an inevitable spillover effect upon their marriages.

Winchester (1997) makes the important fundamental point that 'The opportunities and challenges inherent in being both married and also a minister are so great that it is not surprising that each "estate" – marriage and ordained ministry – is felt to make a "total" claim; and that it may feel intolerable to be attempting to live out two "total claims" simultaneously' (p. 6). It is this bringing together of the two covenants of marriage and ministry – made doubly powerful for those couples who can be described as 'joint' clergy couples – from which many of the more detailed areas of stress arise.

These detailed areas include symbolic and psychological factors as well as very practical and quite mundane ones. Some of the characteristics and peculiarities of being a clergyperson, described in the previous chapter, are so much part of the fabric of the occupation that they also become part of the way in which the general characteristics of clergy marriage are identified. Thus, the fact that the clergyperson lives amongst the people he or she serves; that the vicarage is the property of the Church, which may have quite stringent regulations about what can and cannot be done to it and the fact that it is usually to some extent at least both office/pastoral centre as well as family home are all powerful facts in determining some of the general characteristics of clergy marriage.

Obviously it is also true for many other people in today's changed economic situation that the work place is the home, but the nature of the clerical task is such that it is often peculiarly difficult to separate the two. When for example is a parishioner a friend making a social call, or part of the clergyperson's work situation making a demand on his or her time? More importantly in relation to the internal dynamics of the family, when is father (or if the clergyperson is the woman, mother) present and 'available' as a parent and spouse, and when is s/he emotionally absent even though physically present in the home? These issues will be considered in more detail later in this chapter.

Morris and Blanton (1994) identified five primary stressors upon clergy couples: mobility; poor financial compensation; unrealistic expectations from others and fluid time demands; unclear boundaries between family and work and lack of social support, and they concluded that clergy couples experience stress from all of these factors. Coate (1989) comments that a clergy family 'has to live as if it was in a bubble, encapsulated by its community and watched by it' (p. 188). Thus for anyone marrying a clergyman, it is a choice of living out one's marriage and family life in the public domain.

What people expect of their priest and his or her family is often very different from what they expect of themselves, whether or not they belong to the same faith community. Yet the stresses imposed by these expectations are often largely hidden from the outside world. This may create an intense sense of isolation and unreality for the couple and cut them off from potential sources of help and support.

Many clergy have to experience chronic hostility from their congregations, creating levels of stress and anxiety which are inevitably transferred to the home. The depletion of emotional energy is often severe, with little zest or vitality available for the marriage or for family life. The partner, on the other hand, may experience a painful sense of protectiveness towards their embattled spouse and, because they are often present at meetings or services where their partner is struggling to survive, he or she may have to contend with a flood of mixed emotion as they witness only too vividly their partner's weaknesses, as well as the injustice of the attacks that have been mounted against him or her.

Women who choose to marry clergy may well be making their choice based on some ideals that have been projected onto the clergyman and are longed for and sought, but are not yet achieved in the self. Whilst this is true to some extent of every marriage, the symbolic nature of the clergy role is likely to attract these projections from a partner or would-be partner in a particularly powerful way. Kirk and Leary (1994) make the further important point that, based on their qualitative research with thirty-seven couples, 'clergy for whom the ministry was their first career choice, select their spouses more for the qualities which will enable and facilitate their ministry than for their own personalities' (p. 43). Other complex dynamics may exist for women who have become priests many years after their marriage took place, in trying to deal, on an unconscious level with the threat that the change in their identity may pose to their husband. In this case, the fact that the woman was *not* a priest when the couple were married, may have been an important ingredient in the original partner choice.

Thus for clergy, the passage through the second part of the marital life-cycle described in Chapter 4, when idealization must give way to reality, has an added layer of complexity to it. Each partner must try to sort out whether they have chosen and been chosen by their partner more for their professional than for their personal qualities – and what they feel about that. Whatever idealized expectations that have been held, after the marriage has taken place the ideal can obviously never be fully realized, but the disappointment and frustration has to be lived out to some extent 'in public'. Moreover, as Coate (1989) points out, 'ministers' families have additionally to represent and exemplify the religious tradition for those to whom they minister' (p. 189) and nowhere is this expectation more strongly held than in relation to the way in which the minister conducts his marriage, in good times and in bad.

A further factor which particularly (though not exclusively) characterizes clergy marriages, is the degree of intimacy and confidentiality that must be achieved in relationship to those to whom the clergyperson ministers. How much can work relationships be shared with the partner without breaching confidentiality? And what is the effect upon the marriage if one or both partners need, as part of being effective in their ministry, to create warm, empathic relationships with a range of other people, to the exclusion of their spouse?

This is obviously an important issue for therapists and counsellors too, but again the immediacy, the shared relationship, the all-enveloping experience of living amongst those with whom one's partner is engaged in helping in a wide variety of ways, make the dilemmas about intimacy and shared information much more difficult to resolve. It is one thing to tell or be told about some anonymous person's difficulties; it is quite another for such sharing to take place when the persons concerned are known to the partner and he or she is in some kind of social relationship with them. In a similar way, it is often quite difficult for the clergyperson to discern the right level of appropriate intimacy that will enable important, therapeutic sharing to take place in the work setting without transgressing or challenging the boundary around his or her own intimate domestic life.

The occasions and opportunities for rivalry and competitiveness between the clergy partner and the parish are frequent and powerful and may produce the need to act out the pain irrationally and to regress in quite primitive ways in day-to-day relationships with parishioners. As well as the examples already described, the fact that the home often doubles as an office means that administrators, secretaries and other colleagues may often spend long hours closeted with the clergyperson in the family home, producing a sense of invasion and threat for the partner and children, and inviting the gradual transgression of boundaries in the professional relationship. The fact that the working relationship has been imported into the intimate arena of the home can 'set the scene' for those who should be relating to one another professionally, encouraging them to act out the relationship 'as though' it is personal.

To this needs to be added the more elusive and complex ambiguity which arises from the symbolic role carried by the clergyperson and its meaning within the marriage. The powerful inter-relationship between the sacred symbol and the sexual partnership is perhaps the most complex and potentially stressful aspect of the unconscious material operating within a clergy marriage. Coate (1989) comments: 'I do not think we pay enough attention to the complications on a deep level, of relating to someone in the family set-up at one moment and at the altar the next. It is possible that sometimes the human dimension gets obscured, making ordinary family relationships and perhaps particularly a couple's sexual relationship subject to strange distortion and more than a hint of unreality' (p. 190). Mace and Mace (1980) found around one in five couples in their sample had sexual difficulties some of which seemed to connect with this double-edged relationship. Bearing in mind the significant interconnection of sexual and spiritual experiences (Thatcher, 1993), this is hardly surprising.

Kilpatrick (1994) offers a way of understanding these issues through an anthropological interpretation of blood sacrifice. She talks of 'parallel symbolism' – the way in which the symbolic functions of priesthood were (until 1994) exercised exclusively by men through the medium of the symbolic blood of the Eucharist. This life-giving symbol has its own relationship with the life-giving blood of menstruation and birth, both of which remain essentially and unambiguously female. Part of the struggle over the admission of women to priesthood – sometimes articulated quite explicitly in the debates – was around the rivalrous possession by the genders of this birth/blood symbolism. How then is this 'birthing' experienced within the marriage relationship of a clergy couple, where symbolism and reality must be repeatedly reinterpreted, worked through, lived and understood?

The Eucharist – marked out as the central symbolic act of priesthood – is also a highly sexualized act. It is an intimate and private experience and yet undertaken in a public place often amongst strangers. Thatcher (1993) is bold enough to claim that there is a direct parallel between the words 'This is my Body/Blood' spoken by the representative figure of the priest and the offer of one lover to another of his/her body in the sexual act. The clergy partner sees his/her spouse and lover regularly share him or herself with others in this highly intimate way. Yet s/he hopes to retain with him or her a unique intimacy through their sexual relationship. Again, s/he engages in one kind of intimacy with her partner at the altar and another, parallel kind, in bed. Is it perhaps the close juxtaposition of these symbols that is responsible for not only creating great complexity within clergy marriages, but also encouraging the transgression of sexual boundaries by clergy with people with whom they develop very close liturgical/spiritual relationships?

When this happens, it is not so much perhaps the fact that clergy *confuse* sexual with spiritual intimacy, as is sometimes suggested (Goodling and Smith, 1983; Sandholm, 1989), but that, because of the parallel symbolism between the two, sexual intimacy and spiritual intimacy are to all intents and purposes *the same thing*. This is an area of exploration that is of great potential importance to the well-being of clergy marriage in general and of profound importance too in developing effective prophylactic measures against clergy marriage breakdown. Moreover, these issues may hold particular importance for understanding the dynamics of joint clergy couples and in assisting them with those issues that are unique to them.

The dynamics of clergy marriage

Since the mid-1980s, there have been a number of studies published which have examined clergy marriages empirically, as well as those such as Friedman (1985) which have applied some of the fundamental principles of family theory to the study of clergy family life. This literature has applied work from the general literature on family dynamics, to understanding the specific dynamics of the marriages and family life of the clergy. This enables us to go beyond what are often purely descriptive studies of some of the more obvious features of clergy family life, and try to examine *how* these dynamics actually work.

Three closely interrelated and somewhat overlapping concepts – family boundaries, enmeshment/disengagement and triangulation – have recently received particular focus, through the work of Whybrew (1984), Friedman (1985), Lee (1988, 1995) and others. In relation to the extent to which clergy marriages are able to exhibit high levels of the five variables correlated with marital satisfaction

– similarity, equality, mutuality, androgyny and cohesion – difficulties experienced in relation to these three major areas are likely to be critical.

Boundaries

The psychological boundary around a family or a marriage needs to be permeable without being either rigid and excluding or, on the other hand, diffuse and unable to retain the identity of the couple or family intact. Because of the close identification of family and work in clergy families, boundary problems can be particularly difficult to handle and negotiate. Researchers have discussed two particular problems that may arise – those of intrusiveness (Lee, 1988, 1995; Morris and Blanton, 1994) and boundary ambiguity (Lee, 1995).

The first of these is the most obvious and relates to the difficulty that is very generally experienced by clergy families in maintaining a semi-permeable boundary. The boundary around the marriage and the family is often too diffuse, allowing what may be almost free passage between the family and the outside world. Parishioners may cook in the family kitchen; use rooms in the vicarage for meetings, Sunday school, play groups etc.; people come and go without ringing the door bell; the 'phone gets answered by whoever happens to be passing it at the time. Morris and Blanton (1994) found that this kind of intrusiveness had a deleterious effect upon both marital and parental satisfaction. They comment upon the 'overall sense of disruption and chaos clergy persons feel when their entire world is openly transparent and on display' (p. 194).

Lee (1995) links intrusiveness with Boss's (1977, 1986) concept of boundary ambiguity which identifies the ways in which the psychological absence of a family member, even though physically present, leads to incongruence and consequent confusion on the part of other family members. Since the psychological absence is in itself stressful, both that and the behavioural incongruence are important factors to be considered. Because the majority of clergy work from their home, clergy couples are usually considerably affected by boundary ambiguity in the sense that it is often very unclear as to whether or not the clergy partner is emotionally present for his/her partner and for his/her children or not. The ambiguous nature of what does and what does not constitute work; which people are 'clients' in that they participate in a work rather than a non-work relationship with the clergyperson, and the overlap of working activities and family activities within the confines of the family home, all contribute to boundary ambiguity.

Although not unique to clergy families, the ambiguous nature of the boundary between work and non-work is clearly very different here from someone who 'goes out' to work and 'comes home' from another place, having been engaging with different people in the different activity of 'work' as compared with 'leisure', 'time off' and/or 'family time'. The effect of these ambiguities may be to deprive both the family and the work setting of the benefit of the full engagement of the clergy person and to increase the clergy person's sense of stress and guilt in whichever aspect of his life s/he feels him- or herself to be currently engaged.

Enmeshment/disengagement

A continuum which runs between enmeshment at one end and disengagement at the other, can be used to describe degrees of closeness and distance in a relationship. Either extreme is likely to lead to marital dysfunction, conflict and/or breakdown. In looking at the particular issues that are faced by clergy marriages, both enmeshment and disengagement create particular difficulties. Enmeshment may be expressed through the particular dynamics of the 'two-person career' type marriage described by Papanek (1973) and involving what Finch (1983) has described as incorporation. This will pose a particular threat to those traditional clergy marriages where the wife receives her status, role and many of her day-to-day tasks and functions through sharing in her husband's ministry as a 'clergy wife'. The correlation between the ordained role and its symbolic power discussed earlier, is likely to be significant enough in itself to create an inherent imbalance in the relationship, leading to a fundamental asymmetry which predisposes the non-ordained person to being incorporated into the role of her partner, unless she is able to redress this situation by developing a strong personal and occupational identity of her own.

Despite the many changes that have taken place in the way that the wives of clergy view their role, incorporation within a clergy marriage means that many clergy wives still function as an unpaid curate, excluded from structural power but often exercising latent control over large areas of parish business, and in a way which can never be challenged. This may produce anger and hostility on the part of the congregation, which appears to be unwarranted and irrational to the clergy wife. For her part she may feel exploited and unrecognized, whilst the congregation feels manipulated and controlled.

Within the marital relationship, the wife may take her revenge for her powerless position by being either domineering, manipulative or symptomatic. Alan Bennett's *Bed among the Lentils* and many other examples from fiction provide eloquent illustrations of these processes. Alternatively she may feel progressively more disabled by the projections of other people and by her inability to function in an equally autonomous way or in a way which allows the marriage to foster interdependence between the partners.

Clergy wives have often struggled to position themselves within their marriages and within the influence of their husband's ministry at different places. Many have successfully found an emotionally comfortable place for themselves within their marriages on this continuum between enmeshment and disengagement, often with the help of their own career. Nevertheless, the 'clergy wife', when the term is used in this restricted sense, remains a problematic figure, as Brown (1983) and others have discussed. There may be significant secondary gains for her in being incorporated into her husband's identity, in terms of recognition and a sense of usefulness, affording her power without responsibility. But incorporation inevitably leads to enmeshment and overdependency and often to the anger and depression that is contingent upon the loss of one's own personhood.

In a very different way, the joint clergy couple, where both partners work together in the same parish or other sphere of ministry, may be prone to the same dysfunctional dynamic. In this case, the couple may have achieved an equal association to the ministry, each in his and her own right, but may still be enmeshed, either through overdependency on each other, or because of a lack of external input needed to create the essential space and difference which allows the relationship to flourish and grow, or through the more complex need to be equal and 'the same', rather than being able to grow in intimacy and differentiation simultaneously. Moreover, the dynamic of incorporation may still operate powerfully for couples who are working in the same sphere of ministry and yet have different status – where the husband is vicar for example and the wife an unpaid and subordinate curate within the clergy team.

On the other hand, clergy marriage may be prone to disengagement through the distance created by such an all-absorbing activity as the ordained ministry. The very long hours, and an ethic of constant availability can create a chasm of space between the partners which becomes progressively more difficult for them to negotiate and close. Perhaps the most frequent cry that comes from a clergy spouse is the one which relates to their sense of abandonment by their partner, who must always, it seems, put the needs of others before the needs of his or her husband or wife. There is often a very real dilemma here for the clergy partner, who, whilst wanting to exert a greater claim on their spouse's attention and time, nevertheless feels inhibited from entering into competition with 'God'.

On the other hand, it may be that the *wives* of clergymen who have wanted to resist the dilemmas of enmeshment and incorporation, may find that they have encouraged their marriages to become too disengaged through the strategies they have adopted. The wife's career and other outside interests may, like her clergy husband's, create too great a distance between them for intimacy to flourish. Thus in trying to solve one dilemma, the marriage may be exposed to its opposite.

Disengagement may also be a more likely difficulty for couples where the woman is ordained but the husband is not. This is because it may be easier for a male spouse to resist incorporation than a female one for two reasons. First, there is no role model into which the male spouse is automatically inducted. Second, the husband may be more likely to have developed his own career and to have gained a professional identity of his own, wholly separate from his wife. On the other hand, the asymmetry between clergy wife and non-clergy husband may lead to disengagement. Far from being incorporated into his wife's role, the husband may compensate for his wife's long hours at work and its absorbing nature, by engaging in a parallel increase in his own work commitments, or by finding other interests, including sexual ones, or by decompensating and becoming depressed.

Triangulation

Friedman (1985) has made a thoroughgoing study of the relationship between the three interlocking systems of the clergyperson, the family and the congregation. His seminal work has highlighted the particular difficulties which clergy and their families experience in differentiating themselves emotionally in such a way that they do not succumb to or act out the projections placed on them by others. One reason for the difficulties is the close physical and emotional juxtaposition between work and family, described earlier. As Friedman confirms, 'for clergy, more than for any other professional, work and family systems play all too easily into one another and significant changes in either system may be quicker to unbalance the other' (Friedman, 1985, p. 279).

Friedman argues the relevance of triangulation in understanding the particular difficulties experienced by clergy couples and families in the way that they handle conflict (pp. 36–9). This defensive process, whereby a third party is pulled in to the couple's relationship, to deflect or try to solve its problems, has the effect of hampering the problem-solving efforts of the pair in conflict; creating inappropriate closeness between one member of the pair and the outsider; creating a confused relationship between the other member and the outsider; and disabling the outsider from fulfilling other appropriate roles in the relationship.

For some couples what is triangled into the relationship is not so much another person, but a personal need. The aspiration of the wife for her own career or for a ministry in her own right, for example, may arise out of her increasing frustration with her marriage and may be experienced as a threat to the marriage by her husband. This aspiration may form the third point of the triangle and be used by the partners to create further distance and difficulty between them. Alternatively, often with the help of a counsellor or friend, they may be able to use the threat posed by this new factor to help them face up to the difficulties in their relationship for the first time, with very beneficial results.

Whybrew (1984) has also applied this thinking to the particular triangle formed by the clergyperson, the spouse and the congregation whereby each point in the triangle is viewed as capable of unhelpfully deflecting or detouring conflict between the other two. The Church's influence (as the third party) on the clergy marriage may come from its demands, explicit or implicit, for the clergy couple to model an exemplary marriage in fulfilment of the ordinances of the Church and on behalf of its members. Part of the reason why clergy marriage breakdown often receives such a sensationalized and unsympathetic response, is because of the disappointed idealism with which it has been invested. The Church may also make it difficult for the couple to get help for similar reasons. Thus, the Church tends to put its clergy in the position of 'modelling the final results of functional married life while hiding all the behaviours which would show how to get there' (Whybrew, 1984).

Either the clergyperson or the partner may make an alliance with the congregation against the partner or join together to create a coalition against the congregation, using it as the common enemy to hold the marriage together. The clergy spouse, particularly when it is the wife, is the least well defined member of the triangle and she may need particular help in differentiating herself, so that she can make a relationship with the congregation on her own terms and in her own right. The congregation too needs to engage with the spouse as a person in his or her own right, not as a role, and the clergyperson needs to avoid being the point of exchange through which they relate. When the clergyperson and the congregation are in conflict, each may seek to draw the clergy spouse onto their 'side' of the conflict. There may well be secondary gains for the spouse in participating in the conflict in this way, for in so doing, s/he may either regain his or her partner by the alliance, or, alternatively, punish the partner by siding with the Church.

The arrival of women priests has increased the numbers of women working alongside a male clergy colleague and so inevitably forming a triangular relationship of some kind with him and his wife. This may open up a whole range of fruitful opportunities for identification and growth for the non-ordained clergy wife. In a postal survey of clergy wives in one diocese, several spoke of their delight in this new development and several more of their disappointment that what they had anticipated in the way of a new empathic friendship, with someone similarly distinguished within the parish in terms of her role, had not in fact materialized.

Alternatively, this new kind of triangular relationship may pose a particularly sharp and rivalrous threat to the marriage, because of the many ways in which the male and female priest-colleagues may be drawn into a relationship whose boundaries (as described above) are diffuse and ambiguous. Without openness, care and commonsense, the relationship between the male and female priest-colleagues can quite easily and rapidly gather a momentum of its own, fuelled by the mutual attraction of their shared vocation. The woman colleague's husband, if she has one, may act as an important brake on such a development, particularly perhaps if he too is ordained, and so can the ordained wife. However, this presumes that s/he is not also participating in a collusive *folie à quatre*, disabling them from standing outside the situation or from intervening to put it into reverse. The arrival of women priests within clergy teams and within colleague relationships may require particular sensitivity and vigilance in terms of its effects upon all the marriage relationships involved.

Triangulation is by no means necessarily a dysfunctional process. It may in fact be a useful balancing mechanism for the inherent instability of the pair. Seen in this way, there is every reason to expect that the couple's relationship with the congregation, their clergy role, their religious belief and with God Himself can all be functional, and serve as a means of developing and promoting the marriage relationship, rather than being intrinsically competitive and destabilizing to it. Each of these 'third points', creating as they do a triangular relationship with the couple, can serve to unite the partners at a more profound level and lead them towards greater integrity and shared commitment to the marriage.

8 JOINT CLERGY COUPLES

Let there be spaces in your togetherness.
Kahlil Gibran, *The Prophet*

Because of the novelty of their situation, this research study focuses primarily upon a small group of joint clergy couples, in the hope that it may be possible to examine the characteristics of this population in some depth and to identify some predictors for the ways in which the marital relationship of joint clergy couples may be affected by the fact that both partners are now ordained as priests.

As well as being an unresearched group, joint clergy couples are of particular interest because they are assumed to pose problems for the institution in which they serve. Several American studies have investigated this population. Kieren and Munro (1988), using a very small sample of seven dual clergy couples in the Lutheran Church, contended that whilst representing a new and exciting possibility for collaborative ministry, 'the personal cost of such ministry is very high' (p. 248). Rayburn (1991) found that, compared to clergy married to non-clergy spouses, joint clergy couples experienced significantly more stress from role ambiguity, role insufficiency, role overload and responsibility. Oswald (1985) on the other hand concluded that, given that being a joint clergy couple in professional ministry means being on the frontier of new developments within the Church, the couples in his study appeared 'to be doing well with both the burden and the successes of this form of ministry' (p. 1).

Mace and Mace (1984) commenting on the Churches in the United States in the 1980s remarked: 'the concept of the two-clergy marriage and all its implications for joint professional employment has left some church officials stunned and bewildered' (p. ix). Earlier Mace and Mace (1980) had made the following interesting observations: 'This new form of ministry can pose some knotty problems for the denominations, for the Churches they serve and for the partners themselves. Yet, ideally, this could be for many couples a completely satisfying form of shared ministry, which sweeps away all the inequities and injustices of the past. It would truly represent "companionship marriage" in action at the highest level of united service to others ... We would urge that its newness should not be a ground for prejudice or cynicism.'

In England, various official publications have commented on the practical difficulties of employing joint couples and some hint at the potential problems that may ensue for their marriage. Prior to the ordination of women as priests, but in anticipation of their ordination as deacons, the Joint Ministries Consultation Report (ACCM, 1984) stated bravely that jointly ordained couples 'should not be regarded so much as a problem to be solved as an opportunity to be grasped'. It also sets out a list of the advantages that accrue to joint couples and to the Church (pp. 8–10). But these are matched by an equal number of disadvantages and the document provides ample evidence in its case studies of the practical difficulties which were in practice being experienced by joint couples. One of these was the way in which some dioceses expected joint couples to receive only one stipend and the report itself concedes the need for couples to accept less than full remuneration for two posts when filled by a married couple. It also hints at the way in which 'marital problems may damage each partner's ministry and vice versa'; how 'children may suffer if both parents are ministerial workaholics' and how professional jealousy and competitiveness may undermine the marriage.

In fact much of the intention and tone of this report was positive but two years later a further report (ACCM, 1986) made it clear that in practice many of the concerns which had been identified were still unresolved regarding payment and deployment and that this leaflet was 'designed to aid discussion by throwing light on problematic areas'. It goes on: 'those engaged in joint ministries are likely to experience special difficulties in the course of their working and family life because of the unusual and pioneering nature of their situation'. The tone of the paper is sombre; the sense that joint ministry is problematic prevails.

Moreover, there is little sense in either report that major structural concerns of gender, power, authority, discriminatory practices or ineffective management might need to be addressed, nor any reference to the long and complex history of women's position in the Church or how this might affect both marriage, ministry and the relationship between them. Rather, these reports are acontextual in their approach and emphasis. The challenge posed by joint couples seems to have been framed in terms of how they might best be *fitted in* to the existing institutional culture, structures, expectations and requirements being made of its ministers by the Church. There seemed to be no concept that this new form of professional ministry might have some unique features which could be explored with as open a mind as possible, from the perspective of the underlying theological constructs of marriage and priesthood and in order to reap its potential benefits.

As was noted in the previous chapter, one of the peculiar characteristics of the Church as an institution and thus as an employing body, is the close intertwining of personal and professional issues. Hence the marriages of its employees are not simply a personal matter since the Church professes a strong ideological commitment to marriage as an institution and its clergy are therefore expected to demonstrate their commitment to the Church's teaching by the exemplary manner of their personal lives. These assumptions are enshrined in the Church's official publications. For example, in the report of the Joint Ministries Consultation set up in 1983, the first official recognition of the phenomenon of joint couples in ministry is made and the writers comment: 'Patterns of ministry are symbols, visual statements expressing what the Church believes about Christian community. Joint ministry expresses in a special way both the complexity of women and men ... and also the shared nature of Christian ministry (ordained and lay) which challenges old hierarchical patterns' (ACCM, 1984, p. 5).

This intertwining of the personal and the professional and the setting of very high standards for both leads to considerable difficulties in establishing or maintaining any clear boundaries between the two. Unlike the way in which these matters might be considered within other work contexts, clergy couples in general and joint clergy couples in particular cannot so easily claim that their private lives should be exempt from questions about domestic issues or that, when they are interviewed for jobs, preferment or promotion, inappropriate questions about their domestic responsibilities should not form part of the interview.

The report *Deacons Now* (ACCM, 1991) reviewed the situation relating to women and ordained ministry. It also included a section on joint ministry (pp. 54–9). It identified 159 joint clergy couples, representing 16 per cent of all women who were ordained as deacons. It noted several concerns in relation to joint couples: first, that 'the couple need separate ministerial identities'; second, that the marriage might be 'swamped' if the couples share a common sphere of ordained ministry, and third, if serving in the same area of ministry, there might be a 'blurring of professional confidentiality, a confusion of expectations within the parish and a lack of space and reflection for the couple' (p. 55). On the other hand, where couples were engaged in different areas of ministry there would be difficult decisions when new posts were being considered.

The report also emphasized the need to ensure that sufficient care and 'quality time' is given to a couple's children and it noted, apparently without disapproval, that some dioceses 'question whether both *ought to be* stipendiary at the same time during the period when the couple has parental responsibilities' (p. 59; italics added). As with previous reports, it seemed hard for these authors to be able to show recognition and concern for the potential difficulties faced by joint clergy couples in combining family life with two ministries in the Church, without adopting a 'nannyish' and intrusive approach which would be quite unacceptable today in any other area of employment. There also seemed to be a complete absence of cross-comparison with the ways in which other dual-career couples handle these issues, or any comment on the fact that dual-career couples, as noted in Chapter 4, are increasingly normative and that many of the difficulties, real as they are, have already been faced and tackled in a variety of different ways.

In 1992, the first national conference was held for joint couples when the number of couples was said to be 'over 200 (20–25 per cent of ordained women) and increasing' (Double Vision, p. 2). Again, the report from this conference referred to 'the response of many dioceses to the issue of joint ministry [as tending], understandably, to a cautious pragmatism, aware of financial constraints and the difficulty of finding suitable posts. Those in joint ministry often have to deal with the practical difficulties involved as well as a sense that their vision is not shared by the Church as a whole' (Double Vision, p. 5). Unlike the Church's official publications, the report of the conference makes clear that issues of purpose and meaning were discussed and an effort was made to provide both a theological foundation for this particular form of ordained ministry and to offer some assessment of the way in which joint ministry might contribute to the quality of the marriage as well as to the effectiveness of the ministry.

The report comments that the conference was 'concerned to shew that [joint ministry] offers a sign to the whole Church about how its ministry might creatively develop ... The life of the Trinity as the love of equals in relationship with one another was seen as reflected both in the marriage relationship and in the ministry of the married couple. Such equality, mutuality and complementarity makes greater demands on those involved than clearly delineated roles or a hierarchical understanding of marriage and ministry. It is in the mutual surrender of giving and receiving that a ministry of leadership through service is able to happen. Joint ministry also draws attention to the relationship between sexuality and religion' (pp. 3–4).

The most recent report (ABM, 1995) is entitled *Partners in Marriage and Ministry*. The purpose of this document, the first published since the ordination of women as priests, was 'to encourage discussion of the issues involved, to throw light on problematic areas, where possible, in order to develop greater understanding of this area of ministry by the couples concerned, their advisers, those who work with them, and by diocesan representatives' (p. 3). This document shows a much firmer grasp of some of the issues that are likely to be involved for joint couples. After a reasonably comprehensive check list of questions (pp. 5–7), it addresses issues of selection, training and deployment from both a practical, and an emotional perspective. It commendably advises early and detailed discussion by diocesan authorities with candidates at each of these stages. It also makes some effort to distinguish the needs of joint couples as individuals and as a partnership, trying to do justice to both realities without blurring the boundary between them, or intruding as grossly as some previous attempts across the boundary of what constitutes an employer's proper care and concern, and what constitutes interference and inappropriate control. It stresses the need for forward planning, for detailed job descriptions and for clear agreements regarding the payment of stipends and expenses but it does nothing to engage with a theological or philosophical perspective or with the interesting possibility that the joint clergy couple might also need to be understood as a whole, and as greater than the sum of its parts, with unique gifts to offer that are contingent upon that reality.

The 43 dioceses of the Church of England have made a varying response to joint clergy couples. Some have come to grips with the fact that, now the priesthood has been opened to women, there is likely to be a significant rise in the number of joint couples, requiring vision, forward planning, management and strategies for pastoral care. Others have produced no published policy statement. Some dioceses operate policies which in practice discourage the employment of joint couples so that the issue for them does not have any pressing urgency. In fact, part of the difficulty of describing or analysing this population lies in the very disparate way in which joint ministry is conceived and understood within the Church of England, as well as the many institutional complexities and variations that have arisen since 1994 because of the need to protect those within the Church who cannot accept the ministry of women priests.

The review of this material provides a background for understanding the way in which the particular dynamics of joint clergy marriages are perceived by the Church and by couples themselves. But in the absence of research evidence, many of the beliefs and conclusions about this group are based on speculation and assumptions, unsupported by hard facts. For example, it might well be the case that, far from being particularly at risk, some of the most important ingredients of marital satisfaction are in fact represented in the marriages of joint clergy couples to the same degree as in other kinds of clergy marriages. It may even be the case that some at least of these ingredients will be found at even *higher* levels in the relationships of those couples where both partners are ordained, compared with clergy couples where one partner only is ordained. Moreover, if this could indeed be shown to be the case, we might expect that, because of the likelihood of joint ordination becoming more frequent, marital satisfaction will increase over time as a result of both partners' equal participation in the role of ordained priest.

What specific literature then exists to provide some support for this more optimistic assumption? Two American studies have examined the situation of joint clergy couples in some depth. Some of the findings of one of these (Lehman, 1993) have already been discussed in Chapter 6, as its focus is not confined to joint clergy couples. But part of Lehman's subject group included five men and forty-two women who were serving in what he describes as 'co-pastor' situations with a congregation. Lehman defines the term co-pastor as two ministers working together in an egalitarian relationship as a ministry team, within the same congregation or area of ministry, and who are therefore 'equals in status and authority in their work with the church' (p. 95). This may involve some division of labour, role and function between them, but neither is singled out as the 'senior' minister.

Lehman found that working as co-pastors produced an androgynous effect upon both male and female clergy's ministries. 'Time and again the results of the analysis indicated that there were few (if any) sex differences in ministry style among clergy serving as co-pastors ... There was something about the explicit egalitarianism of the co-pastor arrangement that suppressed most sex differences in ministry style' (p. 192). And Lehman goes on to ask: 'did this type of placement selectively attract persons who define ministry in androgynous terms?' Or, we could equally ask, does this kind of working experience increase the androgynous potential of husbands and wives who work together?

There are difficulties in making comparisons between Lehman's co-pastors and the joint couples in this study. Not all Lehman's co-pastors were married couples and not all the joint couples in this study were co-pastors. But 77 per cent of Lehman's co-pastors were in fact joint clergy couples and about two-thirds of the joint couples in this study did in fact work together, and therefore Lehman's findings are of interest. He comments that 'at least in theory such an arrangement is ideal for couples committed to a marriage partnership, as it allows them to carry the "partnership" ideal into their work as well as other facets of their married life. The co-pastorate allows them to avoid having one partner defined as subordinate to the other' (p. 96). Given that such a large percentage of the co-pastor sub-group of the sample were made up of joint clergy couples, Lehman asks: 'Was the key element [in the absence of sex role differences shewn amongst co-pastors] the fact that most co-pastors were married couples who had been called to serve one congregation as equals?' In other words, was the crucial difference found amongst this sub-group due to the fact that they were joint clergy couples?

Another most interesting study by Rallings and Pratto (1984) repays some careful attention. It is, so far as it has been possible to determine, the only full length book on joint clergy couples, and as such, the nearest parallel to the present study. The authors use the term 'clergy couples' to describe joint clergy couples where both partners are ordained and they undertook their study to test 'some of the theories which may be used to explain clergy behaviours, while offering refutations of some of the more blatant stereotypes which have arisen because of the dearth of empirical data about clergy couples'. Their study sought 'to illuminate how clergy couples – committed to marriage and ministry on a day-to-day basis – were coping with the myriad issues of marriage: intimacy, competition, decision-making, power and so on while caught up in the great flux of values in modern society' (p. 13).

These authors studied a sample of fifty-four couples drawn from three Protestant denominations from the south-east of the United States. The bulk of the sample was drawn from the Presbyterian and the Methodist Churches. Their sample, being interdenominational and drawn from the Protestant Free Churches in America, was obviously different from the three groups of Church of England clergy couples being studied in this research. Nevertheless their work provides some important points of comparison with this study. They summarize the main characteristics of their sample as follows: 'these clergy couples were young, well-educated, and child-oriented. They were largely from the upper middle class and the mothers of one half of them worked outside the home in what the respondents defined as career positions. They were strongly committed to the joint covenants of marriage and ministry. They seemed to enjoy the challenge embodied in this "pioneer venture"' (p. 24).

Almost half the subjects in Rallings and Pratto's sample were employed full-time. When one spouse had a greater time commitment to ministry, it was almost always the husband. 33 per cent of the sample was made up of one partner who worked in parish ministry and the other in some kind of sector ministry or allied work such as religious education, counselling or youth work. Even though many were employed on a part time basis, only 3 per cent of them worked less than 40 hours per week. These couples did not see themselves as competitive with each other. Only 6 per cent used this description of themselves and 21 per cent felt that they were 'not at all competitive' with each other. However, 23 per cent of these couples had not worked very closely together and a further 23 per cent were able to divide their shared work situation on the basis of interest and expertise, and to talk things out between them, if they felt that competition between them was beginning to occur. Even so, the authors comment that 'there seemed to be an undercurrent that these couples were more competitive than they were willing to admit' (p. 34).

The couples in this sample also shared a considerable amount of leisure time together. They did not however share very much worship or prayer time outside their official duties. The interviewers were aware of the couples' 'intense feelings' about this, 'bordering on guilt' (p. 36). The sex-role typology of the sample was also examined, using an adapted version of Scanzoni's Dyadic Adjustment Scale (1976). Four groupings were identified along a 'traditional' and 'non-traditional/modern' continuum. These were: modern wives married to modern husbands (fourteen couples); modern wives married to traditional husbands (nine couples); traditional wives married to modern husbands (seven couples); and traditional wives married to traditional husbands (twenty couples). All four groups expressed a preference for an egalitarian decision-making style in their marriage, which seems to have been their ideal even when the way tasks and roles actually got distributed may have been 'traditional'. Such findings support the many similar findings in relation to the discrepancy between egalitarian views and practice reported by others. However, the presence of one 'modern' spouse of either gender resulted in more egalitarian decision-making taking place, similar to couples where both partners were 'modern'.

75 per cent of the couples thought that they should offer a model of marriage to other couples and that the expectations laid upon them in this regard were therefore reasonable ones. Amongst reasons given by the 25 per cent who did not think that their marriage should be a model for others was the rejection of the idea of 'difference' between them as clergy and the people whom they served, especially the idea that they were on some sort of pedestal.

Amongst the advantages of joint clergy couple marriages given by these couples were those for parishioners: the joint couple 'provided a model of a committed professional team sharing intimacy'. The authors comment that the implication of this statement seems to be 'that commitment and involvement as professionals in work need not threaten the marriage relationship and that this is a valuable model' (p. 49). Other advantages cited for parishioners included being able to offer a choice of genders in counselling, variety in the ministry due to the different gifts of each person, a good bargain for the parish, as joint couples tend to work long hours and act as a backup provision in case of sickness (*sic*). The couples listed ten advantages for themselves and their families. These included 'support of an empathic colleague' and from someone 'who knows exactly what I'm talking about because she's been there' (p. 51); flexible working hours, enabling more time to spend with the spouse and the children; and the common interests and shared values which contribute to the strength and solidarity of their marital relationship.

About one-third of couples could not think of any disadvantages, but a further third commented on the problem of conflict arising out of the different responses to each partner from the congregation. The favouring of one partner at the expense of the other is one type of triangulation which can occur. Alternatively, difficulties may arise contingent upon the couple being experienced as a strongly united power block, standing in the path of the congregation and parish being able to make its voice heard. Others mentioned the unavailability of an unpaid spouse to do all the extra, unassigned tasks! Others again had been affected by the hostility or jealousy of other (non-ordained) clergy wives, who asked 'why are they [clergywomen who are married to clergymen] getting paid for doing the same things I have done all my life without pay?' (p. 53).

Disadvantages for the couples' marriages included those common to most dual-career marriages, those of role strain, task overload and competition between work and family. Couples commented on the difficulty they had in separating their work and their marriage. One respondent commented 'When we go to bed at night, I don't want to go to bed with another minister. I want to go to bed with my wife' (p. 54).

The authors drew attention to the need for these couples to be able to own and handle competitive feelings between them, likely to be an inevitable part of a relationship where a couple has so many joint commitments. They also note the fact that, amongst the differential needs and vulnerabilities of different types of marriage commitments, joint clergy couples, along with other couples who work together in the same job, will have a propensity towards fusion and the need therefore to heed the advice of The Prophet quoted as a heading to this chapter, to 'let there be spaces in your togetherness' (p. 19). They go on to comment: 'We don't know if this much togetherness can be sustained over the long years of marriage. To avoid potential dysfunction, personal time for each spouse needs to be set aside and guarded just as zealously as the couple sets aside and guards time together apart from their work' (p. 68). Although the authors of this study do not make the point, it is also worth noting that a strong cultural imperative of the Church for which the couple is working is its emphasis on family life and the unity and cohesiveness of the family group. This may require the joint clergy couple to be even more conscious of the pull upon them towards fusion.

9 THE COUPLES AND THE QUESTIONS

There are innumerable questions to which the inquisitive mind can in this state receive no answer.
Samuel Johnson, *Letter to Boswell*

Emerging research questions

Three groups of clergy couples agreed to participate in this investigation. One – the group of joint couples – comprised the experimental group and consisted of the majority of joint couples in existence in 1994. The other two groups – traditional couples where the man only was ordained, and couples where the woman only was ordained – were assembled by random sampling and were used as comparison groups throughout the research. (See Appendix A for a description of the sampling method and research methodology.)

As discussed in the previous chapter, the literature on joint clergy couples is a small one. However, the perception of some of these couples is that the Church looks unfavourably upon them, does not understand or value their joint vocation and does little to support them in their effort to be faithful to their joint covenants of marriage and ministry. Moreover, the small body of American literature which does exist suggests the likelihood of there being a greater degree of difficulty and a higher incidence of overt pathology within the marriages of joint clergy couples than in those where clergy are married to a non-ordained spouse. There is therefore some support for the general assumptions made by the Church as to the problematic features of this clergy group.

However, there is also some evidence to suggest that the American studies have followed somewhat uncritically the earlier work done on dual-career couples in general, which found them coping with unmanageable levels of stress and as more likely therefore to have problematic and conflictual marriages. This is in contrast with more recent studies which view dual-career couples as increasingly normative and functional (Rapoport, 1991; Gilbert, 1993; Silberstein, 1993). This is not to say that there are not particular difficulties involved in being a joint clergy couple. The stresses and strains of being clergy and being married may all be experienced in double measure when both partners share the identity of being ordained as a priest.

A recent area of interest, discussed in Chapter 6, has been the work of Francis and his colleagues (1990, 1991, 1992, 1994) who found that both male and female clergy tend to exhibit reverse sex role typing. They have discussed the implications of this for the clergy-person's ministry but not for his or her marriage, nor therefore for the particular type of marriage represented by joint clergy couples. A further interesting area of investigation therefore began to suggest itself, emerging out of Francis's work. But more centrally, the implicit assumption that joint clergy marriages are viewed as being in some way inherently pathological has seemed important to test out. The clinical experiences described in Chapter 2 prompted further questions as to whether these inherent difficulties are exhibited more significantly in joint clergy marriages than they are in clergy marriages of other types.

Because joint couples are a new phenomenon in the Church of England, the nature of a research study into their dynamics can only be exploratory. In relation to clergy marriage *per se*, much has been written and some research has been undertaken, but the subgroup that is of particular interest – joint clergy marriages – is a new phenomenon. It therefore seemed appropriate to adopt a mixed design, employing both quantitative and qualitative methods, as described below, and to adopt Ambert *et al.*'s (1995) suggestion that the research should focus on emerging questions, which could be explored and elaborated as the research developed. (The methodology and design of this study is described in Appendix A.)

These questions have emerged over the period leading up to and after the ordination of women from several different sources. Sources include the clinical and group work already described in Chapters 2 and 3 and, as the study has progressed, the opportunity of interviewing non-clinical couples drawn from the joint clergy group. In addition, more general discussions with clergy about the challenges, difficulties and opportunities afforded clergy couples during this unique period in the Church's history, have helped develop reflections on the different ways in which marriage and the priesthood might interconnect for couples within the three different types of clergy marriage being discussed. As the author of this study, my own subjective experiences during this period, as they relate to my marriage and my priesthood, have also been important in informing and developing reflections on the subject.

Thus, from these different perspectives, the following questions have emerged for further reflection and exploration:

(1) Might it not be the case that, contrary to the fears expressed for these marriages, joint clergy couples will report levels of marital satisfaction no lower than those of other types of clergy marriage, as revealed by the five elements described in Chapter 5?

(2) Might it not be the case that the marital relationship of joint clergy couples will be positively affected by the ordination of women to the priesthood, because of the rebalancing of the marriage in the direction of greater egalitarianism, so that two years after the wife's ordination they may even show *increases* in these five relational elements?

(3) Where the wife is ordained and the husband is not, might it be the case that these marriages will be adversely affected and show decreased levels of these five relational elements two years after the ordination of women to the priesthood, because of the imbalance introduced into their marital relationship by ordination?

(4) Where the husband is ordained and the wife is not, there will, perhaps, be a null effect two years after the ordination of women to the

priesthood since their relationship will not have been directly affected by the ordination of women as priests?

(5) Does the cross-sex role typing of both male and female clergy reported by some researchers, reveal itself within their marriage relationships, and if so, how is the marriage affected?

Hypotheses

Bearing all of these considerations in mind, the hypotheses that were ultimately refined for testing in this study were as follows:

1. In comparison with clergy couples where one partner only is ordained, *joint clergy couples* will exhibit equally high levels of those relational elements that have been shown to be associated with marital satisfaction, and two years after the ordination of women to the priesthood, these will have increased.

2. Couples where the *wife only is ordained* will show decreased levels of these relational elements two years after the ordination of women to the priesthood.

3. Couples where the *husband only is ordained* will show no difference in these relational elements two years after the ordination of women to the priesthood.

4. Male clergy will demonstrate more feminine psychological characteristics and female clergy more masculine psychological characteristics and for *joint clergy* couples this will be demonstrated by greater similarity between the couple in sex role type.

Demographic profiles of the three clergy couple groups

The demography of the three groups of clergy couples was analysed according to age, employment, family composition and background (sibling position, parental occupation, first or second marriage and number and age of children) and the relationship between the developmental course of their marriage and their ministry. The results of this analysis will be presented in two parts. First, the results of the demographic investigation will be described in the rest of this chapter. In the next chapter, the views, attitudes and experience of marriage and ministry of subjects in the three groups will be presented and discussed.

Age differences

The average age of the joint clergy couples group was slightly lower than that of the other two groups. Subjects (both husbands and wives) were most highly represented in the 36–40 age range compared with 46–50 in the traditional group. Amongst couples where the woman only was ordained, the women were most highly represented in the 46–50 range and their husbands in the 56–60 range. The age profile of the joint couples was also slightly lower than that of the total population of clergy for this period in the two English Provinces of the Church of England, as published in the *Church of England Year Book* (1995).

The experimental group of joint clergy couples comprised the total population of joint clergy couples at the time, so no limits were imposed on the age range of subjects. For the two comparison groups, couples who had reached normal retirement age (65) were excluded. Even so, the age profile of both the traditional clergy group and the women only ordained group was higher than that of the joint couples group. There may be several reasons for this. The majority of male clergy in the Church of England in 1993–4 fell between the ages of 47 and 62, so it is to be expected that the traditional couples group, representative of the great majority of married clergy, would be similar. The women only ordained couples were made up of couples where the ordained woman had had to wait to be ordained for some considerable time, so that for many, this next step in her vocation had often had to be abnormally postponed until she was older, due to the bar on the ordination of women prior to 1992. This probably had the effect of inflating the average age of couples in this group.

Although this factor also operated within the joint couples group, it was likely to have been offset by the contrary fact that, since around 1980, nearly every theological college in England began to admit women for training alongside men. This opened up the new possibility of training for men and women together. Since the early 1980s therefore, many couples have had the opportunity to meet during their training years and at the stage in their life course when they would normally be seeking their life partner. They would therefore have been likely to move into marriage and ministry at around the same time and at an earlier age.

Employment profiles

The employment profile of the women in the experimental group of joint clergy couples was somewhat different from the total population of women clergy in 1996, as described in the Report of Diocesan Deans of Women's Ministry (NADAWM, 1997), where less than one-third of those in active ministry were non-stipendiaries. This is presumably because the national report makes no distinction between women of different marital status in terms of employment, nor between women who are part of joint couples and those who are not. 36 per cent of women who were part of joint clergy couples in the present study were in non-stipendiary ministry, but because there is no breakdown in the national report between different groupings, there is no way of knowing how the research sample compares with the employment profile of the 306 couples who formed the total population of joint couples in 1996.

The employment profile of the two groups of ordained women in this study differed quite sharply, with over half of the women only ordained receiving a full stipend compared with only around a third of those women who were part of a joint clergy couple. We might conclude from this difference that it may be more difficult for women whose husband is also ordained to argue their case for receiving a full stipend. It may also be the case that women who are part of a joint couple do not have so pressing a need to argue their case, since they often have a satisfying alternative available to them, through being licensed to their husband's parish as a non-stipendiary priest. It is certainly clear from the responses to questions about diocesan policy in relation to joint clergy couples, that the stated policy in some dioceses is that only one partner should receive a stipend, even though some dioceses are prepared to divide this between both partners. Such a policy creates an inbuilt disadvantage in relation to the marital status of ordained women, which also affects the range and type of ministry that is available to them. Such a limitation also serves to reduce the equalizing effect of ordination, both within the sphere of employment and within the couple's marital relationship.

On the other hand, being part of a joint couple provides opportunities for working together in equal partnership in the same area of ministry which may be less easily available, and perhaps be by nature different for couples in the other two groups. Although some of the couples in both the traditional group and the women only ordained group may have worked alongside each other in parish ministry in an informal way, this kind of 'joint ministry', where the non-ordained spouse works closely with the ordained partner, involves different dynamics and experiences from those of joint couples, as defined for the purposes of this study. Amongst the joint clergy couples, nearly two-thirds of them worked together in parish ministry, even though some of the wives were working part-time. This subgroup of joint couples was therefore exactly comparable with the co-pastors described by Lehman (1993), which were discussed in Chapter 8.

Not all the joint couples could be considered to be dual-career couples, other than in terms of both being ordained, and thus participating jointly in the same vocational identity – a very important fact in its own right. Beyond this however, the great majority of these couples were *also* dual-career couples in the sense that both partners were committed to a vocation which required them to spend a substantial part of the week working outside the domestic sphere, and which held meaning and significance for them in terms of future planning and development. Only around 10 per cent of women and less of the men amongst joint couples were not currently working in ministry or were working in ministry for only a very small proportion of the week. Likewise, amongst the women only ordained couples, the majority of both partners were working for a substantial part of the week, either (in the case of the non-ordained husbands) in their secular work, or in ministry. Some of the women in both groups were non-stipendiary but this does not mean that they were not working, in many cases, a full working week. In contrast, fewer couples in the traditional couples group were dual-career couples. About 45 per cent of the non-ordained women in this group worked part-time and 28 per cent said that they were not working outside the home at present. Only 26 per cent of these women said that they were in full-time work.

The relationship between a person's entry into their vocation or career and their entry into marriage is an interesting one for several reasons. The juxtaposition of two major life transitions may produce an accumulation of stress for the individual and even more so for the couple system itself. Perhaps more importantly, for those couples for whom there is a close juxtaposition of timing between the two, for one or both parties, the entry into each 'state' is likely to be influenced reciprocally by the other. Thus a couple's entry into marriage, where one or both parties have just committed themselves, or are about to commit themselves to a life of service to the Church, is a commitment which carries within it an invisible further commitment to the 'third party' which is represented by the husband and/or wife's vocation. Moreover, the choice of a marriage partner made at the same time as a commitment to ministry may be informed by the future minister's need to find a partner who will be suitable in terms of a clergy spouse.

A further important aspect of the relationship of these two life events is their relative priority in terms of time. For those individuals who were already ordained/licensed before they married, it will have been clear to their prospective partner that they are to marry someone who holds the role and identity of an ordained/licensed person. As was noted in Chapter 7, this is a particularly important point for those occupations, like the priesthood, which have this capacity to 'incorporate' the partner into the occupational role of the other. To know in advance that this will be part of one's marriage is very different from the opposite situation when one or both partners enters into ministry some years after their marriage and who then bring, unilaterally, into the marriage, new expectations, and inevitable new constraints and limitations resulting from both the ordained person's new role and the new expectations placed upon the spouse. Amongst the joint clergy couples there was a significant difference as to whether ordination or marriage had occurred first for husbands and wives, where 45.4 per cent of the men but only 18 per cent of the women had been ordained before they married. Put differently, nearly half of these marriages were confronted with having to accommodate to the husband's call to the ministry and over three-quarters had to deal with what it meant for them as a couple and as a family when the woman made her own decision to go into the ministry at a later date.

The relationship between the number of years that the couples had been married and the number of years that the ordained women had been in ministry (from their original licensing as parish workers or deaconesses) was very similar between the two groups in which women were ordained. The discrepancy between the timing of the two events – marriage and ordination – was however smaller within the joint couples group, as a larger number of these couples had married and got ordained within two years of each other than was the case in the two comparison groups. The two events therefore – marriage and ordination – are more inter-related timewise for joint clergy couples than for male and female clergy respectively in the two comparison groups.

Parental occupation

The parents' occupations of all three clergy groups revealed a very similar profile. Professional and managerial jobs figured by far the highest for the parents of both husbands and wives, ordained and non-ordained partners. The majority of respondents gave their mother's occupation as 'housewife'. Although some of these women would have received professional or other training, and worked outside the home earlier in their marriages, the term 'housewife' in this context meant that for most of the time that the respondent was a child, his/her mother was at home caring for the children and the home as her primary employment.

The mothers of more of the ordained women married to a non-clergy spouse were working professionally and fewer of them were housewives, compared with the mothers of ordained women who were part of joint couples, where the reverse was the case. Comparing the differences between parental occupations of husbands and wives, the wives' parents were more highly represented as professional people than the husbands' parents, apart from joint clergy couples where the reverse was the case – although the differences between them are very small. Perhaps the most striking feature is the very small number of manual workers or white collar workers amongst the parents of any of the three clergy couple groups. In this sense, all three groups come from a very similar social and educational background and this continues to be, as it has been for generations, the professional middle class.

Sibling position

There were no significant differences in the sibling positions of subjects across the three groups. In each group, eldest or only children were the most highly represented sibling positions, particularly amongst the women. In terms of the higher numbers of eldests and onlys in the joint couples group, this supports the findings of Rallings and Pratto (1984) who also found that over 40 per cent of their sample of joint clergy couples were eldest or only children. In relating this finding to Toman's (1976) contention that eldest and only children tended to be high achievers, they concluded that this may well be a characteristic of joint clergy couples.

However, in the present study, *each* group of female subjects, regardless of whether they were ordained or not, shewed a high proportion of eldest or only children (61 per cent joint couples; 56.4 per cent women only ordained couples; 54.4 per cent traditional couples). Moreover, from the findings of the present study, the fact that over half of the non-ordained women and nearly half of the non-ordained men are also eldest or only children suggests that there is no particular relationship between sibling position and the fact of being a clergyperson. Nor do joint clergy couples appear to be more likely to be eldest or only children than traditional or women only ordained couples, a comparison which Rallings and Pratto (1984) failed to make.

It nevertheless remains the case that over half the subjects in all three groups come from the eldest/only position, and even a very conservative interpretation might suggest that there may be some way in which the fact of one or both partners being eldest or only children provides some important and relevant childhood experience for becoming part of a clergy couple in adulthood, in terms of the experience of taking responsibility, and in developing the ability to occupy a unique leadership role within a community.

A more relevant set of comparisons for a comparative study of clergy couples is the match of sibling positions within the couple pairs. Toman (1976) suggests that couples who come from complementary sibling positions enjoy greater marital stability. This is because each partner will have become familiar in their family of origin with the role required of them in their marital partnership. For example, the older brother of younger sisters will get along best with the younger sister of older brothers, both because he will be familiar with some of the demands of the role and because he will be used to living in close contact with the other gender. In the present study, slightly more couples in each of the three groups came from complementary than from similar sibling positions. The biggest difference (although not statistically significant) was in the joint couples group where 40.2 per cent of couples occupied the same sibling position but nearly 60 per cent occupied complementary positions.

Age groups of children

The difference in age profiles between the three groups of couples, commented on earlier, is reflected in, and probably accounts for, the differences in the distribution of their children's age groups. Whilst only 15 per cent of couples where the woman only is ordained have children of eleven years old or younger, traditional clergy couples have over twice as many in this age group – 33.4 per cent, and in contrast with both the comparison groups, nearly half of all the joint couples – 49.4 per cent – are parenting children of eleven years old or younger. In terms of the distribution of adult children between the three groups, 75 per cent of couples in the group where only the woman is ordained, and 54.9 per cent of traditional clergy couples have grown-up children, compared with only 28.6 per cent of joint clergy couples.

As was noted in Chapter 4, the curvilinear interpretation of the life course of marriage, whereby marital satisfaction is found to regress quite sharply during the phase when couples are parenting dependent children, remains well supported by current research, even though other intervening variables, such as the greater sharing of parental tasks between the genders and the greater availability of extended family assistance in some cultures, means that the curvilinear pattern is very probably not as universally applicable as was once thought to be the case. In this study however, the great majority of subjects in all three groups came from a European background and it is reasonable therefore, in observing the different distribution of age groups of children within the three subject groups, to infer differences in the potential levels of stress being experienced in the three couples groups, derived from their parenting responsibilities.

The differences in the numbers of couples parenting children of different age groups suggests that the joint clergy couples are on the whole at an earlier developmental stage in their family life-cycle, and the family experience of these couples is therefore significantly different from that of the other two groups due to their heavy involvement in the care of young children. Half the joint couples are parenting children of eleven years old and younger, compared with 33 per cent of traditional couples and only 13 per cent of women only ordained couples. On the other hand, joint clergy couples are parenting fewer adolescents than couples in the comparison groups – 13 per cent, compared with women only ordained couples (24.5 per cent) or traditional clergy couples (37.2 per cent). Few of the joint clergy couples therefore are as yet coping with the stresses engendered by the potential for conflict between adolescents and their parents. Instead, these couples are heavily involved in the stresses of caring for young children.

Like any other kind of dual-career couple, for those couples where both partners have major time commitments to ministerial duties, this will involve them with the constant juggling of different timetables, continual negotiation about household and child care tasks and the need to cover the care of the children with outside helpers when both parents are necessarily engaged with their work. Of the three groups, the women only ordained couples are least burdened by the potential stresses of dependent children, since the majority of their children are grown up. This may be an important factor in enabling the majority of the women in this group to engage in full-time stipendiary ministry.

10 EXPERIENCE OF MARRIAGE AND MINISTRY

> Grown-ups love figures. When you tell them that you have made a new friend, they never ask you any questions about essential matters. They never say to you, 'What does his voice sound like? What games does he love best? Does he collect butterflies?' Instead, 'How old is he? How many brothers has he? How much does he weigh? How much money does his father make?' Only from these figures do they think they have learned anything about him.
> Antoine de Saint-Exupéry, *The Little Prince*

In addition to these demographic data, a series of questions investigated the subjects' experiences of marriage and ministry, so that comparisons could be made across the three different subject groups and between the groups, before and after the women's ordination. The answers to these questions yielded both quantitative and qualitative data, but, for the sake of clarity, the results will be discussed together in this chapter. The questions covered the following topics: competition between the partners; degree of egalitarianism in the couple's relationship; their relationship with the Church at local and diocesan level; job satisfaction; shared spiritual experience; perceived identity as a clergyperson or clergy spouse; marriage and priesthood as model and symbol and perceived marital satisfaction.

Competition between the partners

Couples in all three groups were asked two questions about how they might handle competition between them in relation to their own jobs or careers. Asked which career would take precedence, nearly half of joint clergy couples (46 per cent), both men and women separately, thought that they would take a flexible approach according to each situation which presented itself. Beyond this 46 per cent, 36 per cent of both husbands and wives said that they would put the husband's career first, compared with 13 per cent of men and 8 per cent of women who would put the wife's career first. Amongst traditional couples, only 11 per cent of wives and 23 per cent of husbands said that they would be flexible, whilst 67 per cent of wives and 59 per cent of husbands said that the husband's career would automatically take precedence.

Amongst the women only ordained couples, 22 per cent of women and 10 per cent of men said they would be flexible. There was a significant difference in this group between the husbands' and wives' responses. Beyond those 22 per cent who would take a flexible response, the *women* in this group were almost *equally divided* between those who said that their husband's career would take precedence (34 per cent) and those who said that their own would (32 per cent). In quite marked contrast, 53 per cent of the *husbands* said that their *wife's career* would take precedence as compared with only 18 per cent who thought that their own would.

Couples were asked whether they would feel comfortable about having their spouse as their 'boss' at work. Husbands and wives in all three groups tended to be equally divided in their responses. Between the groups, however, the women in the joint couples group felt happiest and the women in the traditional couples felt least happy about this idea, whilst the men amongst the joint couples were only slightly happier about it than the men in the traditional group. Both of these results show joint couples taking a more conservative position than traditional couples which is perhaps somewhat surprising considering the new phenomena that they represent.

All three groups were asked whether they thought joint clergy couples would find it difficult to handle competition between them. The responses of the three groups are not therefore exactly comparable as the joint couples were responding in terms of their own experience whilst the two comparison groups were responding in terms of their perceptions of the experiences of others. Amongst joint couples themselves, there was a significant difference in the responses of husbands and wives. The women thought it would either be difficult or very difficult (these two scores combined came to 86 per cent of the responses), compared with 14 per cent who thought it would not be a problem, whilst the men were almost evenly split between those who thought it would either be difficult or very difficult (these scores combined came to 51 per cent) compared with those who thought it would not be a problem (48 per cent). Around two-thirds of both men and women in the other two groups thought that joint couples would have a problem in handling competition between them.

Along with difficulties in relation to the distribution of power and the maintenance of an adequate support structure, Rice (1979) identifies competition between marital partners as one of the three major difficulties with which dual-career marriages have to contend. More recent studies have continued to investigate this variable with some care. In this study of joint clergy couples it was therefore obviously important to try to identify the extent to which competition was experienced as a problematic part of their marriage.

There was a significant difference between the responses given by husbands and wives amongst joint clergy couples regarding the extent to which they thought that competition would be a problem between them. Given that some of the earlier research literature has reported a decrease in both husbands' and wives' experience of marital satisfaction when the occupational status of the wife is higher than that of her husband, the wives' acknowledgement of the potential difficulties in this area is likely to be more realistic than the near 50 per cent of husbands who foresaw no problem. It may be that the husbands were expressing more about their *desire* for what they would like to be the case, rather then facing up to the real difficulties which they might have to encounter.

In terms of career development, joint couples were clearly aiming to be flexible and free from traditional stereotypes, and nearly half the group (and half of each gender) said that they would review each situation on its own merits as they approached their career changes. Given the difficulty of finding jobs that adequately do justice to both partners' developing skills and knowledge, the degree to which a couple can be free of preconceptions, old scripts and covert basic assumptions governing occupational change, the more likely they are to find ways of accommodating to what, at first sight, may be a conflict of needs. But amongst the joint couples, beyond those who would look at each situation flexibly, nearly three times as many in this group – both husbands and wives, would put the husband's rather than the wife's career first.

Obviously this in part reflects an important reality of these couples' situation – around half of them were still caring for dependent children, and the wife was the primary caretaker. Even so, it was striking that very few members of this group, either husbands or wives, both of whom were equally committed to their vocation through ordination, thought that, given a straight choice between the husband's or the wife's career, the wife's would come first. In strong contrast, around one-third of the wives and over half of the husbands in the women only ordained group said that their wife's career would take precedence.

Again, the fact that some of these couples were older, more of them had grown up children than the joint couples group and about one-fifth of the husbands had retired, will partly account for this difference. However, this result, combined with the better showing of the husbands in this group in relation to an egalitarian division of household labour (see below) and the preference of around half of them to be known as the husband of a clergywoman, leaves the impression that the non-ordained husbands of the clergywomen have moved furthest in grasping some of the implications associated with the ordination of their wife to the priesthood, in terms of the way in which this change has resulted in their wife becoming even more heavily involved in the outside world of work.

The fact that fewer of the women in the joint couples group, in contrast to those women in the women only ordained group were in full-time work, either paid or unpaid, may also suggest that joint couples handle competition by avoidance. One way of diluting the threat of competition between the two ordained ministries is to reduce the impact of one of the two careers (invariably the wife's) by engaging in part-time or non-stipendiary work. This effectively removes that partner from the potential competition. The task of protecting the partner and the marriage from the threat of competition was invariably taken on by the wife. In the interview study, one of the wives spoke about her deliberate choice to be only a 'ghost' in the parish, and although she was fully employed in a secular job, the need not to compete with her husband within the same territory was strong. Assumptions of this kind are often supported by diocesan policy, yet it might be more helpful for couples to be given the space and opportunity to examine the reality of these assumptions and the fears which they engender.

In all these ways, the impression is given that joint couples *are* troubled by competition. The women within these couples have also fallen behind their sisters in holding full-time stipendiary posts and fewer of the husbands within the joint couples group would be prepared to put their wives' career first compared with over half the husbands in the women only ordained group.

Egalitarianism

These questions which explored the couples' experience of competition also gave information about the extent to which they perceived themselves as having an egalitarian relationship. Which career will take precedence and whether or not a person could envisage having their spouse as their 'boss' at work obviously also provide information about the couple's egalitarian views. In addition, couples were asked about the way in which they divided the household chores between them and the amount of time which they and their partner spent with their children, as indicators of the sharing of child care tasks, where these were relevant.

Perhaps one of the most surprising features of the comparisons across the three groups were the relatively low levels of equity in division of household tasks evidenced by the joint clergy couples. Over 40 per cent of both husbands and wives in this group perceived the wife as doing most of the household chores compared with only round 6 per cent who perceived the husband doing most. This left around one-third of the group who perceived some shared or equitable distribution between the couple. This differed very little from the way in which traditional couples viewed the distribution of household chores between them – if anything, the husbands in the traditional group perceived a greater shared and equitable division than either the husbands or the wives in the joint couples group.

Yet the majority of the wives in the joint group were in full-time work compared with only a quarter of those in the traditional group. More significantly perhaps, the movement towards the ordination of women to the priesthood had been strongly characterized by a motif of justice and equity between women and men – yet there seemed to be little reverberation of this theme in the day-to-day domestic lives of these couples. Not that the inequities went unnoticed. A considerable number of both the wives and the husbands commented on hassles over household chores with a greater or lesser degree of passion.

In contrast, amongst women only ordained couples, those who perceived the wife as doing most of the chores dropped by half to 20 per cent and instead, over 50 per cent of both husbands and wives perceived the chores as either being shared, equally divided or done primarily by the husband. Again there may be some association between these results and the fact that around a fifth of the husbands in this group were retired, and therefore, maybe both willing and able to shoulder a greater share of household responsibility. But the result may also indicate the greater 'pulling power' of those ordained women who are married to non-ordained husbands in being able to make a claim on their husband for service and time. As in Tesch *et al.*'s (1992) study of joint physician couples, it may be disadvantageous in some respects to know and be known too closely in relation to the stresses and demands of one's job when it comes to arguing the need to offload the woman's 'second shift' of work, after her professional work has ended. There may also be a tacit or even explicit agreement between joint couples that, if they are both going to submit to the pressure to work long hours in their ministerial work, the husband will do so on behalf of his wife, if she in turn shoulders the bulk of the domestic responsibility.

When it came to the couples' perceptions of the time which their partner spent with their children, the perception of husbands and wives in the joint couples group were closer than those in the other two groups. There was a similar finding across the groups in that in each case the husbands were more content than their wives with the amount of time their partner spent with the children, suggesting that in all three groups the women felt that they, rather than their husbands, carried the heavier burden of child care.

Relationship with the Church

The relationship of couples with their congregations (or other areas of ministry) was examined from the two different perspectives of the ordained minister and his or her spouse. All couples were asked if they felt that the demands made by their own or their spouse's ministry were intrusive into their family life. Couples were also asked about their perceptions of the closeness/distance of their spouse's relationship with the congregation. In addition, each partner in the two comparison groups was asked whether they were satisfied with the amount of involvement which the non-ordained partner had in the parish. A fourth question asked whether or not each partner felt supported by the parish. In relation to the couples' perceptions of the diocese, husbands and wives in the joint couples group were asked about the employment policy of the diocese towards joint clergy couples. The traditional couples and women only ordained couples were asked about their knowledge of and views about diocesan employment policy in relation to the needs of their spouse and family.

The couples regarded themselves as having a threefold relationship with 'the Church'. It operated for them on the local level, the diocesan level and on the wider level of the Church nationally or the Church Universal. All three concepts and relationships were experienced as being either supportive or persecutory by different couples. But the most pervasive effect for those where one or both partners was in parish ministry was felt at the local level. Amongst the disappointments experienced over the previous two years by respondents in all three groups, those which related to lack of support or poor working relationships and divisions amongst the congregation or within a sub-group of it, such as the Parochial Church Council, were very frequently cited.

In support of much previous research into the spillover effects between work and family, respondents made it clear that when there was lack of support or even open hostility from the immediate work place – the parish – this took a heavy toll both on partners and upon their marriage. Comparing the two areas of dissatisfaction in ministry that related to the Church, it was the Church at the local parish level, far more than the diocese, that caused stress to respondents. Thus, although many respondents did not know about their diocese's employment policy or perceive any support from it, when asked to comment freely on areas of dissatisfaction in their lives, it was the parish not the diocese that caused them far more difficulty.

Even so, respondents were by no means sanguine about their experience of diocesan structures, in the form of an employment policy towards them. The most obvious finding here was that around half of the clergy and their spouses in all three groups either did not know of their diocese's employment policy or believed there to be none. In addition, small numbers in each group were prepared to say that it was bad, or to give an example of the way that they had found it to be harsh and inappropriate to their needs. Complaints included the ways in which no account was taken of the clergyperson's spouse or children, in relation to his or her career needs or the needs of the children for continuity. One wife in the traditional couples group commented that in her experience of four dioceses, her own career needs had never once been considered when new work was being suggested or offered to her husband.

Joint couples sometimes found that a diocesan policy did indeed exist, but it was one that did not meet their needs. Some dioceses had very clear views about the employment of ordained women who were married to clergymen. Sometimes the policy allowed them to job share, but often it was simply a policy of paying one stipend to the husband, with the wife being expected to work for nothing, simply by virtue of the fact that she was married to a clergyman! This had the very obvious and visible effect of depressing the numbers of full-time stipendiary women clergy amongst joint couples, compared with the higher numbers amongst women only ordained couples. A further blanket policy was operated in some dioceses in that joint couples were debarred from working together in the same parish or other area of work, regardless of their previous experience of working together, or of their personalities, their desires or their particular mix of talents and gifts.

Of the three groups, the ordained women in the women only ordained couples group felt the most supported and the ordained men in the traditional couples group felt least supported by their congregations. This may reflect the fact that, since ordained women are not welcome in those parishes where the three

Resolutions provided by the Act of Synod have been passed, those parishes which employ a woman priest are likely to be doing so with some enthusiasm and after some considered thought. For this reason, ordained women may be experiencing more support and therefore less stress from this source than their male counterparts, whose experience often seems to remain one of lack of parish support or consideration.

Both joint and traditional couples seemed satisfied with the amount of involvement in the parish shewn by their partner, but amongst the women only ordained group, about half the husbands felt dissatisfied in relation to their own performance. From their comments, their dissatisfaction was more in the direction of wishing they could do more to support their wife in her work. However, the great majority of their wives were quite satisfied with what their husbands were doing.

It was difficult to form a very clear impression as to the degree to which couples felt that their own or their partner's ministry or work demands intruded upon their family life, partly perhaps because the question was badly worded. Respondents were given the choice between stating that these demands *often*, *occasionally*, or *never* intruded. All three groups divided up around the one-third/two-thirds mark, in relation to the 'often' choice. But it was unclear as to what the larger percentage who felt that they 'occasionally' intruded really meant. Obviously 'occasionally' might mean 'quite often' or 'sometimes' or only 'very occasionally', given that there were no other choices (other than 'never') on offer.

Even so, the fact that around 37 per cent of joint couples and a slightly higher percentage of women only ordained couples thought that the demands of the outside worlds of ministry and work were 'often intrusive', gives a clear picture of family life often being disrupted and perhaps dislocated by the parish or other work setting. Amongst traditional couples, there was the widest discrepancy between the response of husbands and wives: whilst only 29 per cent of the ordained men felt these demands to be intrusive, 39 per cent of their wives did. It may be that the burden of this intrusiveness, and the irritation of it, falls more upon the person who is less directly involved – the partners and children of the minister rather than on the minister him or herself.

Job satisfaction

The couple's relationship with the Church at both the local and the diocesan level profoundly affected their job satisfaction, and, for some couples, this in turn had a very direct link with their happiness or otherwise as a couple. One couple for example attributed their deteriorated marital relationship directly to the rejection and incompetent handling of the wife's employment needs by her diocese. But there were more subtle effects which were harder to interpret. For example, comparing the areas of dissatisfaction which couples had experienced in their lives over the past two years, there was a marked difference in the way in which ordained compared with non-ordained partners responded in relation to family or marital stress. This area of difficulty was the *most frequently* cited category for non-ordained spouses, both women and men, and the *least often* cited category by those who were ordained. Perhaps most striking of all, joint clergy couples where both partners were ordained did not once cite family difficulties as being an area of disappointment in their lives over the past two years.

On the face of it, there is a perfectly logical reason for this. The question emphasized the couples' experiences of satisfaction or dissatisfaction in their ministerial life. However, it is still the case that non-ordained spouses, most of whom were taking an active part in parish ministry and many of whom fulfilled a ministry in their secular field of work, nevertheless responded in relation to the disappointments they had experienced in relation to their *family life*, regardless as to whether they were male or female. Presumably it cannot have been the case that there were *no* disappointing ministry experiences which impinged upon them and, conversely, none from family life that affected the ministries in some way of joint couples or amongst ordained men or ordained women in the other two groups. The finding is particularly curious since some of the stressful family events cited by the non-ordained partners were ones which must obviously have impinged very heavily on the ordained spouse too – such as major illness in the family, or severe marital tension between the partners.

One explanation might be that, compared to the stresses and disappointments being experienced in the ministry by the ordained partner, the family events which may also have been stressful for them do not come to mind as immediately as those disappointments in the work place. Ordained partners, in contrast, cited as their most important category lack of parish support, poor working relationships and time pressures. It may be that family disappointments, however important, were not experienced as keenly or painfully as the lack of support or open hostility of the person's parish or the ongoing, nagging difficulties of poor working relationships.

However, this discrepancy between the two groups, in their relative weighting of family versus parochial stress, would not have enhanced their cohesiveness as a couple. In this respect, the tendency to ignore all stress that stemmed from the marriage or the family, which is implied in the joint couples group, at least produced a common focus between them. They would, if this were indeed the explanation, have been engaging in the common defensive process of triangling in a third party – in this case the work place – to deflect the tension arising from their marital or family relationships, as described in Chapter 7. Alternatively perhaps the joint couples group really did have fewer disappointments in their family life compared with the other two groups!

Just as striking was the similar reversal that occurred when couples responded to the question about their most satisfying experiences. Ordained respondents most frequently cited liturgical, pastoral, extra-parochial work and teaching, whilst non-ordained respondents most frequently cited personal and family relationships. Beyond that, there were no consistent differences between the respondents in the three groups, nor between the two genders in what they had found most satisfying over the past two years. Within the categories there were some differences in emphasis: obviously the new women priests frequently cited as a satisfying experience, their new ability to preside over the Eucharist as part of their liturgical function. But there were no other gender differences. Men found satisfaction in their pastoral work as much as women, and women found that engaging in diocesan or extra-parochial work, the change process and management responsibilities brought them satisfaction almost as often as men, thus supporting Lehman's (1993) findings that co-pastors do not exhibit gender differences in the way in which they conduct their ministries.

Spiritual experience: shared prayer and worship time

Several questions explored the way in which the couples expressed the religious dimension of their marriages and ministries. The purpose of asking these questions was to discover whether Rallings and Pratto's (1984) finding held good for these couples. They hypothesized that, given the nature of the clergy's commitment, the sharing of spiritual experience through private prayer and worship together would be an important means by which these couples became more cohesive and grew in their level of mutual empathy. They found that not doing so produced a considerable amount of guilt and anxiety.

Couples were asked if they worshipped together on Sundays. Two-thirds of the joint couples said that they did and over three-quarters of the traditional couples, both husbands and wives, said that they did. Of the women only ordained couples, there was some discrepancy between the responses of the wives, of whom 66 per cent thought that they did, and husbands, of whom 80 per cent thought that they did. Couples were also asked if they prayed together, outside the times when their ministerial commitments might dictate that they did so. Around half of the joint and traditional couples, and slightly less of the women only ordained couples did so.

In relation to time taken out for retreat or spiritual renewal, nearly three-quarters of both partners amongst joint couples said that they preferred to go away for a retreat on their own rather than with their spouse. Amongst traditional couples, there was a considerable difference between wives (37 per cent) and husbands (63 per cent) who preferred to go alone. There was an even greater difference between partners amongst women only ordained couples: 83 per cent of the wives but only 17 per cent of the husbands preferred to go alone.

Across the three different kinds of clergy couples, the traditional couples worshipped together more than either of the other two groups. Of the three groups, the joint couples worshipped together slightly less than the women only ordained group (although there was some discrepancy between husbands' and wives' perceptions in this group). One might suppose that sharing worship together would be important for these couples and certainly its loss was something which some subjects, who were part of the joint couples group, noted as something sad which had resulted from the wife being ordained as a priest, and therefore being needed elsewhere on Sundays. Paradoxically, even if logically, the fact of the wife becoming a priest seemed to reduce the number of occasions when the couple could share this activity. Thus, for about a third of these couples, the demands of their ministries had the effect of pulling them in different directions in relation to the sharing of what was for them a very key and very important activity.

But there also seemed the need for separateness in relation to their spiritual lives. The extent to which the three different types of clergy couples prayed together outside their ministerial duties was roughly the same – about half did and half did not. This was a question which was also investigated by Rallings and Pratto (1984) in relation to joint clergy couples, and they were surprised at the low numbers who shared some prayer time privately. However, some clue may be offered by this need for separateness and space by the responses to another question. When couples were asked about their preferences in relation to going away for a period of retreat or spiritual reflection, in relation to whether they preferred to go alone or with their spouse, the ordained person(s) in all three groups preferred to have – perhaps *needed* to have – the space away alone, whereas the non-ordained person preferred to share this time with their partner.

Some of the contrary needs of these couples for space and togetherness may be highlighted here. This may give some indication of the pressing need for those who work in the public sphere of ordained ministry, with little respite from interaction with others, to have time alone and apart from all others, including from their spouse. On the other hand, the non-ordained spouse, who may chiefly bear the experience of feeling that the ministry intrudes upon the marriage, and that time with their spouse is only too limited, may yearn for this chance to be away alone with him or her. For joint couples, where both partners are ordained, there is, in contrast, a high level of congruity in their mutual need to have space alone.

Identity as clergy/clergy spouse

As a result of the ordination of women to the priesthood, several major identity shifts occurred for joint clergy couples and for those where the woman only was ordained. For joint couples, there was a threefold change of identity – for the self, for the partner and for the couple system itself. In examining the question as to whether each partner perceived themselves as being happier as a result of the wife's ordination, 82 per cent of both husbands and wives amongst joint couples said that they were, whilst only 7 per cent said that they were not. (The remaining 11 per cent were not sure.)

Some of the husbands referred to the painful experiences of having to deal with people in their parishes who were opposed to his wife's ordination. Although there may well have been opposition to the ordination of those women whose husbands were not priests, it was obviously experienced at closer range by those husbands who were part of a joint couple and, as priests themselves, and, as perhaps vicar of the parish, they may have had to deal with this opposition at first hand. The blurring of the boundary between what was a professional requirement and yet also a personal pain was undoubtedly a hard juxtaposition to handle.

Couples were asked if they felt more comfortable when they were known to be either a clergyperson or the husband or wife of a clergyperson, in social situations. Amongst joint couples, 18 per cent of the wives preferred to be known as clergy, 29 per cent preferred to be unknown and 47 per cent did not mind. Amongst the husbands, the responses were more evenly distributed. 33 per cent preferred to be known, 27 per cent preferred to be unknown and 38 per cent did not mind.

Amongst traditional couples, 14 per cent of the wives preferred to be known as the wife of a clergyman, 47 per cent preferred to be unknown, and 33 per cent did not mind. Of the husbands in this group, 29 per cent preferred to be known, 28 per cent not known and 41 per cent did not mind. Amongst the women only ordained couples, 27 per cent of the women preferred to be known as clergy, 29 per cent preferred to be unknown and 39 per cent did not mind. Of the husbands in this group, 44 per cent preferred to be known as the husband of a clergywoman, 15 per cent preferred to be unknown and 36 per cent did not mind. When the non-ordained wives in traditional couples were compared with non-ordained husbands in women only ordained couples, there was a significant difference in their responses.

Within the joint clergy couples group, the woman had to assume and grow into her identity as a priest and the husband into his new identity as the husband of a clergyperson. Clearly, this latter role is a far less defined role than all that has, over the last three centuries, developed around the role of clergy wife.

This obvious fact begs the question as to whether, for these husbands, becoming the husband of a clergyperson meant either more or less to them than becoming the husband of a newly appointed surgeon or head teacher of a school. Yet these are not very clear analogies. Their wives had often been in ministry for many years and the question for the wives themselves, in terms of their own identity shift, was often around its identification. 'What exactly *was* different now, compared with how it was before I was ordained?' was the question which some wives found themselves needing to ask. Not surprisingly, the same uncertainty was likely to affect the husbands in this group as to how *their* role might have changed (or not) as a result of their wife's priesting.

For the women in the joint couples group, this question referred, first of all, to the woman's own identity shift. Now that they were priests, were these women still 'clergy wives' *as well*? Had their priestly identity replaced that of clergy wife or was it something 'added on'? The question around whether they were happier to be known or not known as clergy did not exactly address this issue of comparison of the two roles. But one interpretation of the results of the answers to this question might be that the relatively small percentage of wives amongst joint clergy couples who felt more comfortable when known as clergy (18 per cent) might suggest that for some of these, their alternative and more familiar identity as clergy wife was still a more comfortable one.

This may indicate a realism about some of the situational stresses contingent upon being an ordained woman and some nostalgia for a time when life was more predictable and bounded, even if more confined. It was also clear that there were losses as well as gains for those women in joint clergy couples who were able to compare a time when they had been a 'clergy wife' and not been ordained themselves. One clergywoman commented: 'My role was more defined as a clergy wife and less threatening. My "career" then did not really count towards the future; now it has to be taken into account.'

As was clear from the number of positive responses to the role change however, few of the wives or their husbands in the joint couples group could be suspected of wanting to put the clock back. There was realism about the difficulties and the loss, but overwhelming affirmation of the perceived advantage for the couple, the partners as individuals and for the parish and/or other work settings.

Such an interpretation does not necessarily hold good in the different circumstances of the partners from the other two groups. There was a significant difference between the wives from the traditional group and the husbands from the women only ordained group in terms of their identification with the role of clergy partner. Whilst very few (14 per cent) preferred to be known as a clergy wife, only 15 per cent of clergy husbands preferred to be *not known* as such. Whilst wives seemed to be eager to rid themselves of this identity, husbands seemed happy to take on theirs for the first time. Several of the results pointed to the way in which the husbands in the women only ordained group were enormously supportive and perhaps proud of their wife's newly acquired identity and this included being content with being known, for the first time, as the husband of a priest.

Husbands and wives of joint couples were asked to describe the difference in their marriage now, compared with when the wife had been an unordained 'clergy wife'. For a little over half the group, the question did not apply as these couples had been married and ordained within so short a time span that there was nothing with which to compare the present situation of both being ordained priests. Five couples thought that there was little or no difference at all. Twenty-eight husbands and twenty-two wives (a little over one-third of the total) could identify a difference. The responses were divided into five categories and are given in the table on the following page, together with some examples.

Differences between being a clergy wife and a woman priest

1. Relationship is more equal because wife is more able to have her own identity

'I feel more equal in ministry and take more initiative which I think _____ likes.'

'We are now more equal. It has given us a new freedom.'

'My ministry has become recognized in my own right – not seen as an appendage to my husband.'

'The relationship is more free. I have found the space to assert (discover) myself.'

'Her ordination as a priest has contributed to our personal hopes/vision for equality.'

2. Wife is more fulfilled/less frustrated

'I feel more fulfilled.'

'I have developed wider, more diverse commitments.'

'I don't feel the envy, bitterness, anger that I occasionally felt before.'

3. Couple are more fulfilled as a partnership and share more together

'We are more involved in what each other is doing, sharing more.'

'We share more and at a deeper level.'

'We're more of a partnership.'

[Our relationship is] 'more mature, stable, mutually fulfilling'.

[We are] 'busier, but have sense of united purpose and vocational fulfilment'.

4. More stress and more role strain

'I sometimes resent my husband seeming to want me to give more and more time to everything except me.'

'Less time together'

> ### 4. More stress and more role strain (cont.)
> 'The complexity has got worse because now, as a priest, I'm in a double bind of fulfilling nameless and endless expectations for ministry with even less financial resources.'
> 'Probably slightly more stressful in finding jobs that are equally fulfilling'
> 'Increased tensions. Too much pressure'
>
> ### 5. Losses
> 'I am now much less available to my husband's parish – some of them don't know who I am.'
> 'I am not able to help my husband as much as I did. We cannot worship together.'
> 'We work more separately now.'
> 'Very little now in our lives except work to talk about'

Husbands and wives in the joint couples group were asked how an outsider would recognize the difference between them as husband and wife rather than as fellow clergy. Four of the men and seven of the women said that they did not know. Twenty of the men and nineteen of the women said that there was 'no difference' between their behaviour in the two roles which would be recognizable by an outsider. The responses of the rest were divided between the following six categories and are given below with numbers of responses in each category and some examples:

> - 1. Dress (women: 5; men: 9)
> - 2. Little interaction as clergy/primarily marriage partners (women: 5; men: 8)
> - 3. Content/context of discussion (women: 6; men: 3)
> - 4. Emotional expressiveness (women: 21; men: 15)
> - 5. Professional/personal style and authority (women: 10; men: 8)
> - 6. Ontological indivisibility (women: 7; men: 11)

Factors which distinguish personal and professional roles

1. Dress
'Our uniform'
'Dress, liturgy, party manners or whatever'
'Not wearing dog collars'

2. Little interaction as clergy/primarily marriage partners
'Rarely together as fellow clergy'
'In our situation, I always relate to _____ as my wife; we don't really have a large working relationship.'
'They mainly see us as husband and wife. Experiencing her as a priest is still novel and exciting to them.'

3. Content/context of discussion
'I suppose generally speaking people in rural parishes always see you in the "religious position". I'm often referred to as "Mrs Vicar" in totally secular surroundings and when I'm doing ordinary things.'
'They expect us to know what each other knows.'
'I think our behaviour is different and certainly what we talk about is different. In the presence of outsiders – especially parishioners – I suspect we discuss professional matters as fellow clergy.'

4. Emotional expressiveness
'We play more and talk more intimately when off duty.'
'We tend to keep physical distance and don't talk to each other when together as "clergy".'
'We don't live our clergy roles when relaxing.'
'We act very professionally – we would not hold hands at a formal occasion.'
'We voice how we feel about the work when we are alone; we discuss people openly; we let the stress and tiredness come out; we voice our anger, depression or grumbles, or I burst into tears.'

---

5. Professional/personal style and authority

'I tend to defer to him in the parish, as my sphere of ministry is elsewhere – I am his Hon. Assistant Curate here.'

'When I am in charge of a situation, I am more assertive than when he is in charge and I am just helping.'

'We would be quite willing to express opposing views in a ministerial setting – but perhaps a bit less so.'

'At work I would be more definite and prescriptive; my wife would be more conciliatory and understanding.'

6. Ontologically indivisible

'I think we bring our husband/wife relationship into the clergy role – to the discomfort of some and the liberation of others.'

'Most people wouldn't draw a line where our couple ministry ends and our marriage begins.'

'The two intermingle and the outsider would see both aspects going on at the same time to different degrees.'

'We are always husband/wife and fellow clergy at the same time. There is no division. Ministry is about us as people given to a church, not us as husband/wife or priests. My wife is part of the person I am.'

'Ontological. We are both at all times.'

These categories move through a hierarchy from a more superficial level of isomorphy/difference through increasingly more fundamental levels of isomorphy/difference. In comparing the numbers and types of response in each category, it needs to be borne in mind that twenty men and nineteen women gave as their response to the question that there was 'no difference' between the two roles in the way they would be perceived by an outsider. Although this group did not elaborate further, it may be that some respondents in this group also held a fundamental belief in the indivisible nature of the two roles, in common with respondents in group 6.

No data were collected in this research from outside observers to the ordination event. We do not therefore know what the parishioners, the members of congregations, or others who form these clergy couples' social and professional network made of their shifts in identity. It may have been that, in looking in upon joint clergy couples, parishioners wondered why their vicar 'needed' his wife to be ordained; or why she 'needed' this office for herself; or what would the parish lose as well as perhaps gain now that there was no 'clergy wife' in the vicarage to undertake a myriad unnamed, unpaid yet vital and necessary jobs!

A further aspect of identity relevant to joint couples was that of the couples' perceived ministerial style and whether they saw themselves as exercising a style that was different from or similar to that of their partner. The majority of both husbands (88 per cent) and wives (87 per cent) perceived their ministerial style to be different from that of their spouse. Seventeen husbands and thirteen wives responded with extra comment, over and above those who simply said that their styles were different because they had different characters or temperaments, but who did not elaborate further. The responses were sorted into three categories as follows:

Ministerial style

Directive:
I make decisions more 'on the hoof'
I'm more assertive
I'm probably more extrovert
I'm more directive
I'm more proactive and pushy
I go out looking for people, he lets them find him
I lead from the front, he from the back
I'm less pastoral, more directive, more extrovert, less patient
I'm more confrontational

Collaborative:
She's pastoral – I'm managerial
I am less direct and hands-on
My strengths are encouragement and affirmation
She's more of a dynamic leader; I'm more collaborative
She is a better administrator and organizer than I am

Collaborative (cont.):
I get more alongside people
I'm more a co-ordinator
I'm less likely to take the initiative; he's more proactive
I am more delegatory; he's more authoritarian
I am more hesitant; he is more willing to steer people

Mutual:
We've influenced each other a good deal
There is a growing together of leadership styles
We both try to enable and encourage others
We both try to lead from within the people
Neither of us is an 'up-front' person
We are both consensus people

Ministerial and leadership style is an important part of the clergy's identity and it was therefore a question which was asked of the joint clergy couples in relation to their perceptions of a comparison between the ministerial style of their partner and themselves. The question of difference between male and female clergy and within joint clergy couples in particular is an interesting one in the light of Lehman's (1993) findings, that male and female clergy who are not working together tend to be distinguishable along traditional gender lines (*pace* Francis). Contrariwise, he found that co-pastors, most of whom were joint clergy couples, demonstrated far fewer differences in ministerial style.

Although it would be unwise to draw too firm a conclusion from the small number of additional responses offered by subjects to this question, responses were almost exactly equally divided between husbands and wives across the three categories. Thus, although couples perceived differences between their ministerial styles as husbands and wives, there was no overall gender difference. This therefore provides some support for Lehman's conclusion that the fact of working together as co-pastors (which the majority of joint clergy couples in this study did) has the effect of suppressing the gender difference normally associated with ministerial style.

Marital satisfaction

Subjects were asked whether they felt that their marriage relationship had improved, deteriorated or remained about the same over the past two years. Amongst the joint couples, 55.8 per cent of the wives and 50.6 per cent of the husbands thought that it had improved compared with 9.1 per cent of the wives and 5.2 per cent of the husbands who thought it had deteriorated; 33.8 per cent and 42.9 per cent of wives and husbands respectively thought that it had remained about the same. Amongst traditional couples, 49 per cent of wives and 51 per cent of husbands thought that their marriage had improved compared with 2 per cent of both wives and husbands who thought it had deteriorated; 43.1 per cent of wives and 41.2 per cent of husbands thought that it had remained about the same. Amongst women only ordained couples, 51 per cent of both wives and husbands thought that it had improved compared with nearly 49 per cent who thought it had remained about the same. None of these couples thought that their marriage had deteriorated. There were no very obvious differences therefore between the three groups in their own perceptions of marital satisfaction, as they experienced it before and two years after the ordination of women to the priesthood.

Marriage and priesthood as model and symbol

All three groups of couples were asked if they were happy about their marriage being seen as a model of marriage for others. Amongst joint couples, 60 per cent of the wives felt happy about this and 61 per cent of the husbands. Amongst traditional couples, 57 per cent of the wives felt happy and 73 per cent of the husbands. Amongst women only ordained couples, 61 per cent of the wives and 65 per cent of the husbands felt happy for this to be so. Joint couples were also asked if the fact that they were both priests and marriage partners had any symbolic/spiritual meaning for them. Almost exactly half of both wives (49 per cent) and husbands (47 per cent) thought that it had.

These questions about modelling and symbolism were an attempt to examine the core experiences of these couples and to reveal something of their interior understanding of their joint and dual vocations. Whilst all the couples were asked if they viewed their marriage as a model for the marriages of others, obviously only the joint couples could be asked about their perceptions of the symbolism of being both priests and marriage partners. This question asked of the joint couples group was an attempt to get to the heart of the issue of positive difference which joint clergy couples might or might not represent. Put another way, it was an attempt to discover whether a joint clergy couple as an institution constituted something of unique value in its own right – something 'more' than the individual priests/marriage partners of which it was made up, or was a joint clergy couple merely two priests who happened to be married to one another? The answer to the question would affect the expectations one might have upon the Church in shaping policies that would either exploit their potential to the full or simply 'manage' the logistic difficulties that they obviously pose.

Of those seventy-one subjects who replied 'no' to this question about symbolism, some replied that they 'used to think so' but did not think so any more. Others said that they thought this might be so but could not think how. Some respondents said that they had never considered their marriage and priesthood in this way but would want to give it some thought. One respondent replied that he 'had no time for this sort of airy fairy stuff'! (As he was the father of five children under 11, he was probably right!)

The replies of those who said 'yes' were initially sorted into six categories which in turn were categorized into a hierarchy, as listed below. These ranged from those for whom the juxtaposition of marriage and priesthood had 'least meaning' (1 below) through to those for whom it had 'most meaning' (6 below), in terms of it holding for them highly important symbolism of either a psychological or theological nature or both. The replies of some subjects were classified into more than one category.

Of the thirty-eight men and forty-four women who replied in the affirmative to this question, there were twenty-three couples in which both husbands and wives agreed that their joint covenants of marriage and ministry did have symbolic meaning for them. They did not necessarily view that meaning in the same way, although the responses of eleven out of the twenty-three fell with-in the same category. That left thirty-six respondents who had answered in the affirmative, but their partner had not. Some examples of responses within each of these categories are as follows:

Symbolic meaning of being a joint clergy couple

1. Just the way it's always been/practical advantages
'I'm not sure it's priesthood, but more that we are Christians that makes our marriage have a symbolic/spiritual meaning for us.'
'Not sure I understand this – it's just part of who we are.'
'It's just the way it's always been – we wouldn't have met other-wise.'
'Being able to pray together more easily'
'We understand the stresses and strains of each other's jobs.'
'We make a good team, for we have different gifts.'

2. Sacrament of marriage is the primary symbolism
'We can share the deepest, most important things in life – but we have always shared our Christian faith.'
'Difficult to imagine union with someone who was not a priest – despite differences there is a unity at the core'
'I feel this makes us extremely committed to each other and a blessing from God in the way we came together.'
'Intimacy, constancy, unearned love – hallmarks of marriage and relationship to God'
'Affirms interdependence and mutual respect. She is the sex-iest celebrant I know!'
'One of my greatest pleasures is to share the Eucharist with my wife and receive Communion at her hands.'
'I find our partnership more satisfying.'
'I find it in a strange way inhibiting in our personal relationship.'

3. Priesthood adds something to the marital relationship
'There is an element of closeness and understanding which would not be there if we were not both ordained.'

3. Priesthood adds something to the marital relationship (cont)

'We've always felt right for each other – both being priests just adds to that.'

'Our faith adds a deeper dimension to our relationship. I think perhaps we have a more peaceful and relaxed marriage than might otherwise be the case.'

'A feeling of "chosenness and responsibility"'

4. Marriage and ministry have been inextricably linked from the start

'We met during training and neither of us were looking for a marriage partner. Our engagement was – especially for me – very much a matter for prayer and very much a sense of God's pragmatic guidance – to do with our ministries.'

'Since we met at theological college, our callings to marriage and ministry have always seemed to be deeply united and in harmony.'

'We feel that God called us into marriage and ministry together.'

'We believe we were brought together by God to be husband and wife.'

5. Sense of wholeness and unity in the self and/or in the relationship

'In our lives, there is very much a sense that "the whole is greater than the sum of the two parts".'

'Sense of wholeness and a challenge to keep growing'

'We understand each other better – at a spiritual level possibly. I don't think much has changed except there is an area of symbolic completeness in myself.'

'Seems to provide a deeper sense of oneness – unity provides a greater wholeness to each other and each other's ministry'

'We believe we are a working unit for the Kingdom of Christ. The reality is that this unity is always under attack.'

'We have a significant spiritual bond.'

6. Icon or symbol carrying some specific meaning

'That male and female can work together and bring richness and greater depth'

'Both [marriage partners] having a priestly role I think has helped the congregation grow in understanding of the purposes of creation – Christ and His Bride – union as a means of God's grace.'

'We've always thought that a balanced egalitarian priesthood is what God intended and needs for the Church to do the work of the Kingdom effectively, and that our combined marriage/priesthood has been a useful symbol of this.'

'Our marriage can be an icon of marriage/shared ministry.'

'Both marriage and ministry symbolize the Triune nature of God – a community of persons united in love with distinct work to do within the same "being".'

'A type of Christ and His Church'

'A pioneering role, challenging stereotypes'

'As priests we are a sacrament. As a "priest couple" we are a sacrament of marriage (amongst other things).'

'Being human in ministry as a model of humanity in the Church'

Some of the responses could not be confined to one category and so were broken down into several units and then placed into their appropriate categories. These categories were then collapsed into three higher order groupings, giving a more succinct account of the fundamental themes that were of importance to these joint clergy couples, as follows:

1. Continuity with some developmental pattern from the past

Responses in this category ranged over several areas. It included those who saw a connection from the start between their marriage and their ministry – that they were 'doubly called' as one respondent put it. For some this meant that their calling to ministry drew them also, through theological college, to the choice of a marital partner who would be 'right' for them as a future minister and who would therefore support their vocation to ministry both emotionally and with practical help. For others, this link with the past was in the form of an attempt to expiate the guilt of being a survivor of sexual abuse in childhood. Ordination and marriage together provided important symbolism for them of having been healed and accepted for being the person that they were.

2. Expansion of the meaning of the marital relationship

Although some couples made it very clear that the impact of their dual and joint vocations had enhanced and focused both their marriage and their ministry, for many couples, the primary impact of the symbolism of their joint vocations was directed towards the marital relationship. For them, it was a means of increasing their homogeneity and therefore their closeness as a couple. One respondent commented that their joint calling as priests was a sign that they had 'the same values, the same principles and the same beliefs'. Another said that the priesthood 'is a wonderful bond between us and I feel it gives each of us a depth of understanding about the spiritual life and the commitment of the other that is very precious'. Part of the expansion of the meaning and experience of marriage for these couples was the important movement forward into a greater egalitarianism, as a result of the wife being able to be a priest. For many of these couples, the asymmetry of the priest husband and the deacon or non-ordained wife had been hard to integrate into their belief system about either marriage or ministry. The equal partnership that was now possible between them as priests, both mirrored what they already strove for in their marriage and enabled a higher order of equality to be achieved. One correspondent commented: 'It has meant that we are both seen as entirely equal by others in ministry which is what we have always tried to be as marriage partners.'

3. Expansion of the meaning of priesthood

For other couples, the primary dynamic of the symbolism of their joint and dual vocations was in the direction of understanding and living out of their priesthoods more fully. The dual commitment of the couple to priesthood made it possible to expand the symbolism of the interrelationship between priesthood and marriage, in such a way as to assist the work of the ministry in both Church and community. The word 'icon' was used quite frequently, in order to describe the joint meshing together of the two vocations, and the way in which this was on offer to others as a model for integrating different levels of experience. As one respondent put it (who was anxious not to sound pious or 'twee'!) 'it's to do with growth in awareness and appreciation of the sacramentality of ordinary life and relationships'. Some respondents commented on the possibility of modelling some kind of joint parental relationship towards the parish, although this was an ambivalent image that others strongly repudiated, even while wanting to affirm the iconic nature of the possibilities of their dual vocation.

Several respondents tried to express the modelling potential of the interconnection of marriage and ministry and what that symbolized. One commented: 'Ministry is shared. It links male and female. It's not exclusive – it has to share outwards and not be self-contained. It expresses something of the relational quality of ministry and theology.' Another described himself and his partner as 'a cell or small community of faith within the parish'. Several respondents used Trinitarian imagery to describe the symbolic nature of how the inter-relationship of marriage and ministry offered something that was 'more than the sum of the parts' of either. One of these expanded the idea in this way. 'All my ministry, I have believed that Christian/*Trinitarian* ministry is better symbolized by a partnership between men and women, not by one or the other: that this nuclear partnership should be the creative one of a leader sharing in ministry: that there are advantages in this being a marital partnership.' And another respondent commented: 'Both men and women are made in the image of God. The fact that we are married and both priests shows the complete image of God in a small way in our lives.'

There were also some comments on the negative experience of the symbolism. One respondent noted how Christians seem to have more problems with joint clergy couples than people outside the Church. Another noted that the symbolism did not seem to be powerful enough to establish in people's minds the impossibility and undesirability of them always being able to be a clergy spouse for one another. The fact that each partner had his or her own sphere of ministry which must be served, still did not deal wholly with the criticisms levelled at the absence of each from the ministerial activities of the other. There was an implicit recognition of a potential clash between the identity of clergyperson and clergy partner as they exist simultaneously within the person of both husband and wife.

Clearly the couples themselves viewed the symbolism of their relationship in different ways and with different degrees of intensity. Some could not step outside their experience very much because they had never known anything other than both experiences together. They had met and married within the shadow of their vocations to priesthood. Some of these couples would confirm the findings of Kirk and Leary (1994) in relation to their sample of thirty-seven non-joint clergy couples, that their vocations to marriage and to ministry were very intertwined. As in their study, the couples sometimes articulated the inter-relationship in highly pragmatic terms – that the partner was seen as a useful 'helpmate' for the ministry or the fact that the partner was themselves a clergyperson 'oiled the wheels' in significant ways, for they were then able to understand the stresses and strains of ministry from the inside.

The responses of these twenty-three couples, where *both* partners thought that being both priests and marriage partners had some symbolic meaning for them, were reanalysed in order to compare this subgroup with the total group of joint clergy couples. The fact that both partners in this subgroup could identify their dual and joint vocations as carrying some symbolic meaning might suggest that they were more cohesive as couples and closer in their perceptions of their marriage and their ministries.

There were some small but interesting demographic differences between these twenty-three couples and the rest of the joint couples group. The most striking was the difference in their sibling position. Compared with 54 per cent of the joint couples group as a whole, 76 per cent of the subjects in the subgroup were either eldest or only children. This suggests that, in terms of the organizing influence that sibling position has on the personality, these subjects were likely to be more desirous and able to influence their situation and to be happy with what one of them described as 'their pioneering role' as joint clergy couples. They may well have been more conscious of their role and more interested in trying to articulate its latent symbolic meaning.

The couples in the sub-group were also slightly older, had been married longer, and had more grown-up children than the joint couples group as a whole. Therefore they had had more time together to build a relationship around the two vocations and to allow each to influence the other. Their joint vocations had developed the potential of becoming somewhat more integrated. 44 per cent of these twenty-three couples had been ordained before getting married. About half of them therefore had made a primary commitment to ordination before getting married, and this made it perhaps more likely that they would be able to hold on and develop the fundamental meaning of their vocational commitment in the face of the day-to-day vicissitudes of marriage and family life. In a similar way, the fact that more of the children in this sub-group were now grown up might have made it easier for these couples, relieved of the day-to-day pressure of dependent children, to have time and inner space to reflect upon the way in which their marriage and ministry had meaning for each other and were able to be both a mutually sustaining resource and a symbol of such for others.

In relation to comparisons between the sub-group and the joint couples group as a whole across other variables, the differences were not statistically significant, but the trend was consistently in the direction of greater closeness and possibly therefore of greater cohesion between the partners amongst the twenty-three couples. Although only half of the sub-group worked together, they spent more time together; were more critical of themselves than their spouse in relation to shortage of time spent with children; they were more able to make and keep friends; spent more of their holidays with their spouse and more of them took their full holiday entitlement. More of them worshipped together and more of them went on retreat together with their spouse. In terms of those variables which are likely to be divisive for the couple, less of the sub-group thought that competition between them was a difficult problem, and more of them would feel comfortable about having their partner as their boss. There were however no differences between how the household chores were distributed – for both the sub-group and the joint couples group as a whole, the wife did 44 per cent of the chores, whilst amongst the twenty-three couples, fewer shared them or divided them equally between husband and wife.

If this sub-group of twenty-three couples have a tendency to be closer as partners than the joint couples group as a whole, might that suggest that they have moved too far towards the enmeshment of their relationship? This is possible but there was some evidence that these couples were well able also to accommodate difference alongside the closeness within their relationship. 96 per cent of them said that they perceived their style of ministry as being different from that of their partner, compared with the still high, but lower figure of the joint couples group as a whole. Some of them described this difference in ways that made it clear that the difference was of value to them both, enabling learning, movement and growth to take place in their ministries and in their wider perceptions of each other.

The following two chapters describe the way in which an even smaller sub-group were examined in relation to their experiences of marriage and ministry, yielding a wealth of further insights into the meaning of their joint and dual vocations.

11   TWELVE COUPLES TELL THEIR STORY

Connected knowing does not flee difficult alternatives by flight into false innocence (I wash my hands of this mess) or forcible control (send in the troops). Connected knowing emerges from a way of experiencing the world in all its complexity.
Mary Grey, *The Wisdom of Fools*

In order to explore some of these issues in greater depth, twelve joint clergy couples were interviewed. A profile of each couple, together with the methodology used, is given in Appendix B. These twelve couples revealed a great deal about their experiences since the wife's ordination and the way in which their marriage had been affected. They give us a window into understanding the personal significance of the more general findings discussed in the last two chapters and it is these 'windows' which will be described in this chapter and the next. As with the clinical work, these interviews provided a rich source of material for discerning issues of importance to joint clergy couples. They thus contribute to a fuller picture of the experience of marriage and ordination for these couples over the two years since the ordination of women to the priesthood. They are used for comparison and contrast with the results of the quantitative analyses described later in the book.

The interconnection of marital and vocational choice

The calling into ministry for several of the twelve couples had followed a parallel course for the husband and the wife. The husband

and wife of couple no. 8, for example, had both begun to sense their vocations during their teenage years. They had met at university and their decision to marry was taken in the knowledge that both were being called into some kind of Christian ministry. For him this was more obviously a calling into priesthood and in reflecting upon their parallel but different paths, she was able to recognize some jealousy at hearing her husband speak about his vocational journey. Because the way to ordination for her was not open at that time, she had to wrestle to discover what it was that she was meant to do with her life. She commented: 'I couldn't talk about a sense of vocation to the priesthood because I didn't know there could *be* such a thing for me.' This sense of imbalance between them in terms of vocational possibilities had been a consistent theme within their relationship from the beginning, although the imbalance, as described later, had not always been experienced as favouring the husband.

Couple no. 11 were the youngest couple in the group and were still in their first year of being priests when they were interviewed. They met and married while at theological college and were ordained deacons together. For them the choice of their first training parish was limited, first by the policy of the diocese, that they should train in separate parishes, and second by the geographical need to find two parishes near enough to one another, because of being married. In fact they both felt well served in that they had been found two adjacent training parishes in which they were both being given a good training experience.

Couple no. 2 had met at theological college and so their decision to marry was woven into the knowledge of one another as prospective clergy. They were the first joint clergy couple in their diocese and they felt that they had been pioneers without realizing it. Like others, their vocations to the ministry preceded their relationship, but their relationship began at theological college and was therefore inextricably linked with their ministerial vocation. They were both very glad that they had met at the beginning of their ministerial lives because they had been able to grow together along the way, as marriage and ministerial partners simultaneously.

Couple no. 1 had met during their first year of a three-year course of theological training. They were able to describe something of the gentle ambiguity of the way in which acquaintance merged into friendship and friendship merged into a more serious relationship, all within the close-knit community atmosphere of theological college life. This made for an unusual beginning to their relationship. As other couples also commented, they were living very closely alongside each other, seeing far more of each other, and within an environment where work and leisure activities merged together, than would have been normal for many couples at the beginning of their relationship. The college had had one or two other couples who had met at college and gone on to marry, and couple no. 1 assumed that, like them, they would leave college and go and work together.

Diocesan policy changed before they left, however ('the Bishop had had a bad experience of a married couple'!). But in fact, although they did not work together in the same parish, they felt they were given the ideal arrangement which allowed them to develop a measure of independence and separateness in their ministries and, because their two parishes were part of a team, they were also able to be involved in each other's work. They had been ordained deacons together, but after that, felt the imbalance between them keenly, not so much because he was priested and she wasn't but more because his parish seemed obviously a larger and more interesting one. As with couple no. 11, they were having to work out their ministerial roles alongside their very young marital relationship, as they were only a year into their marriage when they were ordained deacons.

Couple no. 12 had met when she had gone to work as the chaplain of a community of which he was a member. Unlike couples who had met at theological college, this couple found that the onset of their personal relationship brought them into collision with the community, as the rules did not allow couples to marry and at the same time remain in community. Their decision to marry therefore meant that they both had to leave. For the husband, this was less difficult as he had already been thinking about ordination as a possible route before he met her, so that this provided him with encouragement to leave and begin his training. But it was a particularly hard choice for her, perhaps because she was at a different stage in her professional development, having finished her training some while earlier and having already worked in a parish before coming as chaplain to the community. She commented: 'I felt

I was doing a good job there and then suddenly having to change just at a point where I was beginning to make a good contribution and also developing in myself. But on the other hand, I suppose at a very deep level in me, I'd always wanted to be married and to be married to someone who was a soul mate ... uhm ... who understood me at a deep level. And so that overrode the situation and of course it didn't affect the fact that I was a deaconess – it just meant I just had to see where the next place of service would be.'

The wife in couple no. 12 was also able to articulate the way in which the fact that they were marriage partners would now irrevocably influence the shape that their future ministries would take. Perhaps more clearly than with any of the couples, the way in which this couple's ministries were exercised was affected by their continuing relationship with one another in the to and fro of an ongoing exchange. At the point when the husband began full-time training, the wife gave up full-time work. She commented on this process of 'exchange': 'This is where Peter began to be the person who was nominated and I became the helper rather than the other way round.'

When couple no. 5 had met, the wife did not know that her future husband was thinking about ordination. This created a considerable problem for her, and therefore for them, as it increased her parents' hostility to the marriage. Hard choices had therefore to be made at the beginning of their marriage, which they both felt, even twenty-four years later, continued to influence their relationship.

For couple no. 4, it was the wife's second marriage. He was already a priest and she a deaconess. Both factors complicated their decision to get married. The wife commented: 'If we hadn't been clergy, we would have been happy to live together and not get married, but because we were clergy this was impossible.' Thus their marriage was to some degree brought about because of fundamental demands made upon them by their ministries. On the other hand, their marriage (because of being for her a second marriage after divorce) might have jeopardized her ordination to the diaconate. Her ordination as deacon therefore had to precede the announcement of their marriage, and therefore dictated the date of their wedding. 'We posted the wedding invitations on the way to my deaconing' commented the wife, and they were married shortly afterwards.

Effects of the wife's ordination to the priesthood on the couple's marital relationship

For some couples, other events had occurred in their lives since the ordination of the wife to the priesthood, which had overtaken that event in terms of their current importance. By the time couple no. 1 were interviewed for example, they had two young children and the wife had now given up work, although she was still licensed to the parish and could, if she wished, be active as a non-stipendiary minister. These major changes in their lives had occurred very shortly before the interview took place and were emphasized by the fact that the two children were brought to the interview and were cared for during its progress by a child care assistant in an adjoining room. Their experience of marriage and ministry and the interconnection between the two had therefore gone through several changes. They were therefore able to make comparisons, not only between their experiences before and after the wife's ordination to the priesthood, but also before and after their adoption of parental roles and her change from being full-time at work within the same work setting as her husband to being full-time engaged in family work with the children and the home.

The two had consequences for one another, in that the arrival of the children had meant that the wife had decided to give up work for the time being in order to devote herself entirely to their care – yet this had come just at the moment when her priesting would have enabled her at last to exercise a full and equal ministry alongside her husband in the parish. There was therefore some sense of disjuncture for this woman alongside her overwhelming joy, and also for her husband who was now without a colleague at all, let alone one who, as a priest, would have become a colleague in an even fuller sense.

Unique among the couples, couple no. 11 had been married a month after the vote had been taken in favour of the ordination of women to the priesthood. They were therefore in a different position from all of the other couples in that they knew, from the start of their marriage, that they would both be able to go forward to the priesthood. As the wife commented, this meant that a fundamental equality in their prospective ministries was built into their marriage from the start. Because both experiences were so recent and so close to one another, it was obviously very difficult for this couple to disentangle one from the other. The wife commented: 'I suppose that because my own view of ministry is such an all-embracing one – it's about me and about who I am – and that's how I've always been in the way I relate to John – my ordination is just part of that and I really can't separate the two.'

Couple no. 8 both felt that her ordination to the priesthood had favourably affected their relationship in redressing this imbalance between them to some extent, although it did not magically change this experience of imbalance entirely. This couple were able to articulate very clearly something of the emotional complexity of being both priests and marriage partners, and the way in which their joint priesthood affected their marital relationship. The husband commented on a sense of diffidence that he felt in their looking after each other or offering care to one another. It was the same kind of diffidence that a member of the congregation might feel in 'caring' for their vicar. As a priest, one had been designated as the 'professionally competent Carer'. How then could one care for the Carer? And how therefore in a marriage between two priests could either care for the other?

They also had strong views about not wanting to work together, or see themselves as having a 'joint ministry', both for the sake of the parish and for the well-being of their marital relationship. Although they had job shared in their first post and this had worked well for them, giving him the opportunity to be fully involved in the care of their first child, they would not want to do so again. They were aware, from their observations of the ministries of others, of the phantasy that congregations can develop around a 'father and mother' and their wish to create a pseudo-family situation, with all the anger that can be generated by such unrealistic and displaced hopes. Unlike many of the couples described in Chapter 10, they were also concerned not to experience themselves as part of a 'joint ministry' for the sake of their own well-being and that of their marriage. The husband commented: 'There's not room for two priests in one family … We don't come as a job lot; we just happen both to be priests.'

The husband's attitude to his wife's ordination and their joint views as to whether or not they were consciously striving towards the goal of egalitarianism in their marriage, materially affected the way in which a couple had approached and experienced the whole ordination process. For most of the couples (though not all), the husbands had been very long-term supporters of the ordination of women and their evident pride and deep emotion at the ordination of their wife was experienced by her as personally affirming and therefore as something that added strength to their relationship. This fact was seen by several of the women as being of the greatest importance in cushioning them from the worst effects of the opposition. In addition some women, such as the wife in couple no. 9, saw the fact that she was married to a priest, and one who was an up-front campaigning supporter of 'the cause', as enabling her to undertake an extremely full ministry in her full-time work alongside her husband.

This couple had a strong commitment to egalitarianism and although they had practised their joint ministries in many different contexts over the years, including a period of time when she was at home caring for their children, the ideal of equality found expression both in their ministerial work and in their shared commitments to the family work of housework and child care. Thus they were able to move easily in and out of all of these tasks and roles in a very flexible way. The wife's ordination had removed another obstacle to their practice of equality in the roles and tasks of ministry and marriage. At the time of the interview, he had just retired as an incumbent and she had begun her first incumbency of a new parish. Their very varied experiences of shared ministry and marriage had now come full circle, with him now at home taking care of the running of the home and she entirely engaged with running the parish. The wife in this case was also able to articulate something of the 'down side' of her full and equal status, in that she was now having to use 'her less dominant skills' in running the parish and confront some experiences that she found 'scary and costly' and which had been previously undertaken by her husband. He too was having to wrestle with the mysteries of the washing machine, one aspect of household work which he had previously left to her! This couple, since her ordination, and more particularly since her induction as an incumbent, were moving from complementarity on towards real interdependence in their relationship.

Couple no. 7 also held a very strong ideal of egalitarianism for their relationship. They had 'always wanted to work together to demonstrate something about working together as equals between men and women in relation to God'. But they had had a less favourable environment in which to practise it, in terms of attitudes, policies and personnel encountered within the Church. They had held high hopes that the Church would enable them to work out an egalitarian relationship in their work setting but had been confronted at the outset by the asymmetry of ordination to priesthood being reserved for him alone. When ordination had become possible for her, it had led to her becoming a rector soon afterwards and he being licensed as a non-stipendiary minister, in what was now 'her' parish. At the beginning of their relationship, they felt that it had been 'hard work' to develop and maintain the egalitarianism that they sought, because of the imbalance in their roles within the Church. They had tried to deal with it by 'sorting everything out each night'. It seemed to take the fun out of their relationship at first, but it had also brought them closer together: they had to take on each other's problems as they related to the relationship itself – they could not get away from them.

For couple no. 1, the wife's ordination to the priesthood had made a very positive difference to both of them. Up until then, she had felt that her own ministry as a deacon in her own right had been unrecognized by the congregation, who could only view her as 'the vicar's wife'. She felt that her priesting made a tremendous difference to the ways others viewed her. The husband described feeling 'a definite sense of relief and release' when his wife was ordained a priest. In that comment may have lain hidden something of the discomfort and embarrassment felt by many men at the gender inequality of ministry, but felt more persistently and unavoidably by those whose wives were most closely affected.

The husband in couple no. 3 had been ambivalent about the ordination in general and about his wife's ordination in particular, although both of them felt that, when the event arrived, he had been fully supportive of her. The rebellious (acting out perhaps) aspect of the movement which he had detected as existing in many women including his wife, and which troubled him ('doing the right thing for the wrong reasons'), gradually seemed to him to have been 'innately and collectively' an essential part of what had to happen. When the person preparing them for marriage asked him not 'how do you feel about marrying someone who might be a priest?', but 'how do you feel about marrying someone who might be a Bishop?', the starkness of the question gave him a new perspective on what was happening: it made him feel 'terribly ordinary'. The primary connection that this husband made with that comment was the way in which his wife's ordination had, in some sense, unbalanced the relationship between them. Because she came from a wealthier and more educated family, he had felt that being a priest had redressed that imbalance. It had helped him 'keep his end up'. His own priesting had given him what he described as a 'singular identity, and to some extent self-esteem'. His wife's priesting was therefore a threat both to that hard won 'singular identity' and to the equilibrium of their relationship.

Although this husband did not make the connection, the words 'terribly ordinary' do perhaps hint as well at another dimension of the experience of having one's wife become a priest, however much in favour the husbands were. There was certainly nothing 'ordinary' about the first ordinations of women to the priesthood, and, for many years to come, there will certainly be nothing 'ordinary' about being a woman priest. It may be that unconsciously, the wife's priesting takes something away from the husband's, simply by virtue of the fact that the event was, and is so 'extraordinary'. There are strong reparative motives in people's choice of career, profession and calling and this is true for the priesthood as much as for any other kind of vocation. In the case of the women, this instinctive reaching out to what will, they hope, heal some of the earlier destructive experiences in their lives has often been quite conscious. But the same process will have occurred for many of the men. Trying to preserve the equal specialness and unique potency of these different experiences for *both* partners is only likely to happen if the couple can acknowledge, own and share some of the centrifugal dynamics that are inevitably aroused.

The husband in couple no. 4 had been more consciously opposed to the ordination of women over a longer period of time. For him therefore, his wife's ordination presented him with an experience that produced powerfully ambivalent feelings in him. Nevertheless he felt that 'in a strange way, her priesting brought us together'. They both recalled vividly sitting together at home and watching the result of the vote. The husband commented: 'We both cried ... I felt that the Church that I'd belonged to had been taken from me. But I also felt relief, partly because the debate was over and the decision was made, partly because the pain that I knew Jenny had been going through was at the end. The Church had made its decision and I felt it was right for me to stay. That's what my head said. It took a long time for my heart to catch up. But that has happened now, more or less.' Asked how she felt about his views, the wife replied: 'I couldn't believe how this person who could sew and cook and do flowers all much better than me – this "new man" – could be saying no!!'

By contrast, the husband of couple no. 2 was conscious of discovering enormous gains through his wife becoming a priest. She had been ambivalent about the idea, as there was no reason why she could not have continued to have done her youth and chaplaincy work as a deacon. But she had had a sudden experience of realizing that the question was more 'why not?' and she realized that her husband had, all along, been hoping that she would go forward. For his part, he had not realized what a dramatic event the ordination would be. He commented: 'It caught me emotionally in a way my own ordination hadn't' and he went on to say that 'it certainly developed our relationship onwards, and that sort of spin off I hadn't anticipated at all ... it's made a more complete ministry for us both, with Mary now being priest – there's a sort of wholeness about it.' The wife of couple no. 6 commented similarly: 'It's brought a lovely kind of unity' to what both of them described as an already very close relationship. 'But it's brought another dimension of unity to the relationship ... being a priest, being able to share that with my husband is very lovely and I value that very highly.'

Couple no. 2 were also very strongly and overtly committed to an egalitarian marriage. She commented: 'we had always worked as equals ... and been seen as equally running the parish and treating each other as totally equal. But then suddenly it's the feeling of really now *being* equal, because we're allowed to do the same things in the sanctuary, although I hadn't felt any lack up till then, I'd felt quite happy doing the role that I was doing. I'd not felt somewhere inside me there was this great yearning to do something else, but having gone past the priesting now, I suddenly realize that now we *are* totally equal – we are able to do exactly the same things, and I think that's part of the difference.'

Because the wife in this couple had been a non-stipendiary minister by choice since the arrival of their children, she saw herself, for the time being, as mainly responsible for the running of the home and for the care of the children. Unlike couple no. 9, therefore, they had not tested out whether their egalitarian ideals would include the division of household labour at the point when she returned to full-time work for the Church. But in relation to their ministries, this couple was able to articulate something of the essence of what was often felt to be a very elusive and subtle change that had occurred for the relationships of these couples when the wife was ordained. For them, it gave substance to the ideal and goal of their marriage, which was that of an equal partnership in all spheres of their life, both ministerially and emotionally. Thus, a major event in the growth of their relationship had been the wife's ordination. Both felt that it had had an immensely significant though indescribable effect on their marriage. He commented: 'we're even better together personally now than we were before ... there's a sense of being even closer ... we're now really co-workers together.' There was for this couple, a deepening integration of their personal and ministerial lives, which had developed over the years from their shared training experiences onwards and which had been profoundly affected by the wife's ordination to the priesthood. Several of the wives would have been able to echo the sentiment expressed by the wife of couple no. 6, in relation to her husband: 'He's more ambitious for me than I am for myself!'

The inter-relationship between marriage and ministry

The way in which the inter-relationship between the couples' marriages and ministries developed, together with the way in which boundaries were handled raised a number of interesting issues. Concepts such as the enmeshment/disengagement continuum; emotional distance regulation, boundary ambiguity and triangulation which were discussed in Chapter 7, help us to interpret some of the material from these interviews relating to this theme.

At the beginning of both their marriage and their ministries, couple no. 11 recognized the potential for clashes between the two. They felt that this was largely because of the unhealthy model of parish ministry that was offered to them, as requiring a six-days-a-week total availability from them. They could see that no marriage would flourish if both partners committed themselves to that full-time. Although people paid lip service to something better, the models that were given them by people at college and, currently by their training incumbents were of a very pressured and full working life, which seemed to come before family life in terms of priority.

Because the experience of both marriage and priesthood was so new to them, it was not easy to know whether the stresses they experienced came primarily from one or the other. The wife for example commented on the difficulty of finding enough personal space for herself – a difficulty which might well have related to the early developmental stage of a new marriage or to finding an appropriate way for her to be a priest. One of the biggest areas of conflict for them had been the sharing of household chores (until they decided to get some paid outside help). The wife, as with most dual-career marriages, whether between clergy or not, had felt keenly the injustice of having to shoulder a bigger share of the family work, when he was 'not pulling his weight'. Here it was the combination of two full-time jobs (rather than the fact that they were both in full-time *ministry*) which made the issue of how to share household chores an important matter at this early stage of the couple's marriage.

Couple no. 1 had experienced several different shifts in the way the boundary between their ministerial work and their personal lives functioned. In relation to the family work of household chores, prior to the arrival of the children, 'the deal had been' that he cleaned the house, she shopped, washed and ironed and they shared the cooking between them. But she still felt she was left doing the greater share of the work. They were however job sharing in the parish at the time, and although she was being paid only one-third of the stipend that was shared between them, she was still putting in an average of seventy hours a week into her parish work. Thus the diocese's unfair split of their stipend, which she said 'hurt her deeply', compounded her feelings about the inequity of their division of household chores. Her husband on the other hand, because of the pressure he was under, always felt that he was doing more than she was in the parish.

Although both partners tended to see the extent to which the other *didn't* fulfil expectations in relation to home and parish respectively, it nevertheless became much harder to avoid conflict over household chores when she stopped work. This of course coincided with the arrival of the children, who created the need to manage the considerable extra dimension of parental responsibilities, which also had to be shared. The couple felt however that the essential difference for them had been the fact that she no longer knew, from the inside, what the parish pressures were like, which got in the way of maintaining one's commitments to the family and the home. Now that she was not herself working in the parish, 'she realizes how many exceptions to the rule there are' and she notices when her husband does not keep the agreed '5 till 7 slot' free of parish duties to be with the children. She commented: 'when we were both working, we were in it together, so it felt, well, "that's life"', when one or other of them were unable to keep a family commitment. The new sense of imbalance between them clearly made a crucial difference to this wife's perceptions of the degree to which the parish intruded into family life, and probably distinguishes a very real difference in perception between those wives who are themselves working as clergy and those who are not, whether or not they are ordained.

Couple no. 1 were also able to articulate something of the difficulties, from both their different perspectives that were created by his ambiguous presence in the home. In Chapter 8, Lee's (1995) work on boundary ambiguity was discussed in relation to the clergy. The wife in this couple commented on the frustration of experiencing her husband 'flitting in and out during the day' but actually being absent when present, because of being at work. This couple were still very new to parenting, so the problem was felt most keenly by both of them in relation to the children. He commented on the difficulty of walking through the house to get something in relation to a piece of parish work in which he was engaged, to be confronted by the request to change a nappy.

This kind of ambiguity as to whether the clergyperson(s) are at work, or 'available' as a spouse or parent is often felt keenly by clergy families because of the ambiguous boundary around both the

working hours and the working space, which for parish clergy usually remains, in part at least, the vicarage. In fact this was not
often mentioned as a difficulty amongst the twelve couples,
although at least one clergy husband had identified the related one
of the intrusiveness of his wife's ministry into his space. The wife
of couple no. 3 was unusual, in relation to a frequently cited griev-
ance in the research and clinical literature, in saying that she had
no difficulties in finding her husband's parishioners in the kitchen
when she returned home from lecturing to her theological students, or in finding a meal being prepared by some parish group.

For some couples, the hostility experienced from the outside
world at different points in their ministries may have had the
effect of pushing them closer together. The kind of defensive triangular dynamics that often operate between husband, wife and congregation, described in Chapter 8, seemed to operate in a special
way for joint clergy couples in their effort to find what was for them
the right emotional distance from one another in their marriage
and their ministry. The diocese, the congregation, a group or individual opposed to the ordination of women, often became the 'distance regulator', mediating but also interrupting the resolution of
their relational dynamics. This 'closeness' may then have become
the closeness of a strong interdependent marriage or a more fragile defensive enmeshment, whereby the couple retreated into the
safety of their inner-relational world. The shading of one into the
other was often very close and there was often some ambiguity as
to how this was experienced.

Couple no. 9 for example described a moment in their ministry
when they were struggling to get the Bishop to acknowledge their
sense of themselves as a full and equal team, at the point when
they were about to be licensed to a new parish. They wanted this
equality symbolized in the wording of their induction. Gradually
they felt that the diocese came to understand what they were striving to embody and the parish got around a bit sooner to seeing that
they were the '"William and Mary" team – almost in a word'. And
yet such an expression, with its symbiotic connotations, emerged
from a reactive need to try to get others to 'hear' what they were
trying to offer, as being something unique and 'more than' the sum
of the parts of which their relationship as ministers was comprised. It was this same couple who, later on in their ministry,

when no longer up against the efforts of the outside world to prise them apart, were able to be comfortable in their separateness and continue the journey of learning new skills and developing new gifts in contexts that were different for each of them.

On the other hand, the congregation might get recruited in to 'filling a gap' in the emotional life of a couple, especially perhaps for those couples who were working in entirely different settings. Couple no. 8 described the complex way in which, in a previous working environment, when the wife was a vicar, her husband would feel considerable jealousy because of the way the needs of his wife's parish often seemed more urgent and pressing than his own. She however was finding a lot of support from the parish, and therefore welcomed their demands upon her, as a compensation for the frequent absences necessitated by *his* job. On the other hand, at the point when the wife was priested and, subsequently moved from her parish ministry, his jealousy became more ambivalent. Up until then, he had had a regular altar and sometimes, in the absence of another priest turning up to celebrate, an extra unexpected one. But after his wife's ordination, he became 'unnecessary' in terms of his liturgical priestly role. In addition, after her move away from parish ministry, he was also deprived of the opportunity of exercising *any* liturgical role, hitherto provided for him, vicariously, via her ministry. This kind of covert blurring between the two ministries and the secondary gains that are contingent upon it, can be exercised in a perfectly functional way, to the mutual benefit of both partners and to the enrichment of both their ministries. Its importance may only become fully apparent to them, however, at the point when it is withdrawn. Part of the anguish experienced by the wife in couple no. 5, for example, related to the fact that, if her husband took the diocesan appointment which was being offered to him, she would no longer have a base from which to exercise her own liturgical ministry.

Similarly, the partners in couple no. 3 were quite conscious of the way in which each of them gained from the very different kind of ministry exercised by the other. For her, a vicarious need was satisfied by the fact that her husband was a parish priest, as well as the helpful closeness it afforded her to the future working environment of most of her ordinand students, giving her added authenticity in the performance of her own job. For him, her theological teaching gave him intellectual stimulation, as well as encouragement to further his own theological studies. As with couple no. 5, the wife became more conscious of the gratification she found in his parochial ministry when he was threatening to change to non-parochial ministry.

This couple had done a lot of thinking about how to keep boundaries between their different areas of work as clergy. On the practical level, they had separate telephones and separate answerphones and never took messages for one another. They were clear that they would never want to work together: 'it would be the kiss of death for us' commented the husband. They worked hard at not being colleagues and almost never went to the same meetings together. On the few occasions when this had happened and it was a group or meeting that the husband was running in the parish, the husband said he had felt confused as to 'who I was in that group with her'. Often, he said, it was when she had challenged something he had said. He finds himself thinking: 'Oh God, I don't know how to deal with this ...' and (if she has corrected him over something he has said) he will find himself thinking: 'Oh dear – everyone will think I'm a fool now.' Inside he will be asking: 'Who am *I* in this and who is *she* in this?' This husband went on to say that 'because we've always gone out of our way *not* to cross into each other's circles when it comes to work, it's quite stark when it *does* appear, but it's very rare'. This suggests the interesting point that, although couples who do not work together may more easily avoid the many pitfalls of intrusiveness, enmeshment and overdependency, when they *do* come up against each other in one or other of their work settings, they have developed fewer tools with which to cope with the experience.

Couple no. 2 were very clear that they *did* want to work together, and reckoned that between them, as incumbent and non-stipendiary priest, they were probably offering the parish a one and three-quarter time ministry. The wife commented: 'we are there to help each other, remind each other, check out things with each other.' They seek professional advice from one another and, for example, he almost always reads his sermons over to her for comment before preaching them. Both would consult each other about working out a strategy for handling a difficult pastoral situation. They felt that the fact that they were both priests allowed them to be very honest with each other about the parish, and to share a lot of their thoughts. However, they were also aware of needing to keep a boundary between their work as priests. They had, for example, a very strict rule of confidentiality and did not share personal information about parishioners with each other, without the person's prior consent.

The husband also felt anxious about 'whether they are seen as a real sort of power house and whether that could be off-putting', both to the parish and to the curate. Adding a slightly different perspective, he wondered how the curate would feel 'with them both being ordained in the vicarage and with him on his own ... how that would feel'. It seemed for this couple, that there were added sensitivities to be considered because they were both ordained, over and above simply being a married couple together in the vicarage when the single curate was on his own. This led them to comment on a further potential boundary problem, whereby the parochial church council or others in the parish may feel that 'us in the vicarage are fixing things, before ever they get to the PCC'.

In terms of the boundary between their personal and ministerial lives, they felt that this was often fuzzy. They had of course nothing to make comparisons with, as, right from the start of their relationship, it had been a working one as well as an emotional one. The work of boundary marker between their private and public worlds was exercised by either of them, as part of the emotional work that needed to be done in the relationship. They did not have strict rules about when parish business should cease but each accepted that the other had the right to flag up a meta rule (a rule about the rules) so that time out or time in from the discussion of parish business would be negotiated as required and as either felt the need. Part of keeping the boundary around their separate identities and separate selves, within what might otherwise have led to some tendencies towards fusion, was having several different spheres of work, including, for the wife, some chaplaincy work outside the parish. Both felt this 'difference' was crucial to the well-being of both their work and their emotional relationship.

Couple no. 1 had had several different experiences of job sharing, including the 'inbuilt inequality' of the husband being the vicar and the wife his curate. This was obviously more problematic prior to her priesting, and it seemed difficult for the congregation then to 'recognize' her as a minister in her own right, rather than 'the vicar's wife'. However their unequal relationship of vicar and curate also introduced 'a certain amount of confusion into their relationship', with him, as vicar, wanting her to work in a particular way, and she not wanting to, but not feeling in a position to refuse. They felt that, in their personal relationship, this dynamic swung the other way round, almost as a kind of compensation, with her making the decisions about 'all the important things', and he being glad to leave them to her.

Couple no. 12 had experienced a particularly complex interweaving of their personal and their ministerial selves and the way in which events within their marriage and their family life had impacted on their ministries and vice versa. There seemed to be two interconnecting themes, the first of which was the alternating pattern of ministry between them. For this couple, ministry had been shared, in the sense that first the wife and then the husband had been the 'up-front' person in ministry and although at one time they had envisaged that in the future, they might have worked alongside one another in a parish, the pattern of one stepping aside, in order to take the supportive and unlicensed role in relation to the other, seemed to have worked well for them instead. In this sense, they functioned more like a non-joint clergy couple, the ministry being recognizably the responsibility of one, but only made possible because of the whole-hearted practical and emotional support of the other. The second theme revolved around the appalling tragedy of losing their first child when she was a tiny baby. The crisis of faith that this created for them was handled in different ways. As the wife expressed it, speaking to her husband: 'You were more able to hang on to your theology than I was.' Turning to the interviewer she continued: 'I found I got to the stage of questioning the whole thing, seeing it as just a wishful thinking mechanism. But Peter held on to a reworked theology which made him able to function as a priest.' The wife found herself in the appalling bind of having lost her faith, but feeling unable to let anyone know and therefore finding very little comfort and support for herself in her struggles. She felt great anxiety as to whether she could admit to her doubts and whether, if she did, this would negatively affect Peter's ministry and people's view of them as a couple. The effect of this for her was that she had no real friends, because the thing that was most deeply part of her and which she needed to share, she felt that 'she wasn't allowed to'.

The couple had moved to a new parish in 1992 just at the point when the ordination of women was making headline news. As people knew that Helen was a deacon, the couple were faced with the difficulty of how to explain the fact that she was not going forward for the priesthood. But the couple were also able to recognize the fact that the primary theme for the inter-relationship of their marriage and their ministry was the alternating pattern of ministry between them – that for them, it seemed to be the case that 'one at a time' was the way in which their ministry had worked out for them so far. But this also had some pragmatic convenience for their relationship. It allowed them to divide the ministerial and the family work between them on traditional gender lines. Peter commented that this pattern at least avoided the domestic conflict which would have had to be faced if both had been 'up-front' at the same time, albeit with different work loads. The fact that only Peter was 'up-front' for the present meant that he did not have the problem of fitting domestic responsibility into his schedule, which he experienced as a 'plus'. However, this was a 'minus' for Helen, who, although she felt fulfilled at one level as a wife and mother, was also taking refuge in the domestic situation whilst feeling acutely the loss of her identity, role and status, and the fulfilment that she would have experienced from living out her vocation.

This couple's experiences brought home in a particularly sharp way something of the costliness and hidden sacrifices involved in the way in which public images and expectations affect the private world of a marriage and create the framework within which it has to find ways of functioning creatively. It is of course also the case that many non-ordained clergy wives also feel the pressure to conform to many overt or half-hidden expectations, including the expectation that they will at least go to church even if they do not take on any of the formally assigned public roles. But because she had been in public ministry herself in the past (and was known to have been), it was more difficult for this wife to have many options as to how she might best handle either her grief or the loss of her faith that had ensued. More crucially, her commitment to the marriage, because of her husband being a priest, meant that certain things necessarily followed. As she commented: 'there was a stage when I wished he wasn't a priest because I would then have been given permission to actually put myself in an atheistic position and be without all these accoutrements and expectations and that may have helped me resolve it quicker ... but I found I couldn't do that, even right inside myself, because I'm so identified with who we are and who Peter is and the whole situation ... and because we've always functioned with me supporting him, right from the beginning ... then suddenly to turn round and say "I'm not going to support you any more, right from the most fundamental level – I'm not going to church" ... that's what it would *mean* you see – and I couldn't function like that in our *marriage* or in our own life at all, so I found it wasn't an option to do it that way – and so I needed to work it out from inside somehow.'

Projective phantasies and symbolic meaning

Perhaps the most difficult of all of these couples' experiences to try to understand, because so elusive, was the way in which the fact that they were now both marriage partners *and* priests carried some symbolic meaning, either for themselves or for others. Some aspects of this idea have been implicitly revealed in the exploration of other themes. Sometimes it was easier to discover more about the way in which the wife's priesting had had symbolic effects for the partners as individuals rather than as a couple. For the wife in couple no. 4 for example, she felt that 'being Reverend Mother is very important to me', a title which she used on her headed notepaper, even though it was a secular job. It carried for her strong resonances of the femininity of priesthood, of *her* femininity and priestliness combined, and of the potential power and authority of the role for someone who described herself as 'a high flyer and going places'. Contrariwise, there was something deeply troubling for her husband in the *symbolism* of admitting women to the priesthood, fundamentally changing the Church to which he belonged, and also changing for him the nature of priesthood, which now could no longer, by definition, continue to affirm unequivocally his own identity as a man.

A powerful symbol, to which several couples referred was that of the icon of a man and a woman together. Couple no. 7 felt that, as a joint couple working together, they could symbolize something of the essential equality of men and women in their relationship with God. Couple no. 5 commented that for them the priesthood was about male and female together, being contained within the wholeness of priesthood. Joint clergy couples gave expression to that symbolism in a particularly clear, overt and powerful way. The wife described them as a 'double blessing' (an expression which has given the title to this study). She saw clergy couples as offering a gift to the Church in their ability to symbolize the wholeness of male and female within the Christian community, echoing St Paul in his letter to the Galatians (3.28). On some occasions this couple had concelebrated at the Eucharist, and their wholeness as a priest couple had felt very powerful at that point.

Phantasies of sexual pairing, parenthood, protection and power are all evoked by priesthood. Does the symbolism of a joint clergy couple, linked together in a priestly, sexual, and, perhaps, parenting relationship make any difference to these phantasies?

Couple no. 1 were able to discuss something of the most intimate inter-relationship of ministry and marriage in relation to the sexual phantasies that can be placed upon the clergy in general and joint clergy couples in particular. They recounted the comment made to a colleague by a Bishop who had said that 'he couldn't abide the idea of a clergy couple being in the sanctuary together, knowing they had been to bed together the night before'. This very stark admission of the problematic nature of bringing together sexuality and spirituality finds a very clear and unambiguous image in the joint clergy couple, which, *pari passu*, may allow it more easily to get resolved. For this couple, there had been, they felt, fewer difficulties in handling the sexual projections of members of the congregation when they were visibly and openly united in both marriage and ministry. As with couple no. 8, they recognized however that the fact of being a joint clergy couple might encourage idealization of them as a kind of 'holy family', a 'horrible idea' as the husband remarked! Couple no. 6's comment that some people are made uncomfortable by 'their double act', some people finding it 'mildly embarrassing sometimes, other people finding it amusing', hints at the defensive need to hide from so direct a statement about what may be both longed for and yet feared.

But the joint clergy couple reveals rather than creates this sexual symbolism. For, as discussed earlier in Chapter 8, multiple phantasies of both a heterosexual and a homosexual nature surround the clergyperson. As with all projections, the more opaque the person or the relationship, the more likely it is to facilitate the phantasies of others. It is likely therefore, that just as the marriage of the clergy in general increases their transparency and makes them more 'real', so marriages *between* clergy increase their transparency still further and 'earth' much of the phantasy material by which they are surrounded. The experiences of couples no. 5 and no. 6 provide support for this interpretation.

The husband of couple no. 5 commented that, in his previous congregation, and prior to his wife's ordination, he had found that the overt, sexual phantasies of some members of the congregation were uncomfortable, pressurizing and demanding. He has felt much freer of these since he and his wife have been more visible as a couple, and particularly as a result of them being seen together liturgically from time to time. It is perhaps as though the up-front demonstration of the couple's union through the spiritual language of the sacrament acts as an analogue statement for their sexual union. It reveals it in a way which cannot be denied and yet because the 'revelation' is made indirectly – in the analogous language of the sacrament – it speaks powerfully to the unconscious.

A different kind of symbolism was projected onto couple no. 4 whose union as a couple and as priests, across the division of those who supported and those who opposed the ordination of women, held significance along this dimension for others as well as for themselves. At the wife's ordination, they described the way in which it took them a long time to find each other during the exchange of the 'Peace' during the service. When they did, they gave each other a really big hug, something that was noted by others at the service, as an image of the coming together of these strongly opposing views. It was as though this couple was viewed as undertaking the healing of a painful, destructive split on behalf of all the Church's members.

The joint clergy marriage also brings out into the open, issues of power, authority and dependency. The husband in couple no. 5 felt that the joint clergy couple demonstrated something about the open acknowledgement of authority, instead of the covert, hidden authority of the 'clergy wife'. A joint couple was, he felt, much less open to manipulation, and it was less easy for members of the congregation to operate the triangular 'go-between' defence so often used in relation to non-ordained clergy wives. This husband spoke from experience, for he had seen at first hand what he described as 'the curious contradiction of external submissiveness and covert power' operating in his parents' (clergy) marriage.

Reparative effects of ordination

In the sense that it helped to repair perceived lacunae in the family's script, or enabled unconscious family mythology to be continued, both partners' ordinations often had connections with their families of origin. As already noted, the husband of couple no. 3 perceived his ordination as helping him to redress the imbalance he experienced in his marriage, because of the disparities between his wife's and his own original families which differed in terms of their class and social influence.

The majority of the couples could either recall or had been told about the existence of clergy or clergy-like figures in their families, even though only two individuals had a parent who was a clergyman. Several individuals commented on the sense of continuity they experienced with these figures when they themselves were ordained. Alternatively, for some, there was a sense of change within the continuity when, for example, the individual moved out of a Baptist or Brethren background, that was experienced as having been strongly influential upon them but also limiting and constraining to some degree.

For some of the women, their ordination was experienced as powerfully reparative. Some had experienced emotional or physical abuse in childhood, which had been compounded during their adult life with the way they had felt abused or misused by the Church. The wife of couple no. 5 had suffered all through her childhood from the criticism and lack of acceptance she experienced from her parents. This related very directly to not being a boy. She felt she had lacked confidence at a deep level. The prospect of becoming a priest had thrown up a lot of hugely painful material for her around facing what it meant to be a woman in authority. She saw the ordination as an immense affirmation of women by the Church, but found accepting it for herself a very difficult thing to do. As she expressed it, there had been abuse of her as a woman and something now was being healed of that abuse, with women and men being accepted as equals, when all her childhood had told her something different – emotionally, psychologically and spiritually. Thus, ordination for this woman was 'a very complete involvement in something'.

For this couple there were, too, complex links between the healing effects of ordination and marriage. The husband had also felt rejected as a child. It had not been OK to be a boy in his family just as it had not been OK to be a girl for his wife. He felt he had been scarred by the experience of being sent away to school at an early age, making him, he felt into a very independent person who hides most of his feelings. He experienced marriage as healing, and throughout most of it, there had been a deep level of relating and rapport between them. Both felt that the now combined and shared experiences of marriage and ordination had meant a coming together for them of these two profound healing experiences and that this had been deeply wholemaking for them.

For the wife in couple no. 4, priesting was also experienced as an affirmation and acceptance, but this time after the rejection she had experienced by her first husband. The experience was complex, because her second husband was opposed to the ordination of women. But in part *because* of this, her marriage to him, was a sign and a symbol that a rejecting Church now accepted her. He, an opponent, had both taken her hand in marriage and laid hands on her at ordination. The process they were required to undertake before she was allowed to go forward for her priesting, was also a healing one. In meeting with a counsellor, she was able to work through her feelings of rejection from her first marriage. She became able to see that experience in a new light and to let go of the feelings of over-responsibility for the way the relationship had failed. The relationship between both their priesthoods and their marriage was clearly very complex for this couple. As with others, marriage had been a healing experience for both of them, but for the husband in a particular way, enabling him to become more his human self rather than only his priestly self. His wife commented: 'I think it was quite scary for him to know who he was when he was not acting as a priest ... I felt that that "flower" – the priest "flower" – had developed ever so well, but that other "flowers" of his life hadn't developed at all because the energy had all gone into the priest "flower".'

For the wife in couple no. 1, her priesting was also experienced as healing. She had lacked confidence, and she sensed herself as someone who, by nature, would always play 'second fiddle'. The hugely accepting and affirming experience of ordination, rebalancing as it did the relationship between her and her husband into a more equal one, deeply affected her own sense of herself as a person, as someone now recognized by others as a person in her own right.

12 ROLE CHANGES AND RELATIONSHIPS WITH OTHERS

I am all at once what Christ is, since he was what I am, and
This Jack, joke, poor potsherd, patch, matchwood, immortal diamond,
    Is immortal diamond.
Gerard Manley Hopkins, '*That Nature is a Heraclitean Fire*'

Relationships with non-ordained clergy wives and with the couple's own roles as clergy partners

Several of the wives amongst the twelve couples interviewed had been married to their clergy husbands for a good many years before they themselves were ordained. It was therefore possible for them to compare these two experiences. The wife in couple no. 6 had felt herself to be happily defined as a 'traditional clergy wife' for the first ten years of their marriage. Yet she felt that the most uncomfortable experiences she had had, when she herself began on the path to ordination, was amongst other clergy wives. The reactions from them fell into two polar opposite categories. On the one hand there was the wife who said with enthusiasm: 'At last, one of us has done it!' On the other hand, many others 'simply couldn't bear it. They felt I had broken the caste ... that I'd sold out ... that by implication I was saying that what they were doing was inadequate. It was really this "breaking the caste" thing. There was often a kind of veiled agenda that I was jealous of John and that there must be something wrong with our marriage if I wanted to be ordained ... uhm ... and I'm sure lots of people worried about how on earth we would manage.'

For some of the women priests in the group, their vocation as a priest had arisen via their prior vocation, or hoped-for vocation, as a 'clergy wife'. This meant that the two identities were felt to be closely interconnected from the beginning. The wife in couple no. 3 for example, recalled that, as a child, she 'saw herself as a vicar's wife'. In some sense, being a clergy wife seemed to be a way that her vocation became articulated for her, within a family culture and at a point in the Church's evolution that did not conceive of the idea of women being ordained. She could clearly remember the moment when she knew that she was going to be a priest and how she could therefore abandon her desire to marry a priest, since she was going to be one for herself. (In fact of course she did both!)

The men did not, on the whole, conceive of themselves in the new and unfamilial role of clergy husband. The husband of couple no. 7 however, because he was non-stipendiary and retired from his secular job, was often at home in the vicarage. He said that he 'takes lots of messages' for his wife. If she is out, he often deals with them himself and finds himself 'becoming her'. He felt, as an ordained spouse, that this was both a legitimate and a productive way of supporting his wife in her running of the parish. The husband in couple no. 2 had given this area some thought. Whilst he did not himself view his partner as a clergy wife, he had had a recent experience of being viewed as a clergy husband. He had met a stranger who knew his wife in her ministerial role. 'You're that woman vicar's husband, aren't you?' was his comment. The husband said that he had really liked that 'label' and found that it gave him a nice feeling. Although he did not explain the feeling further, presumably it related to the equalizing, rebalancing effect that his wife's ordination had had, and the tangible proof that the comment afforded of his wife being seen as a priest and person in her own right. The husband of couple no. 6 spoke of the way in which people would 'phone *him* in order to try and catch his wife, and then use the opportunity to unburden themselves to him. He said that it brought it home to him what his wife had put up with for years, before she was herself ordained and fully involved in her own sphere of ministry.

Several of the women had engaged with the ways in which they were in fact both clergy themselves and the wives of clergy. They had tried to discover what, if anything, this dual identity meant in practice. They had a variety of responses to the sense of being the wife of a clergyman or a clergy wife. Each expression of course suggests a very different interpretation. The wife of couple no. 4 strongly repudiated the role and was rarely seen in her husband's parish. She felt she must seem like a 'ghost' in members of the congregation's minds. 'The whole idea of being Mrs Vicar is appalling' she commented and, interestingly, felt that 'when I'm being Mrs Vicar I feel I'm not being a priest'.

Some of the women had very closely interconnected experiences of ordination and motherhood, which had significance both for their own understanding of priesthood and parenthood and that of their husbands. For the wife in couple no. 3, the two experiences had come together when she had been ordained deacon. She had been heavily pregnant at the time and so had not been required to attend the ordination retreat (a very different diocesan response from that received by couple no. 10!). For the husband of couple no. 3, his wife's experience of being both a mother and a priest meant a new awareness of how motherhood and priesthood 'richly key into one another'. It was the sort of thing he had read about in books, but to experience it at first hand was completely different and had been helpful to his own understanding of what it meant to be a priest.

Employment issues

Almost every possible combination of types of employment were represented amongst these twelve couples, ranging from couples who job shared, to those who worked together in the same parish as vicar and curate with a stipend each, to those where only one of the couple was actively engaged in ministry, the other being retired or full-time at home caring for young children. At the furthest end of the spectrum was couple no. 4, where they were not only differently employed in terms of one working as a parish priest and one as a minister in secular employment, but, in terms of their separate churches for Sunday worship, they were in different dioceses.

One of the most obvious practical difficulties for joint clergy couples is how to organize two jobs which are appropriate and fulfilling to each of the two individuals and also allow them to live together and offer some hope of them being able to achieve a reasonable balance between the needs of their ministry, their family and their own relationship. Their changing needs, dictated by their normal passage through the family life-cycle, will, as for all dual-career families, produce particular stresses at different points and bring their ministries and their family life into greater or lesser conflict, in ways described in Chapter 5. But in addition, as already described, several couples, particularly couples no. 3 and no. 5, recognized that one of the partners had considerable emotional investment in the ministry of the other, thus further complicating employment considerations for them both.

Sometimes the husband and wife had different visions of what it meant to be a joint couple and therefore different ideas about the kinds of jobs they would be doing. For example, the wife in couple no. 10 had a stronger vision than her husband of them working together as a partnership in the same parish. Ironically, the time when they managed to achieve this, in a way that was mutually satisfying to both of them, was when they were both employed by a Cathedral, working together, with the same goals and vision, but undertaking different tasks and duties. But, although satisfying to their partnership needs, these jobs were also limited professionally. They were now in the position of 'having to work their way into jobs in whatever way they can' because of the shortage of ministerial opportunities for a joint couple.

A difficult problem for any dual-career couple is how to manage job moves. Those amongst the twelve couples who were both in full-time employment had tried different solutions. Couple no. 3, for example, had learned something about the emotional complexity involved in making a move, when one of the partners had felt it to have been a unilateral and inequitable decision on the part of the other. The wife had believed that 'they had done deals with each other, and had said "your move now and my move next"'. Because she had thought they had made that kind of bargain, she was angry and upset when he had announced he wanted to look at a non-parochial job. As well as threatening to withdraw from her the vicarious secondary gains she experienced from his parochial job, she had a strong sense of the injustice of what he had done, based on her understanding of the 'contract' that they had made. He commented: 'Looking back on it in terms of praxis – the way it came about – the idea of making a move that would be to *my* career advantage, I think I handled it badly. I don't think I took all the dynamics on board at the time ... I failed to see the things we'd talked about.'

Some of the couples worked in teams in the parish alongside other colleagues. Their identity as a joint clergy couple, and their colleague's views about that, had, therefore, to be taken into consideration. The two couples who spoke most about this aspect of their ministry in some detail were both sensitive to the way in which their colleague might perceive them as a kind of power bloc, from whom he would feel excluded. The husband in couple no. 6 spoke of the way in which members of the congregation would tend to say 'you and Betty' (his wife) rather than 'you and Sarah' (his very experienced and older NSM colleague) when talking about something that needed organizing. He commented that he finds it painful for his colleague as well as annoying for his wife and himself when people regard him and his wife as heading up the team and running the parish.

For some of the older couples, there was a recognition that the new possibilities that had opened up for the wife as a result of her priesting were coming late in her working life. The wife in couple no. 6 commented: 'In a way, my career has come too late – it's part of the price I've paid for being part of this first generation.' This posed the couple with a dilemma, each anxious to forward the needs and hopes of the other, but realizing, because the husband was near, but not quite at, retirement age, these were somewhat in conflict with one another. The wife went on: 'Having come into full-time work late on, I don't want to give it up yet, but I don't think I'd be prepared to sacrifice Jack's ministry for mine.'

Disagreements with diocesan authorities

At the point when they were interviewed, the couples came from eight different dioceses, but most of them had worked in at least one other diocese before the one in which they were currently employed. Thus the experiences that even this small number of couples describe relate to a broad spectrum of diocesan structures and employment practices, some of which differed markedly from one another. One person whom I approached by 'phone to invite her and her husband for interview had had such appalling experiences that she felt quite unable to come and talk about them. The difficulties these couples had encountered with their diocesan authorities were often highly complex and it leads to the realization that these struggles are extraordinarily interesting, beyond the obvious facts of the situations, which often seem on the surface to be simply about very practical matters such as finding two jobs within reasonable commuting distance of each other, or finding two jobs, period.

However, beyond the obvious logistical problems that joint clergy couples pose their diocesan authorities lie covert issues that may not be at all easy to understand, let alone name or discuss. On the part of the couple, the process of working through the issues involved in being both priests and marriage partners *within the marriage* may have taken a considerable amount of negotiation. On the part of the diocesan authorities, the process of bringing the ordination of women to fruition and dealing with the many ongoing issues involved *within the diocese* may also have taken energy and resources, however favourably the particular diocese has been to the priesting of women. For couples and diocesan authorities alike therefore, the process of bringing these delicate matters to one another for discussion, and then having to deal with them in terms of the banalities of cash, housing and pension rights often seems to produce a regressive reaction on the part of either the diocese or the couple or both. One of the wives commented: 'You expect that you might be treated *better* by the Church than by another employer since presumably they are all Christians!' This hinted at the difficulty of squaring the expectations with the reality (and no doubt for the diocese, the difficulty of living out its Christian ideals within the fraught world of staff employment, the need to balance a budget and, perhaps, cope with a resistant congregation).

But joint couples saw themselves as coming with a gift to give and they had some natural expectation that this gift would find a welcoming response. It was often in the first shock of experiencing how differently the Church often viewed them that disillusionment set in. One of the wives commented that she 'longs for the time when joint couples can be seen as something positive for the Church'. She went on to say that the word that usually comes to mind in relation to the Church's attitude towards joint couples is that 'they are a problem to be sorted out'. At no point was this stated more strongly than by a couple who said that they had been told by an archdeacon that as far as he was concerned, joint couples were 'a lethal cocktail'. Such extreme irrationality suggests the presence of strong unconscious forces at work. A possible explanation is that, in a systemic manner, joint clergy couples are made the scapegoat for difficulties being experienced by the Church as a whole. Currently, some of these difficulties might be summarized as being sexuality, finance and staff shortages. Joint couples, as we saw in Chapter 5, bring together the sexual and the spiritual/priestly in a very intense, and potentially alarming way. Moreover, on the face of it, joint couples seem to cost more and, although there is the possible inducement of 'two for the price of one', most clergy couples refuse to comply with that phantasy and instead, present their dioceses with less flexible and less mobile staffing options, or so, at least, it seems.

Something akin to envy seems to be projected onto these couples by some diocesan authorities. One wife commented on the way in which, when she and her husband were asking that her job should take precedence, she was asked to consider 'what she was doing to her husband' by the suggestion that her job, this time round, should be the more senior one. She went on to make the point that, almost invariably, joint couples were dealt with by members of the diocese who were themselves in traditional marriages. Only perhaps one or two Bishops (at the time of writing) are themselves married to clergy. It is therefore very difficult for them to understand, from the inside, what some of the delicate, relational considerations may be for a couple who are both looking for a job move.

The wife just quoted said that she and her husband had told their Bishop that, having finished their two first training posts, they felt that her job should now be the primary one and the one therefore that needed to be arranged first, with his fitted in afterwards. She said that this felt right 'both from within their own understanding of their personal journeys as individuals and from their relationship needs as a couple'. However, 'this was completely overridden by the diocese', who were only prepared to offer the husband a living, licensing her in almost perverse contrast, first to a temporary job as a curate and then to an even less secure situation, without any sense of continuity or possibilities for the future. Couple no. 8 also experienced the diocese's difficulty in accepting the priority of one of the partner's needs (this time it was the husband's) to be considered first in terms of employment, and they also experienced the anger and frustration of the imperviousness of the diocese to their own relational needs.

The wife in couple no. 4 felt that the Church was a poor employer, of both men and women. She was particularly critical of its lack of an equal opportunities policy, which had by no means been resolved by opening the priesthood to women. For her, the fuzzy boundaries, unrealistic demands on its staff, to the detriment of their families, and poor management, all persuaded her that she could exercise her own priesthood more productively in the sphere of secular employment.

Attitudes change over the years and it clearly is not the case, when discussing the experiences of a small group of twelve couples, that one is always comparing like with like. For a couple such as couple no. 6, where the wife trained for the ministry in the late 1970s and was made a deaconess in 1980, her selection conference experiences are probably not typical today. However, this writer has heard stories that come from other women much more recently, that makes this individual's experience worth highlighting, both because of its effect upon her and because it is not so very dissimilar to that of others today, despite much greater awareness of the issues and some emerging good practice. This wife described her whole selection experience as 'very negative', involving endless questions about her relationship with her husband. They seemed to focus on how, because of him being a clergyman himself, could her ordination possibly have a benign effect on their marriage? This kind of approach continued until right up to the eve of her ordination, when she was asked by her Bishop at the end of her retreat: 'Why does a clergy wife want to be ordained?'

On the other hand, the wife of couple no. 9 had had a completely different experience, even though she was made a deaconess in 1975 and had therefore been selected and trained for ministry earlier than the wife of couple no. 6. The wife of couple no. 9 was the first woman in her diocese, who was married to a clergyman, to want to be ordained. She commented: 'some people still say that I was the one who started the rot!' This was however experienced as a very different reaction from that experienced by couple no. 6. For this woman, 'all the doors just seemed to open'. She moved easily through her selection conference, was accepted and found that her previous theological training was affirmed without question in that she now only had to undertake part of the training course. After training, a job was created for her with a full stipend in her husband's parish. The contrast between the women's experiences in these two couples underlines the way in which it is not so much the *period* in time which makes the difference but the *policy and attitudes* of the different diocesan authorities. This in turn must lead to caution in assuming that 'the world is now a different place' for those who are trying to combine marriage and ministry in two joint vocations.

The most extreme consequence of conflict with diocesan attitudes recounted by one of these twelve couples in fact occurred during the months leading up to the 1994 ordinations and is therefore of very recent origin. The conflict was of such intensity that it led to the premature birth of the couple's second child. Another couple, couple no. 10, described the way in which the fact that the wife was pregnant created the most intractable difficulties for her in relation to the diocese. These two examples can perhaps best be viewed and understood systemically, as a symmetrical struggle between the couple and the diocese that moved into a 'runaway' process.

The most striking fact about the twelve couples was their ability to confront the many challenges of their situations, with strength and creativity. Although for some of them, not much had changed in terms of life-style when the wife had been priested, all of them were travelling a complicated route in order to juggle the demands of marriage and ministry more or less successfully. Sometimes this had been done with a lot less support and understanding from their diocesan employers than might have reasonably been expected. Few if any had been looked upon by their dioceses as a 'double blessing', but that does not mean that their dioceses' judgement upon them was sound or valid or that they were not in fact making a good job of both their marriage and their ministries.

What might we learn from these twelve couples? To what extent do their particular experiences support theories of marital interaction in relation to clergy couples and dual-career marriages, and to what extent do they confirm the findings of the quantitative work done in this study? It needs to be reiterated at this point that these couples did not come for therapy. They are not clinical couples and, although in many ways the issues that they were struggling with are not markedly different from the ones being dealt with by the couples described in Chapter 2, it is even less appropriate in relation to these couples to make any evaluative comment upon their chosen ways of living out their marriages and their ministries. Only a few general observations will therefore be made at this point, leaving a more general discussion to the final chapter.

Bearing in mind that joint clergy couples can, to a greater or lesser degree, be described as dual-career couples (depending upon how fully each individual is at any one moment in full-time employment), it is surprising how little the idea of competition as a dynamic within the relationship was discussed during the interviews, although of course it did arise as a topic in other guises. In Chapter 5, both the synergistic and the dysfunctional aspects of competition between the spouses is discussed in relation to dual-career couples and it is an issue that has been considered in American studies of joint clergy couples (see Chapter 9). Only two or three couples talked openly about the potential for competition within their relationship or the actual experience of it. But the infrequent *acknowledgement* of competitive feelings, coupled with the frequency with which couples had experienced struggles with employing authorities and personnel, suggests that some displacement of these feelings may be occurring. Given the stresses involved in handling the many new aspects of their ministerial and family lives during the first two years after the wife's ordination, it would feel much safer for these couples to displace angry and conflictual feelings onto 'the diocese' or some other outside recipient, thus more easily preserving the integrity of the marital relationship. This is not however to deny *either* the very real difficulties some of these couples had experienced with the Church as an employer, *or* the obvious and impressive strength, health and resilience of their marital relationships.

Every ministerial choice, on the human level, is hedged around by limitations, in the sense that no individual has total freedom in seeking out an area of ministry for which they feel best suited. Thus clearly, clergy who are married to non-ordained spouses will be limited in their freedom to move into some areas of ministry by the fact that their wives cannot easily move jobs, or a critical moment has been reached in the school careers of one of the children. The claims of ministry and family often clash. The question at issue here is whether or not couples in joint ministry face *more* complicated considerations, especially at the beginning of their ministries and whether the fact that they are married to a fellow clergyperson places more limitations upon those choices.

These struggles with diocesan authorities often seemed to revolve around unrealistic expectations on the part of one side or the other. In summary, it seems unreasonable on the face of it, for a clergy couple to complain about not both being employed, if two jobs do not exist. It would be unreasonable for two doctors, married to one another and both seeking employment, to complain for the same reason. However, there are particular considerations which complicate the situation for the joint clergy couple and make their apparent 'unreasonableness' more understandable. First, the dual and contradictory expectation on the part of the Church that the house 'goes with the job' *and* that the priest must be resident in his/her parish, immediately limits the flexibility of those couples who both want to work as parish priests. It is becoming accepted that one of the pair may in fact have to commute to their parish, but this still leaves them with the difficulty of finding parishes near enough to one another to make this a possibility without creating a completely unviable situation for the family. Second, it will be argued later in this chapter, and again towards the end of this study, that clergy couples are not merely a peculiarity of ministry, reflecting the *ad hoc* decision to marry of two individuals who happen to be priests. They represent a form of ministry in its own right that requires that the Church creates for it a new 'shape' within which it can function. This is required, both for the sake of the Church and for the sake of the couple. Third, this suggests that, for those couples who are jointly selected for training (an increasingly frequent occurrence), the Church might reasonably be expected to take a medium to long-term view in its recruitment policy, so that these joint couples at least might expect that selection and training would be followed by the offer of employment possibilities, likely to enable this particular form of ministry to flourish.

Until these ideas are grasped more fully, many joint couples find that the most manageable solution seems to be for one to be employed in a parish and the other in a sector or diocesan ministry. It was the choice made by several of these twelve couples, carrying with it, as we have seen, the advantage of providing the non-parochial partner with opportunities for the liturgical expression of his or her ministry if that was what was wanted. In particular, as one wife put it, if *one* of the pair can get a job with some regular time boundaries around it, this can stabilize both partners and offer some chance for them to balance the demands of their ministerial and their family lives.

The diocese for its part may be unreasonable in expecting a joint couple to undertake two jobs (where two posts are already established) in exchange for one stipend. Only the rather poor argument that a 'stipend' is not a salary, but the means whereby the Church enables its ministers to undertake ministry, prevents this organizational behaviour being considered as nothing short of derisory. This is particularly true when it is combined with the inequitable gender assumption that the woman rather than the man should forgo her stipend. The offer to a joint couple of a stipend for one partner, with the other being licensed as a non-stipendiary minister, is a very problematic solution when this is being used as a way of arriving at a compromise between what the couple really want and what the diocese feels it can offer. The difficulty for the couple is that, whereas in other occupations, there is either a job on offer or there isn't, the non-stipendiary licence falls into a grey middle area between the two. Non-stipendiary ministry is a perfectly valid form of ministry to which many priests are called but not when it is offered and taken as a fudge to get around such difficulties as the lack of a post, shortage of money, denial of women's right to equal employment status, collusion with a parish's hostility to a woman in a leadership role, etc., etc. In these circumstances, being an NSM carries many negative connotations which have to be dealt with in some way within the couple's marriage. Several couples in this group described the ongoing difficulties of dealing with imbalances in their relationship of various kinds, which were in some cases exacerbated by the Church's employment policy.

On the other hand, the fact of being a joint couple allowed these twelve couples an enormous range of possibilities for their growth as individuals and as a partnership. The positive side of the lack of clarity in the Church's response to joint couples is that it enables these couples to work out a multitude of different ways of connecting their ministerial and their family lives – experimenting with balancing their roles in different ways; adapting their ministries to the stage that they are in the life-cycle and in relation to the needs of their children and encouraging one another along their separate but interrelated ministerial journeys. The image of the dance has, for many years, been a classic image in the family therapy literature describing the dynamics of family and couple interaction. It seemed a very apt image for these twelve couples, as they moved in and out of different expressions of their ordained ministry, one in relation to the another.

The steps of the 'dance' were easier to discern for some couples than for others. Job sharing was one quite straightforward pattern, even if anything but straightforward in the living of it. But there were other patterns too, which, in a less overt and less clearly articulated way, enable the couple to move in and out of each other's ministries, one stepping aside while the other's ministry came to the fore. This allowed the couple to adjust their involvement in ministry to fit in with the needs of their families, with the differing needs of each of them to undertake the 'hands on' care of children, and with the changing and evolving sense of their vocations. The impression is that of ministry which is deeply shared at a profound level of understanding, regardless of differences in the contexts in which it is exercised.

In fact it would be important to underline the point that no simplistic glance at the degree of difference between types of ministries in which the partners were involved would say anything very much about the quality of the relationship between the two. For some couples it was very important both to be working together in the same parish, alongside one another, sharing pastoral concerns and responsibilities and participating each week in a shared liturgical event. Others felt the need to work in different spheres of ministry, but felt it essential to worship together on Sundays. Others needed to work under what they described as 'the same umbrella' perhaps in the same parish team but in different parishes. Others again needed to work in quite separate kinds of ministry and in quite separate places. But these needs had clearly changed for couples over the past two years and showed every sign that they would continue to change and interweave, allowing each to develop different aspects of themselves, both personally and ministerially.

The way the dance was danced may also have been significantly affected by the stage in the life-cycle and in their working lives that the couples found themselves to be, at the point when the wife was priested. With their working lives ahead of them, a couple may have needed to struggle together and in opposition to one another, in order for each to define what was essential to their development as individuals, and in the process, create what would enable the relationship to flourish. At the mid-point, and again towards the end, the issues and tasks for the couple would have been different. Twelve couples is obviously too small a group from which to draw any conclusions, but even within this number, there is a sense in which the wife's priesting is mediated differently for them, according to *when* it has occurred in the couple's life course.

These were the different steps and sequences used at different moments in the creation of the dance. Far more significant is the underlying commitment to the dual covenants of marriage and ministry and the relationship between them, involving, as it clearly does for these twelve couples, a strong investment in each *and* in the investment in each made by the other person.

The closeness/distance dimension has particular significance for any dual-career couple, but, as has been noted in earlier chapters, it has added dimensions for joint clergy couples, who are sharing on a multiplicity of different levels of experience – spiritually, sexually, procreatively (in many cases), vocationally and for some, occupationally via the same work setting. For couples whose natural tendency and desire it is to work closely together, the danger for them is that of enmeshment and overdependency, with the consequent avoidance of difference and the stifling of growth and development for each person as an individual. Clinging together in an undifferentiated 'glob' of marriage and ministry in the face of a world that is often perceived to be hostile may become the temptation! On the other hand, for those couples whose natural tendency is to guard their separateness and define themselves in contrast to the ministry and approach of the other, the dangers for them are those of disengagement, lack of cohesion and a reduction in opportunities for growth in mutuality.

Some of the twelve couples were clearly more attracted towards one relational solution than the other. Being either too close or two distant has its dangers and may reduce the ability of the couple to nurture their relationship *in its own right*. Finding an optimum place along this closeness/distance continuum remains a challenge for all married couples, but, because it is such an obvious difficulty for the joint clergy couple, it may in fact be less easy to avoid working at the problem.

The issue that seemed to reveal most conflict between the couples was the issue of egalitarianism, as represented by the equal division of the tasks of outside work and family work (household chores and child care tasks combined). This is not surprising considering that one of the most repeated and consistent findings of research into dual-career couples is the way in which couples hold strongly to an ideal of egalitarianism for their relationship, but find the reality hard to deliver in practice (see Chapter 5). The difficulty increases in proportion to the number of children being cared for by the couple. One or two of the couples were able to describe their division of work both outside and inside the home as done on a 50/50 basis. One or two had completely (or almost completely) reversed their previous traditional gender role division, because the husband had stopped full-time work, whilst his wife had increased her ministerial responsibilities. But several of these twelve couples had experienced conflict to a greater or lesser extent, both within the relationship, over how family work was divided or handled between them, and, on the more general level, of experiencing the gap between their reality and their ideal.

Sometimes the couple described the conflict as having been very sharp between them in this area, but as having been side-stepped, by the organization of outside help with child care, household care or both. In the detailed reviewing of the video material, the underlying unease between husbands and wives was more often discernible through their embarrassed laughter, jokes or their non-verbal movement or facial expressions. There was perhaps a painful awareness for some of them that, whilst, for the women, a huge stride towards egalitarianism had been taken by the Church, the more mundane step away from the kitchen sink had yet to be fully achieved.

The degree to which the couple perceived the wife's priesting as representing a significant watershed moment in their relationship was quite difficult to tease out. This was in part because the couples varied according to whether they took primarily a functional or an ontological view of what ordination meant. Some, almost despite their more functional inclinations, nevertheless felt that the wife's priesting had introduced a very remarkable change into her life as an individual and into the relationship. The comparison between the period before and after her ordination was further complicated by the fact that for some of the women and for some of the couples, the moment of greater change was the moment when the wife was ordained to the diaconate, as this represented her entry into holy orders *and* was accompanied by a series of very visible symbolic changes in both dress and function. Thus, both functionally and ontologically, ordination to the diaconate, seven years earlier in most cases, was remembered as a greater moment of change.

Additionally, ordination to the priesthood had only taken place two years ago, a very short time in which to experience the fruits of change. Moreover, other very crucial life events had also taken place during this period, making it difficult for the couple to determine whether they or the fact that the wife had been ordained priest, were responsible for any changes that they felt had occurred. Given the presence of all these factors, it was all the more remarkable that some of these couples were able to talk about the wife's ordination to the priesthood as bringing about major beneficial changes in their relationship and in how they viewed each other as partners.

13 CLERGY COUPLE DIFFERENCES

We must encompass contradictions and make our peace with them.
Ruthellen Josselson, *Ethics and Process in the Narrative Study of Lives*

The final part of this study consisted in the investigation and comparison of the three groups of clergy couples with one another, and in relation to changes which might have occurred in their marriages during the two-year interval which had elapsed since the ordination of the women as priests. The purpose of this part of the study was to determine as objectively as possible whether the couples shewed difference or change in levels of those relational ingredients of similarity, androgyny, cohesion, equity and mutuality which have been shown to be associated with marital satisfaction. It is to this material that we will now turn.

The extent to which the hypotheses (described in Chapter 9) could be upheld was tested using three psychometric tests. These were selected to examine the dynamics of the three clergy couple groups and the change that might occur after the women's ordination, in order to determine the extent to which the five selected ingredients of marital satisfaction identified in Chapter 5 could be observed or inferred from the results of these tests. The tests were administered to all three groups of clergy couples, just before and two years after the women were ordained. The results of these investigations are described in this chapter. (See Appendix C for a description of the tests.)

Sex role typing

As discussed in Chapter 6, one of the particularly interesting suggestions that has been made about the personality make-up of both clergymen and clergywomen, has been the way in which both genders appear to exhibit higher levels of sex-role characteristics that are stereotypical of the other gender (Francis *et al.*, 1990, 1991, 1992, 1994). Bearing these reported sex typing differences in mind, one of the interests of this study was the way in which clergy might exhibit differences in their sex-role classification according to the three different types of marriage which they inhabit.

Accordingly, one of the four hypotheses that was advanced was that the clergy in the three groups would exhibit higher levels of those characteristics which are stereotypically associated with the other gender and that these would be reflected in different degrees of similarity between husbands and wives across the three different types of clergy marriage. In other words, it was hypothesized that in traditional couples, there would be similarities between husbands who were clergy and their non-ordained wives on those variables that are associated with femininity; that there would be similarities between wives who were clergy and their non-ordained husbands on those variables that are associated with masculinity and that there would be similarity on both masculine and feminine variables within joint clergy couples.

The results of the tests done on the first occasion, before the women were ordained, were mixed. When ordained men from the joint and traditional couples combined were compared, as whole groups, for femininity with non-ordained men from the women only ordained couples, no significant difference was found. However, when the masculinity level of the ordained women from the joint couples group and from the women only ordained couples combined, was compared with the non-ordained wives in the traditional couples group, the trend was in the predicted direction but did not reach statistical significance. Thus, in terms of an intergroup comparison of masculinity and femininity between clergy and non-clergy, the results did not confirm the hypothesis. Although the direction of the means when the groups were tested on the first occasion suggested that ordained women might be more masculine than their non-ordained counterparts, ordained men did not exhibit higher levels of femininity than their non-ordained counterparts, in the way we might expect from Francis's findings. This result therefore lends only weak support for Francis's findings and for the first part of the fourth hypothesis of this study.

The results of the comparisons of selected items from the Bem Sex Role Inventory gave stronger support for the hypothesis on sex-role reversal, as did the intra-couple comparisons for similarity (see section below on similarity). Husbands and wives in traditional couples saw themselves as similar in respect of 'sympathy' and 'sensitivity' to others (classified by the BSRI as feminine) but not similar in relation to leadership dimensions. Likewise, husbands and wives in the women only ordained couples saw themselves as similar on the masculine dimensions of 'assertiveness', 'having leadership qualities', 'acting as a leader' and 'being independent'. Joint couples saw themselves as similar on the masculine dimensions but not on the feminine dimensions. In respect of the joint couples therefore, it seems that the women clergy, in line with their sisters in the women only ordained group, were displaying more masculine qualities than the male clergy were displaying feminine qualities. This may have been because the effort to achieve ordination for women was still so recent – an effort which had often required of them the exercise of leadership, independence and assertiveness to a high degree.

When the couples were tested two years later, the results of comparing the groups as a whole of ordained subjects with non-ordained subjects in terms of their levels of femininity and masculinity were more clear cut. When ordained men from the joint and traditional couples combined were compared for femininity with non-ordained men from the women only ordained couples, no significant difference was found. Similarly, when the masculinity level of the ordained women from the joint couples group and from the women only ordained couples combined, was compared with the non-ordained wives in the traditional couples group, the means for these two groups had converged. In other words, there were no observable differences between ordained and non-ordained subjects in terms of their levels of masculinity and femininity. Thus, in terms of an inter-group comparison of masculinity and femininity between clergy and non-clergy, the results did not confirm the hypothesis.

Although the direction of the means when they were tested on the first occasion had suggested that ordained women might be more masculine than their non-ordained counterparts, there were no differences between them when they were tested two years after the women were ordained. Similarly, ordained men did not exhibit higher levels of femininity than their non-ordained counterparts on either occasion. If ordination had any effect on the women in relation to their sex-role characteristics, it thus *reduced* the difference between them and the non-ordained group of women in the study.

The results of the comparisons of intra-couple levels of similarity, however, continued to give some suggestive support for the hypothesis (see next section). Similarly, the results of comparing selected items from the Bem Sex Role Inventory gave some support to it, especially in relation to ordained women married to a non-clergy spouse. Both partners in the women only ordained group now perceived the ordained wives as being more 'assertive', 'acting more as a leader' and 'having more leadership abilities' – in other words, they continued to perceive themselves and be perceived by their husbands as being stronger in these masculine qualities; equal with their husbands in terms of the masculine qualities of 'independence' and 'having a strong personality' but stronger than their husbands in terms of the feminine qualities of 'sympathy' and 'sensitivity to others'.

On the other hand traditional couples, whilst perceiving the husband as acting more as a leader, continued to view husbands and wives as equally sympathetic and sensitive to others – in other words they continued to view the male clergyman as being equally expressive of these feminine qualities as the wife. For joint couples, the observable change was more in terms of the increased perception of the wife's masculine qualities than vice versa (movement both ways in both husbands' and wives' levels of femininity and masculinity respectively would have been needed in order fully to support the fourth hypothesis), but whilst the male clergy continued to be perceived as being less sympathetic and sensitive than their wives, none of the other (masculine) qualities were viewed as being expressed at a different level between the genders.

Obviously it was the women in both groups who had been the primary recipients of the potentially change-inducing experience of ordination, and who had exercised their priesthood for the first time over the two years since the first testing. It is not unexpected therefore that the women should show the greatest changes over the two years since ordination, in comparison with the two groups of couples where the husband was himself a clergyperson.

Sex role classification

The clinical literature has linked different sex-role classifications with marital satisfaction and with individual psychological adjustment. In particular, androgyny has been correlated with both, in contrast with the undifferentiated classification which has been correlated with marital distress. It was obviously of interest therefore to examine the levels of the androgynous and undifferentiated classifications in all three groups of couples and to compare these with the norms established by Bem.

As compared with Bem's norm of 30 per cent, the ordained women in the joint couples group were almost exactly similar (28 per cent); the ordained women married to non-ordained husbands were somewhat less androgynous (21 per cent) and the wives in traditional couples were considerably less androgynous than the norm (17 per cent). Husbands in joint couples were more androgynous than Bem's norm for males of 20 per cent registering a level of 25 per cent. Husbands in the traditional group were higher still (28 per cent) whilst the non-ordained husbands of clergywomen were very comparable to Bem's norm (21 per cent).

We might however have expected that androgyny would have accounted for a higher percentage of the classification of sex-roles amongst clergy couples, since being androgynous is consistently correlated with marital satisfaction (Chapter 5) and if clergy generally have more functional marriages than the population at large (Chapter 7). In the event, with the exceptions of the non-ordained clergy wives and the ordained women married to a non-ordained spouse (both of which groups shewed a lower level of androgyny than the norm), all the other groups of both male and female clergy are very comparable with Bem's norms. There were no statistically significant differences between the three groups of clergy couples, nor any observable consistent trend that distinguishes them. Androgyny accounted for a slightly higher percentage of the distribution of classes amongst joint clergy couples but the comparisons with the other two groups are too close to observe any trend.

The male and female subjects in the three groups were compared again two years later both with the normative data and with the results of the first testing. There were no significant differences between the results of the first and second testing, and thus no difference could be discerned in relation to sex-role classification that might have been attributable to the effect of the independent variable of ordination. As compared with Bem's norm of 30 per cent, the level of androgyny in all three groups was still somewhat lower. It had in fact fallen for women in joint couples and risen for both the ordained women married to a non-ordained spouse and for non-ordained women in the traditional couples group. All three groups of women were also higher than the norm in terms of being undifferentiated, suggesting that it was more difficult for the women, whether they were ordained or not, to develop both high and equal levels of masculine and feminine qualities. On the other hand, the men in all three groups, again irrespective of whether they were ordained or not, were all slightly above the norm for androgyny and below the norm for being undifferentiated. Both of these differences, which had been discernible on the first occasion, were even more clearly demonstrated on the second.

An interesting difference does therefore begin to reveal itself in comparing all the males and all the females across the three groups with Bem's norms for males and females respectively. The male subjects in all three groups were considerably lower than the norm for masculinity and considerably higher for femininity; whilst the female subjects in all three groups were lower than the norm for femininity and higher than the norm for masculinity. Thus, whilst no significant differences in sex typing revealed themselves in the comparisons between ordained and non-ordained subjects (as discussed in the previous section), when viewed as whole gender groups in relation to the normative data, there did appear to be some consistent differences between these subjects and the norm.

It raises the interesting possibility that when clergy couples are examined for differences in sex typing, it may not be the fact of ordination *per se* that creates the difference, but the fact of being part of a *clergy couple system* embedded in the wider system of the Church, together with the many unique contextual features which characterize the make-up of that *wider system*. In other words, perhaps it is the case that there is something about being part of a clergy marriage, which, as discussed in Chapters 7 and 8, has many distinctive features to it, that creates the difference that makes the difference for these couples. Some implications of these findings will be discussed in the final chapter.

Similarity

Similarity between husbands and wives is another relationship variable which has been shown to be correlated with marital satisfaction. The level of similarity between husbands and wives in each group was therefore examined on the basis that the same sex-role classification, regardless of whether it was low or high, has been shown to be a very important variable for a couple to share, since sex-role stereotypes influence both behaviour and cognitions about relationships.

In terms of both androgyny and masculinity levels, husbands and wives in joint couples were significantly more similar to one another than were husbands and wives in traditional couples. In other words, joint couples shared the same (quite high) level of androgyny, whilst husbands in traditional couples were considerably more androgynous than their wives.

The other comparison to reach statistical significance was the difference between the androgyny level of women only ordained and traditional couples – the husbands and wives in women only ordained couples being more similar to one another than were the husbands and wives amongst the traditional couples. Logically there is no particular reason why this might be so, other than perhaps the powerful effect that preparing for ordination may have had on changing the functioning of the individual partners in the women only ordained group in comparison with the traditional couples group, which, of the three groups, was not directly affected by the independent variable of ordination.

Other comparisons were not statistically significant, but the trend was in the predicted direction in almost every case. Husbands and wives in joint couples were more similar to one another because, as predicted, each clergyperson is likely to have a larger share of psychological characteristics associated with the other gender than is so of the population at large. This will make a couple, where both partners are ordained, more similar than a couple where one partner only is ordained. In relation to all three classifications, masculinity, femininity and androgyny, this trend held good in comparisons between joint clergy couples and both the other couple groups, except for the comparison on femininity with traditional couples. Here, the husbands and wives amongst the traditional couples were more similar to one another than within the joint couples.

Predictably too, in the comparisons between husbands and wives in the women only ordained and the traditional couples group, the women only ordained couples were more similar in terms of masculinity and the traditional couples were more similar in terms of their femininity. As these levels of similarity did not reach significance, the results give only weak support for the hypothesis concerning sex type reversal – but because of the trend, there is some support here for the view that both clergymen and clergywomen are nearer to the norm for the other gender, and therefore in terms of femininity and masculinity respectively, they are more similar to their non-ordained partner who exhibits more typically in relation to his/her gender norms.

Similarity between spouses was also tested by the FES. The profiles of all three groups show a high degree of similarity of response between husbands and wives, particularly between those in the traditional couples group. There were no statistical differences between the results of the groups. These however were inter-group comparisons and do not in themselves reveal the level of similarity or otherwise within couple relationships themselves. This was revealed however by the incongruence scores within the three couple groups. Again there is very little difference between them, although they show the women only ordained couples, followed by the joint couples, displaying more incongruence between the scores of husbands and wives than do the traditional couples. In this respect, the prediction that joint couples would reveal a greater degree of similarity than the other two groups was not confirmed.

The level of similarity between husbands and wives within the couples in each group was also examined two years after the women's ordination. There were only two significant results, but the trend, with one difference, remained in the predicted direction. Unlike the first occasion, women only ordained couples showed more intra-couple similarity than joint couples in relation to their level of masculinity. This is however consistent with other observable effects that occurred in the two years after ordination for the ordained women in this group. In comparison with the ordained women in the joint couples group for example, more of them have full-time and stipendiary posts, and more of them therefore are competing with men in the wider spheres of professional ministry. They are, in other words, taking and using opportunities to exercise the more masculine sides of their personalities.

Not surprisingly therefore, there is, on the second testing occasion, a significant difference in level of intra-couple similarity between women only ordained couples and traditional couples in terms of masculinity. Husbands and wives within joint couples too remain more similar to one another, as would be expected, compared with husbands and wives in traditional couples. In all other respects, the results remained the same as on the first occasion, except that the differences in levels of intra-couple similarity between joint couples and women only ordained couples in terms of androgyny were not now significantly different.

Similarity between husbands and wives as whole groups was again tested by the Family Environment Scale. The profiles of all three groups showed, if anything, an even higher degree of similarity of response between husbands and wives regarding the perceptions of couples of their family environment. There were no statistical differences between the results of the three groups but the husbands and wives in each group had very similar perceptions to one another. The following two figures show, by way of an example, the high degree of similarity in the perceptions of family life of husbands and wives of the joint couples.

On the second occasion too, the incongruence scores revealed that both joint and traditional couples fell below Moos's norm, showing a higher degree of intra-couple similarity than the norm for four-person families. In contrast, women only ordained couples revealed less similarity in perception of their family environment than the norm, though they have moved slightly nearer to the norm than they were when first tested. Thus, two years after ordi-

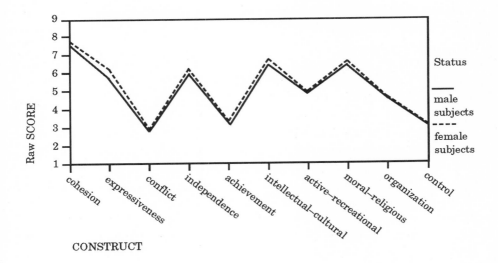

Figure 13.1 Profiles for joint couples group. Time 1

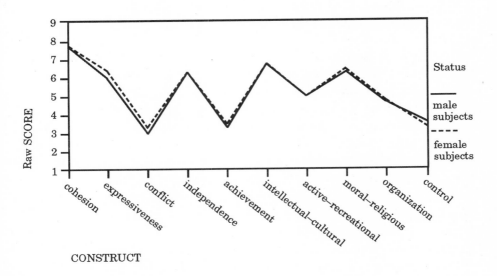

Figure 13.2 Profiles for joint clergy couples group. Time 2

nation, joint couples have become more congruent in their perceptions than they were before – husbands and wives of one another. They are also slightly more congruent in their perceptions than were traditional couples. In this respect, the prediction that joint couples would reveal a greater degree of similarity than the other two groups was confirmed.

Mutuality

Mutuality is a bi-directional element of relationships which has been shown to be correlated with marital satisfaction. Its definition and importance was discussed in Chapter 5. As might have been expected, the distribution of scores for mutuality for all three groups of clergy couples was skewed, in that the majority of scores for each group fell above one standard deviation above the mean, i.e. above average for the population at large. This shows three groups of clergy couples all demonstrating high levels of this important relational ingredient and, if we accept the connection between mutuality and marital satisfaction, as providing some hard evidence of this in their marriages.

The scores of all three groups of female subjects was compared with those of all the male subjects, and there were no differences between them in relation to the extent to which they demonstrated mutuality. Men and women scored equally. However, when the genders were compared within their three respective groups, women were found to score slightly higher in terms of mutuality than men in both the two comparison groups, but not when husbands and wives in the joint couples group were compared. Joint couples scored both highly and similarly with one another. Since all three groups demonstrated a high level of mutuality, it was not surprising that no significant differences were found between the three groups, when the groups as a whole were compared with one another. However, there was a slight trend in the predicted direction, with joint couples scoring more highly than both traditional couples and women only ordained couples and to that degree, demonstrating a slightly higher level of mutuality between them.

Because mutuality is a concept made up of six distinct elements (see Appendix C), the degree to which each element contributed to the total amount of mutuality demonstrated was examined for the joint couples group in terms of differences between husbands and wives. (See Figure 13.3.)

This revealed that husbands demonstrated significantly higher levels of empathy (the process by which one person experiences the feelings and thoughts of another and simultaneously knows her/his own different feelings and thoughts); authenticity (the process of

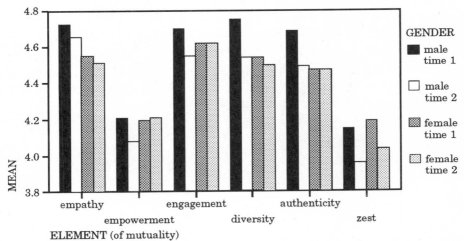

Figure 13.3 Mean scores for each element of mutuality

coming closer to knowing and sharing one's experiences with another) and diversity (the process of openly expressing and receiving or 'working through' different perspectives, opinions and feelings) within their marriages compared with their wives.

Interpreting this result requires some caution. It is set within the context of a high level of mutuality (demonstrated by the high levels of all six elements) expressed by both husbands and wives. However, the fact that there is this difference between husbands and wives in their expression of these three elements suggests that husbands are making a greater contribution towards the total mutuality score than are wives.

The results of the second testing occasion were similar to those of the first. There were no significant differences within either the gender, the group or the couple comparisons. Compared with the first occasion however, the levels of mutuality had decreased slightly in each gender and each group with the exception of the men in the traditional group. Levels were still high, in that the majority of couples scored above the mean for their group. Since all three groups again demonstrated a high level of mutuality, it was not surprising that no significant differences were found between the three groups, when the groups as a whole were compared with one another.

When the six elements contributing to the total amount of mutuality were examined for the joint couples group, only the element of diversity was found to show significant difference between husbands and wives on the second occasion. This revealed that husbands demonstrated a significantly higher level of diversity within their marriages compared with their wives. Thus, apart from this one element, husbands and wives demonstrate a very high degree of similarity in the levels expressed of each element that goes to make up mutuality.

Cohesion

The term cohesion is used throughout the family studies literature as an overall description of the degree to which family members are bonded with one another through experiences of warmth, nurturance, time together, intimacy and consistency. The Family Environment Scale measures a couple's perception of cohesion by the degree to which they rate themselves as being high on cohesion itself and on expressiveness, and as being low on conflict.

In fact all three couples groups demonstrated high levels of cohesion and expressiveness and low levels of conflict, indicating that in terms of their inter-personal relationships within the family, that they were all well functioning units. Nor were there any perceptible differences between the three groups on these dimensions. Not surprisingly, all three groups also scored highly on those items which went to make up a moral and religious emphasis and also represented, through the intellectual/cultural construct of the FES, a high degree of interest in political and social commitments.

All three groups scored low scores for conflict, competition, organization and control. These two last constructs indicate the degree to which family activities and responsibilities are structured and planned and the extent to which the family makes use of set rules and procedures to run their family life. The fact that these clergy couples scored low on these two latter dimensions might indicate some level of disorganization and confusion within the family system, but the fact that they also scored high on cohesion and low on conflict makes it more likely that their low scores on these dimensions indicate flexibility, interdependence and the ability to work creatively with family life situations as they arise, beyond the limitations of a rule-bound system.

The only significant differences between the groups was in relation to the dimensions of independence and their active social and recreational life. Joint couples scored lower on both. The lower scoring on the dimension that gives some indication of involvement with the outside world in ways that are unconnected with work, might relate to the fact that half of these couples have very young children which precludes much involvement with the outside world as far as the adults are concerned. The lower score on independence is interesting in that it might suggest that these couples are less able to function as separate individuals and more prone to the kind of fusion that has been suggested as being a particular predisposition of this kind of couples type.

All three couples groups again demonstrated high levels of cohesion and expressiveness and low levels of conflict on the second testing occasion, indicating that in terms of their interpersonal relationships within the family, they continued to be well functioning units. There was in fact only one change that had occurred during the two years which separated the testing of the three couples groups. On the first occasion, all three groups had rated their family environment as low on organization. On the second occasion, the joint couples continue to rate organization as low, but the two comparison groups now rated it as high.

In summary, no perceptible change seems to have taken place in terms of the cohesiveness of these couples as a result of the ordination of the women in the two groups where the wife was ordained. This suggests that no deleterious effects have occurred for these two groups in relation to their perceptions of their family environments.

They remain just as cohesive as family units and as able to handle conflict appropriately. They also perceive themselves as remaining low in terms of their need to achieve and compete, factors which are likely to reduce the potential tension between their aspirations and the imperatives and norms of their vocation. However, the joint couples remain low in their ability to be independent, which might again raise a question as to the ability of these couples to function sufficiently strongly as individuals within their couple relationship.

14 TOWARDS THE FUTURE

> The wisest know that the best they can do ... is not good enough. The not so wise, in their accustomed manner, choose to believe there is no problem and that they have solved it.
> Janet Malcolm, *The Journalist and the Murderer*

This study set out to investigate the effect of the ordination of women to the priesthood on the marriages of a sample of those married women who were ordained priest in 1994. In particular, it has examined the effect upon that small minority of couples in which, since 1994, both partners have been ordained priests. These joint couples have been the cause of some concern; the belief being that the stresses attendant upon all clergy marriages might well be experienced in double measure by those couples where both husband and wife are clergy. These couples have also been felt to be problematic to the Church for practical reasons because of the difficulty in establishing a coherent employment policy which will serve the needs of the organization without damaging the couple's relationship.

In many ways it is not surprising that the concern felt by the Church for the marriages of its clergy should be felt in double measure in relation to those couples where both partners are ordained. When these marriages do break down, the Church witnesses the distress of two people for whom it held a very direct and immediate responsibility as an employer, over and above its pastoral concern for the marriages of every Christian. Not only is the Church faced with the marriage breakdown of two of its clergy at once, but the parish or other work setting served by the couple is affected in double measure. If both have been working together in the same parish, there will be multiple levels of dislocation, as both clergy are lost simultaneously. If the couple were working in two distinct work settings, both setting has to come to terms with what has occurred and its implications for the Church's ministry in those places. These are indisputable facts. But whether the fact of being a joint clergy couple means that one's marriage is *more* prone to breakdown in the first place is, of course, a different question altogether, and one which this study has sought to investigate.

What then, if anything, changed for those couples, as a result of the women becoming priests? Did the events of 1992 and 1994 which allowed and implemented the ordination of women to the priesthood produce any fundamental changes for women and men in their marriage? The answer from this research in terms of change has to be 'it depends'. Reading the subjective accounts of many of these respondents – both those who were interviewed and those larger numbers who commented upon the changes they themselves perceived, we might well conclude that there had in fact been quite considerable beneficial changes for many of the couples and especially for those in the joint couples group. On the other hand, in relation to the more objective measures of change represented by the quantitative analysis, we would have to conclude that not much seemed to have changed at all.

Those who saw the ordination of women as spelling disaster for Church and for family life alike can in no sense feel that their forebodings have been realized. The very stability of the marriages of the couples who went through this process testifies to the continuity and coherence of the experience for them on a personal level. The fact that ordained women have not in so doing jeopardized their marriages lends support at least to the first hypothesis of this research. The fact that their equal recognition as priests alongside their male colleagues does not appear to have had many quantifiable additional benefits for the dynamics of their marriages and family lives may be cause for some disappointment. However, a two-year time span is a very short one, and probably much too short to be able to capture the more subtle secondary effects of such a momentous change.

Some of the particular stresses that are likely to be faced by these couples have been noted, and the ways in which dioceses have tried to support joint couples in their marriage and ministry, or have failed to do so. The best of dioceses have been genuinely concerned to honour the joint covenants of marriage and ministry which these couples have espoused and to which they are wanting to give expression in one very particular way. The worst of dioceses have seen them as a threat – as 'a lethal cocktail' – as one of the couples in the interview study were described by one Archdeacon. The intention underlying this study has been to clarify a few of the ways in which the marriage relationships of joint couples might be similar to or different from those of traditional couples where the husband is ordained to a non-ordained wife and to those couples where the wife is ordained but not the husband. In so doing, the hope has been that it might have become possible to remove some of the fears and misconceptions that seem to surround joint clergy couples and to lay a better foundation for policy and planning on the part of the Church, as well as for informed and considered choices on the part of the couples themselves.

This study has not needed to demonstrate that joint couples are 'better' than other clergy couples in relation to any point of comparison, nor that they experience a greater degree of marital satisfaction or a lower level of stress. It will have been enough to show that the marriages of joint couples are not *inherently more problematic* than those of other clergy couples, nor more prone to breakdown, so far as it is possible to predict these matters. In trying to make a prediction, five parameters, derived from the psychological literature on the determinants of marital satisfaction, were used – cohesion, similarity, androgyny, egalitarianism and mutuality – and three clergy couple samples were tested to see if they showed marked differences as to the degree to which they exhibited these five relationship factors. Again, it needs to be reiterated that the study did not have to demonstrate that joint clergy couples exhibited *more* of these qualities than other clergy couples – simply that joint couples did not seem to exhibit *less* of them than clergy couples of the other two types. If the study has demonstrated that, then it will have made one modest contribution to our knowledge of clergy marriage and more importantly, it will have debunked some of the myths that have, in a remarkably short time clustered around the idea and reality of joint clergy couples.

Four hypotheses were advanced. In brief these stated that:

(1) Joint couples would not show lower levels of the five ingredients correlated with marital satisfaction and that two years after the ordination of woman to the priesthood, these levels would have increased.

(2) Women only ordained couples would show decreased levels of the five ingredients two years after the woman was ordained to the priesthood.

(3) Traditional couples would show no difference two years after the ordination of women.

(4) Ordained women and men would both show higher levels of those psychological characteristics associated with the other gender and that, as a result, marriages where both partners were ordained would be more androgynous.

The hypotheses were tested both quantitatively and qualitatively. In short, few statistically significant differences were shown to exist between the three clergy couples and no change could be shown to have occurred in the marriages of any of the three groups which might have been attributable to the effect of the independent variable of ordination. Nor were the findings of other researchers into the sex-role reversal of clergy upheld. On the other hand, the trends of almost every result were in the predicted direction.

The results were therefore mixed in relation to the hypotheses that were advanced at the outset of the study. By showing that there were no measurable differences between the marriages of joint couples and other clergy marriage types, the primary hypothesis was supported. No evidence was found that these marriages might be more vulnerable and that must be good news, both for the couples themselves and for the Church. On the other hand, there was no evidence either that the marriages of any of the three groups had improved in any dramatic way over the two years following the ordination of women to the priesthood in terms of the amount of cohesion, mutuality, egalitarianism, similarity or androgyny that they exhibited.

But neither had they deteriorated. In particular, the second hypothesis, that predicted that the marriages of ordained women married to laymen might well deteriorate, was also not supported. There was no evidence to suggest that these marriages had changed for the worse over the two-year interval which separated the two tests and that too must be good news. On the contrary, all three couple groups exhibited high levels of mutuality, cohesion and partner similarity both before and two years after the ordination of women. This must be good news in relation to the quality and stability of clergy marriage in general, despite the fears often expressed and the very real stresses upon it.

In relation to joint clergy couples, the primary focus of this study, there were some pointers from the results of the study which are suggestive of both their strengths and their weaknesses. On several of the quantitative measures, joint couples demonstrated higher scores than those in the comparison groups and few if any results showed joint couples as scoring less well in relation to the degree of cohesion, mutuality, egalitarianism, similarity and androgyny exhibited in their marriages. Because the husbands in the joint couples group scored higher than the norm in terms of androgyny on both occasions (as did the husbands in the traditional couples group), these marriages are well served by one of the partners contributing a high level of this variable to the relationship. In contrast with the comparison groups, joint couples showed a consistent trend towards a greater degree of intra-couple similarity than did couples in the other two groups. Again, this is a good prognosis for their marriages.

On the other hand, the fear that is sometimes expressed about couples of any kind who seem to be highly similar and cohesive is the fear of fusion – the fear that the individuality of each partner may become erased, to the detriment of each and ultimately to the impoverishment of the relationship itself. There were some indications that the joint couples in this study had a tendency in this direction. Their scores for independence fell below the norm on both occasions and the more general descriptive data showed clergywomen in this group less strongly represented than the ordained women in the other group in terms of full-time stipendiary posts, or in holding independent leadership positions in parishes as vicars and rectors. In practice, some of these women may not have had to make very much of a shift from being vicar's wife to vicar's curate, so that the implicit hopes of ordination to the priesthood, in terms of its equalizing effects and the new potential avenues for the expression of their vocation, were in many cases not fully realized. There was no evidence that joint clergy couples were more egalitarian in their domestic life, nor that they had made much headway in job sharing arrangements that would have brought a greater experience of equality into the work place.

On the other hand, joint couples were clear that they valued the differences in their working style, and the small sub-group of couples who held very similar views about the symbolic meaning of their joint commitment nevertheless also regarded their working style as very different from one another. Joint couples, in contrast to the other two groups, looked for space apart from one another when they went away for a period of retreat.

In relation to ordained women married to non-ordained husbands, far from confirming the second hypothesis, that they would fare less well than their sisters who were part of joint clergy couples, there were several indicators that these women were doing very well in terms of the higher degree of egalitarianism that had been achieved in their marriages, the strong level of support they were receiving from their husbands, and the solid commitment that they showed towards the realization of their vocation.

Two major sets of studies, Francis and colleagues (1990, 1991, 1992, 1994) and Lehman (1993), examined gender difference amongst male and female clergy and came to different conclusions. In this study the results were mixed. Whilst Francis found support for sex-role reversal amongst clergy, Lehman, on the contrary found that, apart from co-pastors, male clergy were more masculine than female clergy in relation to their use of power, their empowerment of others, their mode of decision-making and the ethical legalism they employed in their pastoral and other face-to-face work. There was quite strong support in this study for Lehman's finding that being a co-pastor – i.e. working together in parish ministry, which the majority of the joint couples did – resulted in less sex-role typed behaviour. But there was less support for the reversal of gender characteristics in ordained men and women generally found by Francis *et al*.

There were, however, some interesting findings in relation to the sex-role classification of the clergy couples and a comparison between these and the norms for the population at large. In summary, they suggest that men and women in clergy couples, whether ordained or not, are untypical in their sex-role characteristics. In step with Francis's conclusions (but for different reasons), the men in this study are less masculine and more feminine than the norm, whilst the reverse is true of the women. The determining factor is not however ordination, but seems instead to be the fact of *being part of a clergy couple*. Francis *et al.* made their comparisons of ordained men and women with norms for a general population of non-ordained men and women respectively – not with the particular population represented by the non-ordained spouses of the clergy. It may well be therefore that therein lies a crucial difference between the two sets of comparisons, and which leads to substantially different findings.

The second interesting observation that can be made from the results of comparing the sex-role classifications of the subjects in this study with the norm, is the sharp difference that is revealed between the women and men in terms of their levels of androgyny and their undifferentiated state. Women are lower on the former and higher on the latter than men, and this occurs on both occasions, before and two years after ordination, for those who were ordained. Bearing in mind the fact that being androgynous has repeatedly been shown to be highly correlated with mental health and with marital satisfaction, whilst being undifferentiated is characteristic of high levels of mental distress, the continuing imbalance between women and men in terms of this element of sex-role classification is suggestive of some particular vulnerability for women in the Church, whether they are ordained or not.

The vulnerability to stress of the women in these couples does not indicate of itself a vulnerability in the marriage. High levels of both masculinity and femininity and especially of the balanced mix represented by androgyny can be contributed by one partner sufficient to enable the marriage to be highly satisfying and stable. As Peterson *et al.* (1989) have pointed out, two androgynous persons married to each other are the most satisfied but one androgynous partner will contribute significant beneficial effects to the relationship. What these results may however indicate is that, despite the ordination of women to the priesthood, women continue to bear the brunt of the 'shadow' side of the Church's lived experience.

In the responses of subjects to the question asking which experiences had been most disappointing over the last two years, both husbands and wives, where the wife was ordained, still cited the wives' experience of rejection, the difficulty of finding appropriate jobs, the role strain between ministry and domestic life and the unhelpful nature of diocesan policy. All these were offset for most respondents by the joys of having been ordained or of having an ordained wife, but these negative experiences nevertheless impinged more powerfully and immediately on the women than on the men. It may be, too, that the interaction between the couple system and the system of the Church in which it is embedded – characterized as it remains by strongly patriarchal structures and traditions – means that those women who are part of its ministry, by virtue not of ordination but by being part of a clergy couple, thrive less well than do their husbands.

In terms of comparisons between different types of clergy marriage, there may well be some very good reasons why joint clergy couples may fare even better than other clergy marriages. As was noted in Chapter 7, a considerable number of researchers have pointed to the vulnerability of clergy marriages to the disruptive effects of intrusion, incorporation and boundary ambiguity. Resisting the incorporation of one partner into the career or vocational demands of the other, withstanding the intrusion of the effects of that career or vocation and handling the boundary ambiguities that arise from the spillover between work and family, all remain problems for partners of those who are involved in all-enveloping vocations or careers such as politics, business, journalism, scientific research or the Church. The more enveloping the career of one of the marriage partners, the more important it is for the other partner to hold a counterbalancing involvement of their own, which is equally magnetic, absorbing and able to confer identity and self-worth on the individual and bring interest and zest to the relationship.

The paradox may be that for many couples, the *same* career, or a closely parallel work interest, may hold out the best chance of the couple avoiding the damaging effects of intrusion, incorporation and boundary ambiguity, because, although all of these dynamics continue to occur – and may occur even more intensely for couples who share the same career – they tend to be converted into the service of the relationship rather than standing in opposition to it. The competitive tendencies of the couple are more likely to be synergistic and provide energy and impetus to each other's ministry and, if they are working together, competition is more readily transformed into pleasurable co-operative effort. The similarity of work interests and work pressures builds empathy and understanding between the partners and also forces them to confront these pressures more energetically. As one of the couples in the interview study made clear, things became more problematic for them when the wife gave up her ministerial duties for it was then that she found the ministerial demands of her husband's work intolerable. Until then, the demands made by her own ministry had had a counter-balancing and equalizing effect which had brought symmetry and egalitarianism to the relationship.

There were some significant demographic differences between the three samples which are also likely to have affected the outcome of levels of marital satisfaction. The joint couples for example had a much higher proportion of young children and they were therefore coping with the concomitant high levels of stress associated with this factor. Despite this being the case, their showing in relation to the five chosen indices of marital satisfaction was, as already noted, equal to and in some cases higher than those shown by the other two groups.

For some of the women only ordained couples, ordination had come to them as a new opportunity now that their children were independent or now that a natural end had come to the person's first career. It thus represented for one partner a new beginning with new possibilities for realizing hope and meaning for the self that had not been fully realized before. For some couples this may have been experienced as a rebalancing within the partnership, especially where one, usually the woman, had been prevented from exercising many of her gifts in work outside the home because of child care preoccupations. For others, especially represented by some of the clinical families, the new possibilities which were opening up for one partner seriously unbalanced the relationship, either because they were seen as an already favoured partner again being favoured with a new extension of the self, or because ordination came just at the moment when the other partner was experiencing some serious loss of status or self-esteem in the world of work or elsewhere. However although these were concerns for some of the clinical situations described in Chapter 2, they were not born out by the findings of this study for women only ordained couples in the sample as a whole.

Perhaps the major finding of this study is how well the couples in all three groups were doing in terms of their marriages at what was a very unsettled and transitional phase of the Church's history. These results will hopefully set in context some of the anxiety which the Church has shown in relation to clergy couples in general and joint couples in particular. However, this does not mean that we should be sanguine about the obvious difficulties that joint couples may face in doing full justice to their dual commitment to their marriage and their priesthood.

Some of these difficulties arise out of the inter-relationship between the joint couple and their colleague and diocesan network. Any significant pairing relationship within a group can evoke powerful feelings in the group as a whole. Some of the respondents from the joint couples group described painful experiences of hostility from colleagues in their teams and deanery chapters. The envy that may be evoked in others by the unique expression of shared personal and ministerial life, demonstrated so obviously and visibly by a joint clergy couple, may be in sharp and painful contrast to the isolated or conflictual experience of many clergy, married and single alike. Such feelings of envy and longing may also be aroused in members of diocesan hierarchies, who are in no way immune from the experiences of isolation or conflict in their personal relationships that are felt by other clergy. This may lead them, perhaps quite unwittingly and unconsciously, into dealing with joint couples in punitive and destructive ways.

The Church continues to find difficulty in fully addressing the needs of all its clergy for support in both their professional and personal lives. The long awaited report of the Working Party and Consultation set up after a General Synod debate in 1993, in order to address the way in which clergy marriage might be better supported, seemed to be rather tentative (Winchester, 1997). It notes the identity of the Working Party that produced it as being 'informal' only and it offers its conclusions in terms of 'suggestions' rather than 'recommendations'. This is unfortunate, because the Report has much of value to say both in relation to the prophylactic support of clergy marriage and in terms of the professional help and counselling that is needed when clergy marriages experience unmanageable difficulties. It has curiously little to say, however, in relation to clergy marriages where the woman is ordained, nor to the particular group that comprises joint clergy couples.

The fact that the majority of couples in all three groups were doing well in their marriages does not mean that there is room for complacency. As shown in Chapter 10, very high percentages of clergy in all three groups and their non-ordained spouses either did not know what the diocesan policy was with regard to themselves and their families, or believed there to be none, or had experienced it as bad or unsupportive in some way. A very obvious improvement that could be made without undue difficulty would be the systematic effort to develop and to disseminate a clear and coherent policy with regard to the employment of different kinds of clergy – both joint clergy in joint couple marriages and those married to a non-ordained spouse and their families. Such a policy needs to take due account of the differential needs of the careers of non-ordained spouses and of clergy children's schooling. These needs and those of the Church will not always cohere, but an enormous step forward would have been taken in reducing the level of family and marital stress if dioceses could at least be perceived as *trying* to take account of these factors, and entering into a fully informed dialogue with all parties concerned. At both diocesan and parish level, the Church could do more to support the marriages of all its clergy. Dioceses should provide:

- a culture that believes support and assistance in ministry to be a proper expectation
- consistent, ongoing monitoring of the inherent stresses involved, through the provision of well qualified work consultants who can offer regular support, encouragement and advice
- opportunities to participate at all levels in the policy and planning of development and change, especially in areas which affect the deployment of staff
- an open, consistent and well publicized employment policy
- the dissemination of information and knowledge about consultancy, time management, group process learning, stress management training and counselling services through a local directory or information sheet

- the implementation of an equal opportunites policy in recruitment and employment
- the provision of appropriate resources in terms of money and personnel for confidential access to counselling for clergy couples and individuals, through the appointment of advisers in pastoral care and counselling
- a vicarage whose layout enables the clergyperson to maintain a geographical boundary between his/her office and the family home. It should also take all appropriate measures to make the house safe and secure.

The parish should:

- ensure a welcoming and collaborative atmosphere in its relationship with its clergy
- take seriously its promises and obligations undertaken at the induction of a new incumbent to work with and alongside its clergy in undertaking the common task of the Church
- develop knowledge and skill in understanding the way in which parishes and parish groups may both idealize and denigrate its clergy for their own irrational and unconscious reasons
- honour the clergy's efforts to keep boundaries around family time and family space
- be open to getting outside consultancy help to monitor the relationship of clergy and congregation, so that difficulties can be addressed before they become acute.
- provide a separate telephone line (with an answer phone) in the vicarage for parish business.

In relation to joint clergy couples, the findings of this study show how the Church needs to give great freedom and respect to joint couples to enable them to arrive at what may be their own unique solution to the challenges that they face, alongside providing them with a great deal of support and a variety of models, ideas and examples for living out their dual commitment. Joint couples are offering the Church a precious gift, which is more than the sum of the parts of their marriage and their ministry. They need to experience the special, glad welcome of the Church for what they have to offer. Alongside the important recommendations made in the

Winchester Report (1997) for full, professional counselling services and for an integrated system of clergy support, joint clergy couples in particular would be better served by an attitude of respectful curiosity and optimism on the part of Church leaders, than by the anxious and defeatist attitudes that they so often encounter.

The ordination of clergy wives as priests in this first wave of joint clergy couples has not resulted in the disasters which some predicted. In many ways, the ordination of the wife has 'ironed out' the serious impediment of injustice and inequality experienced so critically by some of these couples, as the interview study demonstrated so clearly. Managing the two covenants of marriage and ministry on a day-to-day basis, however, requires new thinking for a new situation. For Church authorities as for the couples themselves, it requires endlessly innovative solutions to the many practical problems of how to manage the interrelationships of two priestly vocations, with a strong personal relationship and the demands of a family. It requires opportunities for the couple to understand and nourish their double experience of unity so that the extra dimension of spiritual unity between them is fully brought to birth, and becomes usable in the service of both their marital relationship and the Church they are called to serve.

Along the continuum of intimacy without fusion and differentiation without isolation, the special vulnerability of the joint clergy couple is that of being drawn towards fusion. This means that their individual personhoods will be in danger of getting lost in the closeness and multiple overlaps of their joint working and marital commitments. There were some indications that women clergy in joint couples played less of a part in the outside world of ministry than their sisters who were married to a non-ordained spouse. Fewer of them received full stipends and fewer of them ran their own parish. There was also a sense that clergywomen who were married to a non-ordained spouse had had to assert themselves more and struggle harder to gain a foothold in ministry, whilst the women in joint couples could, if they wished, shelter within their husband's ministry in a way that was not dissimilar to a non-ordained clergy spouse, if he or she so wished. The difficulty of facing up to and confronting the seduction of dependency (or the equally magnetic pull of counterdependency, its opposite) is one which inevitably lurks within and around a joint clergy couple.

These are ever-present dangers for all couples who work within the same profession. But they have an added force for joint clergy couples, because the agency itself for which they work, the Church, is characterized by a culture of dependency and by a powerful valency which inherently encourages union and fears differentiation. Moreover, the strong doctrinal emphasis on the permanence and stability of marriage and the overriding importance of the family, imposes a hidden agenda upon all clergy marriages to be exemplars for the commodities of marriage and family life which are so important a part of the Church's brief. The need for clergy couples to have interests and commitments outside the Church and, to some degree at least, separate from one another, will be an important part of any prophylactic provision which clergy couples organize for themselves.

An important finding in this study was the disappointing level of equity that existed amongst joint clergy couples in relation to the sharing of household and child care tasks between the couple. There is consistent research evidence to suggest that inequitable sharing of domestic family work between couples, where both have a considerable occupational commitment, is associated with lower levels of marital satisfaction, particularly for the wife. Moreover, many of the more general written comments made by both partners in all three groups of couples, drew attention to protracted unresolved tensions surrounding the sharing of household work.

Such tensions are always likely to be harder for those couples where both partners have a substantial work commitment outside the home, and they are likely therefore also to affect those couples within the traditional group and the women only ordained groups where the wife and husband respectively has his or her own career. But because the great majority of joint couples were both heavily engaged in ministry of some kind, whether stipendiary or not, such inequities are likely to have a consistently deleterious effect upon their experiences of both their marriage and their ministry. A concerted and sustained attempt to develop a more egalitarian sharing of these domestic duties and/or to organize appropriate and effective outside help, would undoubtedly reduce stress in these marriages and probably substantially increase both marital satisfaction and fulfilment in the ministry.

So far as the particular focus of this study is concerned, the needs of joint clergy couples with regard to finding employment that is suitable both to their gifts and talents in ministry and to their needs as a couple and a family, all of this dimension needs to be given a much higher priority by the Church. This is not to deny that joint clergy couples do raise some knotty logistical problems for the Church as an employer. The couple has to be helped to find two jobs, in close enough proximity to each other to allow them to live in one house. If these are both parochial jobs, this will mean that one parish will not have a resident priest. If the jobs are in the same parish, both their clergy will be away for days off and holidays at the same time and both will probably leave their posts together, leaving the parish either bereft or severely reduced in its clergy provision during the interregnum.

When joint couples work together in the same parish or other work setting, many other issues arise in relation to the opportunities for collusion and manipulation. A parish may feel that the strong coalition between the couple makes them too powerful to oppose and at the same time disempowers the parochial officers and structures. Alternatively, the couple may be experienced by the parish as too fragmented, and the parish may create fearsome phantasies of the power which it and/or its individual members have, to inflict damage and destruction on the couple's relationship. In reality, a joint clergy couple makes overt for the parish to understand what is the latent and often unmentionable power block introduced by many a traditional clergy relationship. Where both partners are ordained, the 'clergy wife' no longer holds power without responsibility; instead she is accountable for her actions and influence through the same structures and framework that govern her spouse.

Joint clergy couples need to feel that they and the Church are 'batting on the same side', not in opposition to one another, as so often feels to be the case. To enable joint clergy couples to have the freedom to honour themselves and each other as individuals as well as their marriage as a relationship that is more than the sum of its parts, they need the 'permission' of the Church not to be 'totally available' and not to lose credits when they take proper times off – daily, weekly and annually. They need to feel that the Church can and will put energy into finding jobs for each partner that genuinely develop the gifts of each person within the particular stage of the life-cycle that both the individual and the relationship is at, viewing this as an investment by the Church which is likely to bring significant returns. The findings of researchers reported in Chapter 4, which show that negative work experiences exert a harmful effect on marriages (and vice versa), need to be taken seriously by parishes and dioceses alike.

In their study of joint clergy couples, Rallings and Pratto (1984) found that ministers who were part of a joint clergy couple wanted 'to be seen and treated as unique individuals with unique gifts and personalities. They want to live in situations where these talents can be fully utilized but they also want to live with their spouses. Certainly this poses problems for congregations and Church executives with regard to placement and advancement. All that clergy couples want ... is a sincere up-front effort to deal with the problem situations ... to help them honour their joint covenants of marriage and ministry' (pp. 62–3).

There are various ways in which the Church, as an employer, could better meet these hopes. Rallings and Pratto (1984) make several suggestions, including establishing the principle of equal pay and the clear understanding that whatever remuneration is available is shared jointly by husband and wife. They recommend a norm of regular in-service training opportunities for the couple jointly for those who are working together in the same area of ministry; the easy availability of counselling for the couple's relationship on a growth/enrichment basis not in response to crisis, and perhaps most important of all, an involvement of joint couples in the policy making of the Church at diocesan and national level in relation to recruitment, deployment and issues of ongoing support.

Joint clergy couples still only number around 400 in England, so they are not likely to represent a great 'wave of the future' in the ministry of the Church. Yet their numbers will certainly increase and having in mind some avenues through which they can be helped to realize the full potential of their practical and symbolic gift to the Church, could only be helpful in advance of this time. As McKieran-Allen and Allen (1973) point out, 'In ordained ministry and marriage, two signs of God's grace stand side-by-side in Christian community' (p. 182). The Church has in its midst a resource of great value which deserves care and encouragement to allow the potential of these couples to flourish and to enable them to become both for themselves and for the Church, the double blessing that they are.

APPENDIX A: METHODOLOGY

Design

The research described in this book employed a mixed design, using a range of quantitative and qualitative methods. The intention was to conduct a longitudinal study of joint clergy couples – the experimental group – (in so far as time constraints allowed) in order to measure the effect of the independent variable of ordination on the quality of their marital relationship and to combine the rigour of quantitative methods with the greater depth afforded by a qualitative approach. (See Appendices B and C for quantitative instruments and qualitative methodology.)

This mixed design has allowed for the testing of the research questions, using conventional statistical analysis of the data yielded by the quantitative measures, together with the wider additional perspectives afforded by the qualitative material. The latter has fleshed out the meaning of the statistical analysis and allowed for other dimensions of these clergy couples' experience to be revealed and considered.

Participants

1. Experimental group

The experimental group was comprised, theoretically, of the total population of joint clergy couples, working in the two English provinces of the Anglican Church. The original hope was to have obtained this total population for the research. The most recent available figures for joint clergy couples is 306 couples (28 per cent) out of a total population of 1,076 women who are both married and ordained (NADAWM, 1997). However, in 1993–4, when the subjects were initially contacted, this figure was estimated at around 240 couples. All known couples were contacted, with the help of a mailing list compiled by Double Vision, a national network set up in 1992 to act as a support and meeting point for joint clergy couples. Of the 240 couples contacted, 101 agreed to participate, an estimated 40 per cent of the total population of joint clergy couples. The attrition rate, after the two-year interval, was 24 per cent, leaving 77 couples in the experimental group when they were tested again on the second occasion.

2. Comparison groups

Two other kinds of clergy couples – those where either the man or the woman was ordained – were used as comparison groups with the joint clergy couples. These were recruited as follows:

(1) *Male partner ordained married to non-ordained wife ('traditional')*
This group was obtained by taking every 60th man's name from *Crockford's 1993–4 Directory*. Excluded from this sample were Bishops; men working abroad or in Scotland, Wales or Ireland; men born before 1930; men who had been former clients; and men married to ordained women.

(2) *Female partner ordained married to a non-ordained husband ('women only ordained')*
This group was obtained by taking every 10th name from *Crockford's 1993–4 Directory*. Excluded from this sample were: women working abroad or in Scotland, Ireland or Wales; women born before 1930; women who gave their title as 'Miss'; women who had been former clients; and women married to ordained men.

This yielded sixty-four male clergy married to non-ordained wives and fifty-three women clergy married to non-ordained husbands willing and eligible to participate. The attrition rate, after the two-year time interval, was 20 per cent and 25 per cent for the two groups respectively, leaving fifty-one and forty couples at time two in the two comparison groups.

Procedure

Couples were first contacted in the autumn of 1993. This was about a year after the Church of England had voted in favour of ordaining women to the priesthood but before the first ordinations actually took place. Couples were sent a letter asking them if they would be prepared to participate in a piece of research, the aim of which was to study the effects of the ordination to the priesthood of women on their marriages, with particular reference to joint clergy couples. It was explained that they would be required to complete four questionnaires on two separate occasions.

Questionnaires for the experimental group were mailed in time for them to be returned before the first ordination ceremony took place on 14 March 1994. Re-testing took place approximately two years later, during the course of 1996. On both occasions, the research instruments were sent by post and the couples were asked to complete them independently of their partner. Subjects in the two comparison groups were given the same instructions and were tested in the same way.

APPENDIX B:
THE INTERVIEW STUDY

Participants

Twelve couples from the experimental group of joint clergy couples agreed to be interviewed. It was felt that twelve couples (around 10 per cent of the experimental group) would allow sufficient variety to provide illustrative material of some of the issues involved in being a joint clergy couple. The couples were interviewed during the spring of 1996, almost two years after the first ordinations took place.

From amongst all of those who had originally expressed their willingness to be interviewed, a selection was made (on the basis of cost and convenience) from couples living in or adjacent to the Home Counties. In order to find twelve couples who were able to be interviewed at times and places that were possible both for them and for the interviewers, every couple who lived in Greater London and the Home Counties (twenty-seven couples in all) was invited for interview. This allowed for an adequately varied group of couples to be recruited, in terms of their age, life-cycle stage, seniority in and type of ministry being exercised, views about the priesthood and about the relationship of priesthood and marriage.

Couple no. 1

This couple had been married for nearly seven years. The husband was 35 and the wife 37. They had met at theological college and they had both been ordained deacon together. Prior to ordination, he had worked as a social worker and she as a teacher. He was the middle child of three and the child of a clergy family; she was the younger of two children. Their vocation to ordained ministry therefore preceded their relationship with each other, although their marriage, which took place while they were still at college, occurred just over a year before their ordination to the diaconate. When they were first contacted, the husband was the vicar of an urban parish and the wife worked full-time as the parish deacon in her husband's parish, but at the time of the interview, she had given up work to care for their two children.

Couple no. 2

Couple no. 2 had been married for ten years. The husband was aged 40 and the wife 35. They had met at theological college, the husband being one year ahead. He was therefore ordained deacon one year before she was ordained deaconess. They married a few months after she was made a deaconess and now had two young children. Prior to ordination, he had worked as a surveyor and she had been a student. He was the elder child of two and she the middle of three. Neither were children of clergy families. At the time of the interview, he was the vicar of a suburban parish in a 'new' town and she worked with him as part of the parish team on a part-time, non-stipendiary basis.

Couple no. 3

This couple had been married for nearly nine years. The husband was aged 39 and the wife 46. They had trained at different colleges and both were ordained as deacon and deaconess respectively two and three years before their marriage. Their vocations to the ordained ministry therefore fully preceded their relationship with each other. They had two young children. Prior to ordination, he had worked in the helping professions and she as a teacher and lecturer. He was the fourth of five children and she was the eldest of six. Neither were children of clergy families. At the time of the interview, he was the incumbent of an urban parish and she taught theology.

Couple no. 4

This couple had been married for six years. The husband was 52 and the wife was 47. It was the wife's second marriage, her first having ended in divorce, and she had three adult children from that marriage. There were no children from the current marriage. They had trained at different colleges and at different times, he having been a priest for twenty-five years and, she having been a deaconess and then deacon for fourteen years. They therefore met and married a considerable time after both had begun their ministries. Prior to ordination, he had been a primary school teacher and she had had several different jobs, in nursing, book-keeping and music. Both were eldest children and neither were from clergy families. At the time of the interview, he was the vicar of an inner city parish and she was working as a minister in secular employment, managing a voluntary sector organization.

Couple no. 5

Couple no. 5 had been married for twenty-four years. He was aged 48 and she 52. They had four adult children. He had entered upon his training for ordination in his mid-twenties and had been a priest for twenty-four years. She had been made a deaconess eight and a half years earlier, having previously been employed as a teacher, lecturer and play group organizer. Their entry into the ministry was asymmetrical. He had been ordained seven months before they had married, so that for her, marriage meant a parallel acceptance of being a clergy wife. For him, his wife's vocation came much later and was therefore a factor that was introduced into their marriage relationship long after it had begun. He was the third child of four and she was the elder of two daughters. He was the child of a clergy family; she was not. At the point when they came for interview, he had just been appointed to a senior post in their diocese, having previously been employed as the vicar of a medium-sized parish. She already held a senior diocesan appointment.

Couple no. 6

This couple had been married for 27 years. He was aged 57 and he 61. They had two daughters, one in her late teens and one in her early twenties. He had been ordained for thirty years and they first met when he was a young curate in the parish where her family started to worship. She therefore 'became the curate's wife' and saw herself in the role of clergy wife until her own vocation to the ordained ministry began to emerge and she was made a deaconess in 1980. She had therefore been in the ministry for fourteen years. Prior to ordination, she had been a librarian and also worked for the media. He was the youngest and she the eldest in their families of origin and neither of them were children of clergy families. At the time of the interview, he was the rector of a team ministry and she held a senior diocesan appointment.

Couple no. 7

Couple no. 7 had been married for seven years, this being the husband's second marriage, his first ending with the death of his wife. He was aged 66 and she 52. There were no children of the marriage, nor did he have children from his first marriage. They had trained for ordination separately, and both had been ordained seven years ago, just after they married. The two events were therefore very closely interconnected. For the husband, his priesthood came as a second 'career' after spending his working life as a University lecturer. Prior to ordination, the wife taught religious education in a secondary school. He was an only child; she the middle child of three. She was the child of a clergy family; he was not. At the time of the interview, she had recently become the vicar of her parish, whilst he was part of her staff team, working as a non-stipendiary minister.

Couple no. 8

This couple had been married for fifteen years and had two young children. He was aged 39 and she 40. They had met and married prior to training for the ordained ministry at the same college and had been made deacon and deaconess the same year, eleven years earlier. Their vocations therefore came after their commitment to each other in marriage. Prior to ordination, he had been a research student and she had been a librarian. Both were eldest children and neither were children of clergy families. At the time of the interview, he held a senior appointment in the Church whilst she was a residential canon at a Cathedral.

Couple no. 9

Couple no. 9 had been married for thirty-three years and had three adult children. The husband was aged 60 and the wife 55. He had also been ordained for thirty-three years, his ordination taking place a few months before they married. Thus the wife's entry into marriage was also an acceptance of the role of clergy wife. However, although she did not train for full-time ministry until thirteen years later, she read for a diploma in theology the same year that her husband was ordained. Prior to ordination, he worked in a variety of jobs, including managing a business, and she taught religious education. He was the eldest child and she the second child. Neither of them were children of clergy families. At the time of the interview, he had just retired and she had just become an incumbent of a small parish in a new town.

Couple no. 10

Couple no. 10 had been married for six years and they had two very young children. He was aged 37 and she 36. They had trained at different colleges but had met on their ordination retreat, when he was preparing to be ordained priest and she to be ordained a deacon. They married one year later, so that their marriage came out of a joint knowledge of the vocation of each of the partners. Prior to ordination, he had worked as a research scientist and as a teacher, and she had also been a teacher. Both were eldest children and neither came from clergy families. At the time of the interview, he was team vicar of part of a large new town and she held a temporary part-time parochial post in a parish nearby.

Couple no. 11

This couple had been married for just over a year. They had met at theological college and their marriage preceded their ordinations by seven months. The two experiences were therefore closely interconnected. He was aged 29 and she 28. Prior to ordination he had worked first as a research student and then as an assistant warden of a night-shelter. She had worked as a chaplain's assistant and as an assistant manager in a hostel for young offenders. She was the eldest and he the youngest child in their original families and neither came from a clergy family. At the time of the interview both were employed as stipendiary curates in adjacent parishes, one suburban and one serving a large housing estate. Both were in their first posts, having been ordained together as priests the previous year.

Couple no. 12

Couple no. 12 had been married for nine years and had three young children. He was aged 40 and she 46. She had been made a deaconess fourteen years earlier whilst it was some years later that he embarked upon his own theological training. They were ordained deacon together. At the time of the interview, he was the vicar of a country parish whilst she described herself as a housewife, taking an active part in supporting her husband's work, but mainly behind the scenes. She intended to remain a deacon. He was the youngest and she an only child and neither of them came from a clergy family. Prior to ordination, he had worked as a community worker and she as a teacher.

General observations on the interview sample

The ages of these joint clergy ranged between 28 and 66, the average age being 43. The number of years they had been married ranged between 1 and 33, the mean number of years being 11.5. The number of years that the individuals had been ordained was equally wide, with seven couples being ordained at or within two years of one another, and four at a much greater distance apart.

With nine of the couples, at least one of the partners was ordained within two years of getting married. For three couples, both partners were ordained within one year of their marriage so that for these couples, these two major life decisions were closely interrelated.

Six couples had more than one child aged eleven years or younger for whom they were caring alongside doing their jobs, and so they were engaged in that high stress period of family life that involves, as we noted in Chapter 5, particularly tough dilemmas for the dual-career couple. Of these six couples, one partner (the wife) had given up work temporarily to look after the children; one (the wife) was working part-time and one (the wife) was working as a non-stipendiary minister, thus enabling some greater flexibility in terms of her hours at work and family commitments. Only two couples in this group were managing to work full-time in two very demanding full-time jobs and also care for their children. Like others among the twelve couples, they made use of a considerable amount of outside help in relation to child care and care of the home. Four couples had older children who had now left home and two couples had no children. In one case, this marriage was a second marriage and the other partner was therefore a step-parent to (grown-up) step-children. In terms of their families of origin, only three individuals were children of clergy families. During the course of the interviews however, other 'clergy like' people such as Free Church preachers, missionaries, committed churchgoing relatives or even a parent who had felt called to the ministry but who had not been accepted, all obviously had had an influence on the individual's choice of vocation. Some individuals had clergy further back in their family history and felt that they were affected in some way by shared family mythology around the clergy. Fifteen individuals were either eldest or only children in their original families. In three couples, both partners were eldests or onlys; in five couples, men who were youngest or near youngest children in their families of origin had married women who were eldests or onlys and in four couples the reverse was the case. Thus the partners in nine out of the twelve couples were from complementary sibling positions.

The range and types of ministries being exercised was also very wide. Eleven were in full-time parochial ministry (eight men and three women). One (a woman) was a residentiary canon. One (a woman) was in paid part-time parish work. One (a woman) was a lecturer on an ordination course. Two were non-stipendiary ministers (one man and one woman). One (a woman) was employed full-time as a minister in secular employment. Three (two women and one man) held senior diocesan posts and they, together with the residentiary canon, were members of the Bishop's staff meeting. These four were therefore party to the decision-making centre of the diocesan machinery and privy to very confidential material about other clergy, some of whom might include their partner's colleagues, or even their partner him/herself. Two of the parochial ministers were still in their first training posts. One (a man) held a senior position in the Church's central organization. Two (men) were Rural Deans. Three were not working in any formal way for the Church at present, two of whom described themselves as housewives (one of which had elected not to be ordained as a priest) and one was retired. Of those working full-time in parochial ministry, two of the women and seven of the men were incumbents and the settings for their parochial ministry and that of the two who were in training parishes included a rural parish or group of parishes (two); an urban or inner city parish (three); a suburban parish (five); and large housing estate parish (one).

The interview questions

The following areas were explored with each couple:

> How and when the couple met in relation to their respective vocations?
> The effects of their families of origin on their choice of partner and vocation?
> Their experience of change in their family and marriage over the last two years since the wife's ordination?
> Their experience of how the Church views them as a joint clergy couple?
> Whether they experienced their marriage as more or less stressful since both became priests?
> The effect of doing the same kind of job on their ability to be both close and separate?
> Problems/possibilities that their joint priesthood might pose for them in the future?

Interviewing procedure

Ten of the interviews took place at Birkbeck College. They lasted for approximately one and a half hours, and were preceded by a short period of introduction and explanation of the overall purpose of the research project over a cup of coffee. The interviews were conducted by a male and female co-interviewing team and were video-taped. Two took place in the couple's own homes. These were conducted by the female interviewer alone and were audiotaped.

All the couples recorded their assent to the interview being recorded, over video and audiotape respectively. Couples were assured that the material would be treated with absolute anonymity, fully and appropriately disguised where necessary to prevent recognition, and that subjects would be shown any anonymous quotations from interviews to be used for publication, for their prior approval. In the event, it was decided to send all twelve couples the full transcript of the descriptions of the themes, so that they could see and comment on the way in which the material they had provided had been used. The couples' comments were then incorporated into what became, in some cases, a revised and richer interpretation of the material, with the inclusion of the subject's later reflections on the material of the interview.

Analysis and presentation of the data

The interviews yielded tapes of high technical quality and all ten videos and both audiotapes therefore provided data which the researcher was able to analyse in detail. Analysis of the interviews was undertaken in two ways – first by case and then by theme. Eight major themes were extracted from the material. Wherever possible, direct quotations from the interviews were included, in order to illustrate a particular theme in the couple's own words.

Appendix C:
The Psychometric Tests

The three psychometric tests chosen were the Family Environment Scale (FES); the Bem Sex Role Inventory (BSRI) and the Mutual Psychological Development Questionnaire (MPDQ). Taken together, they combine to give a rich source of data, which builds from the intra-personal through to the inter-personal through to the family system perspective. Considerable possibilities of cross-correlation between them exist.

The FES assesses the social environmental characteristics of all types of families along three dimensions of family life: inter-personal relationships, personal growth and basic organizational structure (Moos and Moos, 1986). Within these three dimensions, it assesses the degree to which a family or couple demonstrates cohesion, expressiveness, the ability to handle conflict, independence, an achievement orientation, an intellectual/cultural orientation, an active/recreational orientation, a moral/religious emphasis, organization and control. The validity and reliability of FES has been well demonstrated in measuring change over time in relation to a wide variety of families and couples.

The BSRI was designed by Bem (1974, 1981, 1993) to provide an instrument for establishing a sex-role classification and for undertaking empirical research into psychological androgyny. The BSRI contains 60 personality characteristics, 20 of which describe stereotypically feminine behaviours, 20 describe stereotypically masculine behaviours, and 20 are filler items. The important feature of the BSRI is that it treats masculinity and femininity as two independent dimensions rather than as two ends of a single continuum of gender. This makes it possible to classify subjects into four discrete classes:

Masculine: scoring high on masculine and low on feminine items
Feminine: scoring high on feminine and low on masculine items
Androgynous: scoring high on both masculine and feminine items
Undifferentiated: scoring low on both masculine and feminine items

As a psychological test of an individual's propensity to adopt sex-role stereotypes in their attitudes and consequent behaviour, the BSRI has been shown to be highly reliable. Lenney (1991) comments: 'the BSRI is the most frequently used measure in sex-role research and is most often used as a standard to which other instruments are compared' (p. 582).

The MPDQ has been developed recently by workers at the Stone Center for Developmental Studies at Wellesley College, Massachusetts. It offers a research tool that emerges from a congruent theoretical base, is applicable to the study of marriage and allows the possibility of combining the systemic, feminist and marital foci of this study. The MPDQ focuses on two key elements of inter-personal relationships – mutuality and interdependence. It is derived from a relational perspective and it emphasizes the relational processes of reciprocity and connectedness. Genero *et al.* (1992) define mutuality as 'the bi-directional movement of feelings, thoughts and activity between persons in relationships' (p. 36). They suggest that 'mutuality involves a shared sense of relationship that transcends the immediate and reciprocal exchange of benefits' (p. 37). They identify six key elements of mutual interactions – empathy, engagement, authenticity, empowerment, zest and diversity. These have been operationalized into the following working definitions:

Empathy – the process by which one person experiences the feelings and thoughts of another and simultaneously knows her/his own different feelings and thoughts.
Engagement – the focusing on one another in a meaningful way.
Authenticity – the process of coming closer to knowing and sharing one's experiences with another. Seeing and recognizing the other for who he/she is and being seen and recognized for who one is.
Empowerment – the capacity for action that emerges from connection within a relationship. To participate in an interaction in such a way that one simultaneously enhances one's own capacity to act as well as the other's.
Zest – feelings of vitality, aliveness, energy, enjoyment and gusto.
Diversity – the process of openly expressing and receiving or 'working through' different perspectives, opinions and feelings.

Leads to an increased sense of connection and enlargement of the relationship rather than the dissolution of that connection.

The authors and others have found that perceptions of mutuality yielded by the questionnaire correlate significantly with measures of social support, relationship satisfaction and cohesion. Likewise, low mutuality scores have been found to be associated with significantly higher ratings of depression and vice versa (Genero *et al.*, 1992). The MPDQ has good test/retest reliability and a high degree of correlation between mutuality and measures which test relationship satisfaction and cohesion.

BIBLIOGRAPHY

ABM (Advisory Board of Ministry) (1995) *Partners in Marriage and Ministry: A Practical Guide for Husbands and Wives Engaged in Professional Ministry Together, and for Their Advisers*, ABM Ministry Paper 11, Church House, Westminster, London.

ACCM (Advisory Council for the Church's Ministry) (1984) *Joint Ministries Consultation*, Occasional Paper No. 16, Church House, Westminster, London.

ACCM (Advisory Council for the Church's Ministry) (1986) *Joint Ministries – A Practical Guide for Husbands and Wives Engaged in Professional Ministry Together and Their Advisers*, ACCM, Church House, Westminster, London.

ACCM (Advisory Council for the Church's Ministry) (1991) *Deacons Now*, ACCM, Church House, Westminster, London.

Altrocchi, J. and Crosby, R. D. (1989) 'Clarifying and measuring the concept of traditional versus egalitarian roles in marriage', *Sex Roles*, 20, 639–48.

Ambert, A. M., Adler, P. A., Adler, P. and Detzner, D. F. (1995) 'Understanding and evaluating qualitative research', *Journal of Marriage and the Family*, 57, 879–93.

Antill, J. K. (1983) 'Sex role complementarity versus similarity in married couples', *Journal of Personality and Social Psychology*, 45, 145–55.

Barling, J. (1990a) *Employment, Stress and Family Functioning*, London: Wiley.

Barling, J. (1990b) 'Employment and marital functioning' in F. D. Fincham and T. N. Bradbury (eds), *The Psychology of Marriage*, New York: Guilford Press.

Baucom, D. H., Notarius, C. L., Burnett, C. K. and Haefner, P. (1990) 'Gender differences and sex-role identity in marriage' in F. D. Fincham and T. N. Bradbury (eds), *The Psychology of Marriage*, New York: Guilford Press.

Belsky, J., Spanier, G. B. and Rovine, M. (1983) 'Stability and change in marriage across the transition to parenthood', *Journal of Marriage and the Family*, 45, 553–56.

Bem, S. (1974) 'The measurement of psychological androgyny', *Journal of Clinical and Consulting Psychology*, 42, 155–62.

Bem, S. (1981) *Bem Sex Role Inventory Professional Manual*, Palo Alto, CA: Consulting Psychologists Press.

Bem, S. (1993) *The Lenses of Gender*, New Haven: Yale University Press.

Berger, P. and Kellner, H. (1964) 'Marriage and the construction of reality', *Diogenes*, 38, 1–24.

Bernard, J. (1972) *The Future of Marriage*, New York: Bantam.

Blanton, P. W. (1992) 'Stress in clergy families: managing work and family demands', *Journal of Family Perspective*, 26, 315–30.

Boss, P. (1977) 'A clarification of the concept of psychological father presence in families experiencing ambiguity of boundary', *Journal of Marriage and the Family*, 39, 141–51.

Boss, P. (1986) 'Psychological absence in the intact family: a systems approach to a study of fathering', *Marriage and Family Review*, 10, 11–39.

Brehm, S. (1985) *Intimate Relationships*, New York: McGraw-Hill.

Brown, S. (ed.) (1983) *Married to the Church*, London: Triangle.

Bryson, R., Bryson, J. and Johnson, M. (1978) 'Family size, satisfaction and productivity in dual career couples', *Psychology of Women Quarterly*, 3, 67–77.

Byng-Hall, J. (1973) 'Family myths used as defence in conjoint family therapy', *British Journal of Medical Psychology*, 46, 239–49.

Byng-Hall, J. (1995) *Rewriting Family Scripts: Improvisation and Systemic Change*, London: Guilford Press.

Carr, W. (1989) *The Pastor as Theologian*, London: SPCK.

Church of England Year Book (1993) London: Church House Publishing.

Church of England Year Book (1995) London: Church House Publishing.

Cluff, R. B., Hicks, M. W. and Madsen, C. H. (1994) 'Beyond the circumplex model: a moratorium on curvilinearity', *Family Process, 33, 455*–70.

Clulow, C. (ed.) (1990) *Marriage: Disillusion and Hope*, London: Karnac Books.

Coate, M. A. (1989) *Clergy Stress: The Hidden Conflicts in Ministry*, London: SPCK.

Craddock, A. E. (1991) 'Relationships between attitudinal similarity, couple structure, and couple satisfaction within marriage and de facto couples', *Australian Journal of Psychology*, 43, 11–16.

Dicks, H. V. (1967) *Marital Tensions*, London: Routledge and Kegan Paul.

A Double Vision (ed.) (1992) *Conference Report for Ordained Couples Held at Swanwick* (17–19 February).

Dowell, S. and Williams, J. (1994) *Bread, Wine and Women*, London: Virago Press.

Ekhardt, B. N. and Goldsmith, W. M. (1984) 'Personality factors of men and women pastoral candidates', *Journal of Psychology and Theology*, 12, 109–18.

Epstein, C. F. (1973) *Woman's Place*, Berkeley: University of California Press.

Erikson, E. H. (1968) *Identity, Youth and Crisis*, London: Faber.

Ferreira, A. (1963) 'Family myths and homeostasis', *Archives of General Psychiatry*, 9 November.

Finch, J. (1983) *Married to the Job: Wives' Incorporation into Men's Work*, London: George Allen and Unwin.

Fletcher, B. (1990) *Clergy under Stress: A Study of Homosexual and Heterosexual Clergy in the Church of England*, London: Mowbray.

Frame, M. W. and Shehan, C. L. (1994) 'Work and well-being in the two-person career: relocation stress and coping among clergy husbands and wives', *Journal of Family Relations*, 43, 196–205.

Francis, L. J. (1991) 'The personality characteristics of Anglican ordinands: feminine men and masculine women?', *Personality and Individual Differences*, 12, 1133–40.

Francis, L. J. (1992) 'Male and female clergy in England: their personality differences, gender reversal?', *Journal of Empirical Theology*, 5, 31–8.

Francis, L. J. and Pearson, P. R. (1990) 'Personality characteristics of mid-career Anglican clergy', *Social Behaviour and Personality*, 18, 347–50.

Francis, L. J., and Rodger, R. (1994) 'The personality profile of Anglican clergymen', *Contact*, 113, 27–32.

Friedman, E. H. (1985) *Generation to Generation*, New York: Guilford Press.

Gasson, R. (1981) 'Roles of women on farms – a pilot study', *Journal of Agricultural Economics*, 32, 11–20.

Genero, N. P., Miller, J. B., Surrey, J. and Baldwin, L. M. (1992) 'Measuring perceived mutality in close relationships: validation of the mutual psychological development questionnaire', *Journal of Family Psychology*, 6, 36–48.

Gilbert, L. A. (1993) *Two Careers/One Family: The Promise of Gender Equality*, London: Sage.

Gilbert, L. A. (1994) 'Current perspectives on dual-career families', *Current Directions in Psychological Service*, 3, 101–5.

Gilligan, C. (1982) *In a Different Voice: Psychological Theory and Women's Development*, Cambridge, MA: Harvard University Press.

Glenn, N. D. (1990) 'Quantitative research on marital quality in the 1980's: a critical review', *Journal of Marriage and the Family*, 52, 818–31.

Goodling, R. A. and Smith, C. (1983) 'Clergy divorce: a survey of issues and emerging ecclesiastical structures', *Journal of Pastoral Care*, XXXVII, 277–91.

Gottman, J. M. and Levenson, R. W. (1988) 'The social psychophysiology of marriage' in P. Noller and M. A. Fitzpatrick (eds), *Perspectives on Marital Interaction*, Philadelphia: Multilingual Matters.

Graham, E. (1995) *Making the Difference: Gender, Personhood and Theology*, London: Mowbray.

Greenacre, R. (1993) 'Epistola ad Romanos', *The Tablet*, 20 March.

Griffith, J. L. (1986) 'Employing the God–family relationship in therapy with religious families', *Family Process*, 25, 609–18.

Haraway, D. (1988) 'Situated knowledges: the science question in feminism and the privilege of partial perspective', *Feminist Studies*, 14, 575–99.

Heaton, T. B. and Pratt, E. L. (1990) 'The effects of religious homogamy on marital satisfaction and stability', *Journal of Family Issues*, 11, 191–207.

Hebblethwaite, M. (1984) *Motherhood and God*, London: Geoffrey Chapman.

Hochschild, A. (1989) *The Second Shift*, New York: Aronson.

Horsman, S. (1989) *Living with Stress*, Sheldon, Exeter: Society of Martha and Mary.

Houseknecht, S. K. and Macke, A. S. (1981) 'Combining marriage and career: the marital adjustment of professional women', *Journal of Marriage and the Family*, 23, 35–44.

Howatch, S. (1987) *Glittering Images*, London: HarperCollins.

Howatch, S. (1988) *Glamorous Powers*, London: HarperCollins.

Howatch, S. (1989) *Ultimate Prizes*, London: HarperCollins.

Howatch, S. (1990) *Scandalous Risks*, London: HarperCollins.

Howatch, S. (1992) *Mystical Paths*, London: HarperCollins.

Howatch, S. (1995) *Absolute Truths*, London: HarperCollins.

Hulson, B. and Russell, R. (1991) 'Psychological foundations of couple relationships' in D. Hooper and W. Dryden, *Couple Therapy*, Milton Keynes: Open University Press.

Jung, C. G. (1925) 'Marriage as a psychological container' in *Collected Works*, vol. 17, 187–201.

Kieren, D. K. and Munro, B. (1988) 'Handling greedy clergy roles: a dual clergy example', *Pastoral Psychology*, 36, 239–48.

Kilpatrick, L. (1994) 'Menstruation as ideology: social and symbolic meanings of women's blood in contemporary Britain'. Unpublished thesis, University of Sussex.

Kirk, M. and Leary, T. (1994) *Holy Matrimony? An Exploration of Marriage and Ministry*, Oxford: Lynx Communications.

Lasch, C. (1979) *The Culture of Narcissism: American Life in an Age of Diminishing Expectations*, New York: Norton.

Lee, C. (1988) 'Toward a social ecology of the minister's family', *Pastoral Psychology*, 36, 249–59.

Lee, C. (1995) 'Rethinking boundary ambiguity from an ecological perspective: stress in protestant clergy families', *Family Process*, 34, 75–86.

Lehman, E. (1993) *Gender and Work: The Case of the Clergy*, Albany, NY: State University of New York.

Lenney, E. (1991) 'Sex roles: the measurement of masculinity, feminity and androgyny' in J. P. Robinson, P. R. Shaver and L. S. Wrightman (eds), *Measures of Personality and Social Psychological Attitudes*, vol. 1, 574–660, London: Academic Press.

Mace, D. and Mace, V. (1980) *What's Happening to Clergy Marriages?*, Nashville: Abingdon.

Mace, D. and Mace, V. (1984) 'Foreword' in E. M. Rallings and D. J. Pratto (eds), *Two-Clergy Marriage: A Special Case of Dual Careers*, Washington, DC: University Press of America.

Mackey, R. A. and O'Brian, B. A. (1995) *Lasting Marriages*, Westport, CT: Praeger Publishers.

McKieran-Allen, L. A. and Allen, R. J. (1973) 'Colleagues in marriage and ministry' in J. L. Weidman (ed.), *Women Ministers*, San Francisco: Harper & Row.

Malony, H. N. and Hunt, R. A. (1991) *The Psychology of the Clergy*, Harrisburg, PA: Morehouse Publishing.

Marsh, H. W. and Byrne, B. M. (1991) 'Differentiated additive androgyny model: relations between masculinity, femininity and multiple dimensions of self-concept', *Journal of Personality and Social Psychology*, 61, 811–28.

Martin, T. W., Berry, K. J. and Jacobsen, R. B. (1975) 'The impact of dual career marriages on female professional careers', *Journal of Marriage and the Family*, 37, 734–42.

Menges, R. J. and Dittes, J. E (1965) *Psychological Studies of Clergymen: Abstracts of Research*, New York: Nelson & Sons.

Mickey, P. A., Wilson, R. L. and Ashmore, G. W. (1991) 'Denominational variations on the role of the clergy family', *Pastoral Psychology*, 39, 287–94.

Millar, F. E. and Rogers, E. (1988) 'Power dynamics in marital relationships' in P. Noller and M. A. Fitzpatrick (eds), *Perspectives on Marital Interaction*, Philadelphia: Multilingual Matters.

Moos, R. H. and Moos, B. S. (1986) *Family Environment Scale* (2nd edn), Palo Alto, CA: Consulting Psychologists Press, Inc.

Morris, M. L. and Blanton, P. W. (1994) 'The influence of work-related stresses on clergy husbands and their wives', *Journal of Family Relations*, 43, 189–95.

NADAWM (National Association of Diocesan Advisers in Women's Ministry) (1996) *The First Two Years* (published by NADAWM).

Nicola, J. S. and Hawkes, G. R. (1985) 'Marital satisfaction of dual-career couples: does sharing increase happiness?', *Journal of Social Behaviour and Personality*, 1, 47–60.

Olson, D. (1976) *Treating Relationships*, Lake Mills, IA: Graphic Publishing Company.

Olson, D. H. (1993) 'Circumplex model of marital and family systems, assessing family functioning' in F. Walsh (ed.), *Normal Family Process* (2nd edn), New York: Guilford Press.

Oswald, R. M. (1985) *Couples in Professional Ministry*, Washington, DC: The Alban Institute.

Pahl, J. (1989) *Money and Marriage*, London: Macmillan.

Papanek, H. (1973) 'Men, women and work: reflections on the two-person career', *American Journal of Sociology*, 78, 853–72.

Peterson, C., Baucom, D., Elliot, M. and Aitken, P. (1989) 'The relationship between sex role identity and marital adjustment', *Sex Roles*, 21, 775–87.

Pollock, A. D., Die, A. H. and Marrot, R. G. (1990) 'Relationship of communication style to egalitarian marital role expectations', *Journal of Social Psychology*, 130, 619–24.

Rabin, C. (1996) *Equal Partners – Good Friends*, London: Routledge.

Rallings, E. M. and Pratto, D. J. (1984) *Two-Clergy Marriage: A Special Case of Dual Careers*, Lanham, MD: University Press of America.

Rapoport, R. and Rapoport, R. N. (1971) *Dual Career Families*, Harmondsworth: Penguin.

Rapoport, R. and Rapoport, R. (eds) (1991) *Working Couples*, London: Routledge.

Ray, J. (1988) 'Marital satisfaction in dual career couples', *Journal of Independent Social Work*, 3.

Ray, J. (1990) 'Interactional patterns and marital satisfaction among dual-career couples', *Journal of Independent Social Work*, 4, 61–73.

Rayburn, C. A. (1991) 'Clergy couples and stress: clergy married to clergy', *Psychotherapy in Private Practice*, 8, 127–30.

Rice, D. (1979) *Dual-Career Marriage – Conflict and Treatment*, New York: Free Press.

Richmond, L. J. (1985) 'Clergymen, clergywomen and their spouses: stress in professional religious families', *Career Development*, 12, pp. 81–6.

Rizzuto, A.-M. (1979) *The Birth of the Living God*, Chicago: Chicago University Press.

Rogers, A. L. (1991) 'Stress in married clergy', *Journal of Psychotherapy in Private Practice*, 8, 107–15.

Sandholm, G. L. (1989) 'The changing face of marriage and extramarital relationships', *Journal of Pastoral Care*, XLIII, 249–58.

Sanford, J. A. (1982) *Ministry Burnout*, London: Arthur James Ltd.

Sayers, S. and Baucom, D. H. (1989) 'Sex role identity and communication among maritally distressed couples'. Unpublished manuscript.

Scanzoni, J., Polonko, K., Teachman, J. and Thompson, L. (1989) *The Sexual Bond: Rethinking Families and Close Relationships*, California: Sage.

Silberstein, L. R. (1992) *Dual Career Marriage: A System in Transition*, Mahwah, NJ: Lawrence Erlbaum Associates.

Silberstein, L. R. (1993) 'Dual career marriages', *Sex Roles*, 28, 631–53.

Skynner, A. C. R. (1976) *One Flesh: Separate Persons: Principles of Family and Marital Psychotherapy*, London: Constable.

Solomon, M. F. (1989) *Narcissism and Intimacy*, London: Norton.

Spanier, G. (1976) 'Measuring dyadic adjustment: new scales for assessing the quality of marriage and similar dyads', *Journal of Marriage and the Family*, 38, 15–28.

Spitze, G. L. and Pleck, J. H. (1984) 'Nonstandard work schedules and family life', *Journal of Occupational Behaviour*, 7, 147–54.

Spitze, G. and Waite, L. J. (1981) 'Wives' employment: the role of husband's perceived attitudes', *Journal of Marriage and the Family*, 43, 117–24.

Surrey, J. L. (1984) *Self-in Relation: A Theory of Women's Development*, Work in Progress, no. 13, The Stone Center for Developmental Studies, Wellesley, MA: Wellesley College.

Tesch, J., Osbourne, J., Simpson, D., Murray, S. and Spiro, J. (1992) 'Women physicians in dual-physician relationships compared with those in other dual-career relationships', *Academic Medicine*, 67, 542–44.

Thatcher, A. (1993) *Liberating Sex: A Christian Sexual Theology*, London: SPCK.

Thomas, D. L. and Cornwall, M. (1990) 'Religion and family in the 1980's: discovery and development', *Journal of Marriage and the Family*, 52, 983–92.

Toman, W. (1976) *Family Constellations* (3rd edn), New York: Springer.

Towler, R. and Coxon, A. P. M. (1979) *The Fate of the Anglican Clergy*, London: Macmillan.

Walrond-Skinner, S. (1976) *Family Therapy – The Treatment of Natural Systems*, London: Routledge and Kegan Paul.

Walrond-Skinner, S. (1987) 'Feminist therapy and family therapy: the limits to the association' in S. Walrond-Skinner and D. Watson (eds), *Ethical Issues in Family Therapy*, London: Routledge and Kegan Paul.

Walrond-Skinner, S. (1988) *Family Matters: The Pastoral Care of Personal Relationships*, London: SPCK.

Walrond-Skinner, S. (1989) 'Spiritual dimensions and religious beliefs in family therapy', *Journal of Family Therapy*, 11, 47–67.

Walrond-Skinner, S. (1994) 'So far in this world' in S. Walrond-Skinner (ed.), *Crossing the Boundary: What Will Women Priests Mean?*, London: Mowbray.

Weisfeld, G. B., Russell, R. J. H., Weisfeld, C. C. and Wells, P. A. (1992) 'Correlates of satisfaction in British marriages', *Ethology and Sociobiology*, 13, 125–45.

Whybrew, L. E. (1984) *Minister, Wife and Church: Unlocking the Triangle*, New York: The Alban Institute.

Winchester (1997) *Support for Clergy Marriage: A Consultation Paper*, Rotherham: Diocesan Church House.

INDEX

ABM 109

abuse 11–12, 14, 30–1, 156, 183, 184

ACCM 105–6

Act of Synod 136–7

ambivalence 12, 15, 19, 28–31, 33, 47, 58

androgyny 33, 62, 66–9, 80, 86, 98, 202, 206–9, 219–21, 223, 245

anger 2, 14, 18, 23, 28–9, 35, 76, 79, 90, 96, 100, 145, 148, 166, 193

anxiety 6, 21, 33, 35, 46, 48, 59, 93, 140, 178, 226

asymmetry 57, 156, 238

Bem, S. 66–7, 204–7
  Sex Role Inventory (BSRI) 204, 245, 246

boundaries 25, 69, 75, 93, 95, 97–8, 104, 107, 110, 142, 171, 172, 173, 174, 177, 193, 197, 228
  ambiguity 98–9, 171, 173, 224

breakdown (of marriage) 45, 62, 97, 99, 103, 217–19

careers ix, 1, 10, 20–1, 40, 42, 45–7, 73, 75, 83, 99–102, 112, 130–3, 136, 144, 169, 227, 230, 239
  see also dual-career couples; two-person careers

child care 45–6, 50–2, 56, 58, 128, 133–4, 165, 167, 200–1, 225, 230, 242

childhood 11, 15, 22, 24, 31, 78, 126, 156, 183–4

Church ix, x, 1–3, 8–12, 14–19, 23–6, 28–31, 33, 35–7, 42, 46, 49, 55, 63, 76–81, 83, 86–7, 89–90, 92–3, 105–12, 115, 116–18, 120, 123, 129, 135, 138, 148, 152, 155, 157, 168, 170–1, 179–84, 187, 189, 191–3, 195–8, 201, 208, 217–20, 223–4, 226–32, 233, 235, 240, 243

clergy wife 21, 99–101, 103, 143–5, 149, 183, 186–8, 193, 238–40
  see also vicar's wife

Coate, M. A. 77–8, 79–80, 93–4, 96

cohesion 33, 62–3, 66, 69, 86, 89, 98, 159, 200, 202, 214–15, 219–21, 245, 247

colleague(s) 12, 17, 29, 32, 50, 53, 95, 104, 176, 190, 218, 226, 243

competition, competitiveness 30, 46, 53, 57–9, 84, 88, 95, 101, 104, 106, 112–13, 115, 129–33, 160, 195, 215, 225

complementarity 42, 62, 109, 167

congregation 13–14, 32, 83, 85, 93, 100, 102–4, 111–12, 114, 135–6, 148, 155, 166, 168, 174–5, 178, 181, 183, 188, 190–1, 221, 232

connection in relationships 40, 43–4, 66, 246–7

co-pastor(s) 84, 111–12, 122, 139, 150, 139, 222

coping 66, 89, 112, 117, 127, 225

deacons, diaconate 1, 4, 11, 15, 16, 19, 24, 27–30, 34, 36, 75, 106, 108, 156, 162–4, 168, 179, 188, 194, 198–9, 201, 236–41, 243

dependency 13, 15, 17–18, 45, 91, 100, 176, 182, 229–30

depression 22, 59, 76–7, 79, 88, 100, 147

dioceses 15, 36, 104, 104, 106, 108, 110, 122, 135–6, 138, 162, 172, 172, 189, 191–5, 197, 218–19, 227, 231, 238

discrimination at work 50

disengagement 69, 97, 99, 101, 171, 200

Double Vision 108–9, 234

dual–career couples ix, 49–59, 64, 87, 90, 108, 115, 117, 122–3, 128, 131, 172, 189, 195, 199–200, 224–5, 242
see also joint clergy couples

egalitarianism 33, 55, 59, 64–5, 68, 71, 83, 88, 111, 113, 118, 129, 132–3, 155, 156, 166–8, 200–1, 219–22, 225
emotional distance regulation 25, 171
empathy 25, 33, 39, 41, 44–5, 54, 66, 140, 213, 225, 225, 246
employment 19, 22, 46, 50–2, 56, 105, 108, 110, 120–2, 125, 135–6, 139, 188–9, 191, 193, 195–8, 217, 227–8, 230, 238, 243
enmeshment 40, 69, 97, 99–101, 160, 171, 174, 176, 200
equal opportunities 51, 193, 228
equality 2, 4, 25, 53–5, 59, 64–5, 109, 145, 156, 165, 167–8, 174, 181, 222
see also inequality
equity 50, 53–4, 62–5, 68–9, 133, 202, 230
exemplar, clergy as 78, 86, 103, 107
extroversion 82

faith
see also religious belief
community of 157
crises of 79–80, 178–9
Family Environment Scale (FES) 209, 245
femininity 13, 67–8, 81, 90, 180, 203–5, 207–9, 223, 245
see also gender
feminism 44, 62, 66–7, 83
Francis, L. J. 72, 81–2, 84, 117, 150, 203–4, 222–3
Friedman, E. H. 97, 102
friendship 65, 77, 104, 163
fusion 44, 115, 177, 215

gender x, 14, 18, 21, 28, 35, 37–8, 40, 44, 54–7, 65, 67–8, 71, 74, 79–85, 87, 89–91, 96, 106, 113–14, 126–7, 131, 139, 150, 168, 179, 197, 200, 203, 205, 207, 209, 212–14, 220, 222, 245
see also androgyny; femininity; masculinity
Genero, N. P. *et al.* 66, 246–7
Gilbert, L. A. 49, 54–6, 117
Gilligan, C. 44
God 27, 36, 77, 80, 83, 87, 89, 101, 104, 153–5, 157, 168, 176, 181, 232
guilt 10, 12–13, 15–16, 33, 48, 58, 80, 90, 99, 113, 140, 156

homogamy 62
hostility 32–3, 93, 100, 114, 164, 174, 193, 226
housework 19, 50, 52, 55, 58, 133, 160, 167, 172–3, 200, 230

identity 11, 14, 16–17, 22, 24–5, 31–3, 37, 41, 44, 47, 49, 53, 67–8, 72, 89, 94, 98–101, 117, 122–3, 129, 142–5, 149–50, 158, 169, 179–80, 188, 190
incorporation 99–101, 224
inequality 54, 168, 177, 229
intimacy 17, 39, 54, 66, 95, 97, 101, 112, 114, 153, 229
introversion 72, 79, 82
intrusiveness 98, 137, 174, 176

jobs
changing 57, 189
satisfaction 50, 53, 57, 77, 129, 138
see also careers
joint clergy couples x, 5, 9, 16–17, 25, 39, 42, 49–50, 52–58, 60, 86–8, 90, 97, 105, 108, 110–12, 115, 116, 118–27, 130, 131, 133, 135, 138, 141–3, 149–50, 152, 155, 157–9, 161, 174, 181, 189, 191–2, 195, 199, 203, 207, 209,

219, 221–2, 224, 227–32, 233–5, 236, 243

Kirk, M. 42, 77, 94, 158

Leary, T. 42, 77, 94, 158
Lehman, E. 82–4, 111–12, 122, 139, 150, 222

Mace, D. and V. 96, 105–6
marital dissatisfaction 51
marital satisfaction 33, 42, 45, 47, 50, 52–55, 58, 61–5, 67–9, 73, 80, 86, 97–8, 110–11, 118–19, 127, 129, 131, 151, 202, 206, 208, 212, 219–20, 223, 225, 227, 230
masculinity 55, 67–8, 81, 203–5, 207–10, 223, 245
  see also gender
model, of marriage 6, 103, 114, 151–2
mothers 13, 15, 22, 29, 31, 56, 91, 93, 112, 124–5, 166, 179–80, 188
Mutual Psychological Development Questionnaire (MPDQ) 245–7
mutuality 43, 55–6, 62, 66, 69, 86, 98, 109, 200, 202, 212–14, 219–21

NADAWM 80, 121, 233

ordination ix–xi, 1–4, 6, 8–9, 11–30, 32–6, 38, 42, 49, 61, 73, 75–6, 79, 85–7, 91, 106, 109, 111, 118–19, 121–5, 129, 132, 134, 142, 145, 148, 151, 156, 159, 161–2, 164–71, 174, 182–8, 191, 193–5, 201–2, 204–8, 210, 212, 214, 220, 223–4, 226–32, 233, 236–41, 243

parenting 14, 44, 65, 74, 91, 173, 181, 188
parishes 15, 18, 25, 37, 74, 86, 93, 95, 98, 100, 104, 108, 113, 114, 122, 124, 132, 135–40, 142, 144,

146–9, 157, 162–3, 165–8, 170, 172–7, 179, 187–90, 194, 196–7, 199, 217–18, 221–2, 227–9, 231, 236–41, 243
power 2–3, 14–15, 17–18, 20, 22–4, 29, 31, 33, 35, 37–8, 44, 47, 53, 55–6, 73, 78, 79, 83–4, 89, 92–6, 99, 101, 107, 112, 114, 169, 177, 180–3, 190, 208, 222, 224, 226, 230–1

qualitative research x, 9, 42, 94, 118, 129, 218, 221, 233
quantitative research x, 62, 118, 129, 195, 233

Rabin, C. 64–5, 68
Rapoport, R. and R.N. 53, 117
regression 12
religion 87, 109
religious belief 63, 87–8, 104
roles 14, 17–21, 24, 28–30, 32, 40, 43, 45, 47, 51–7, 59, 63, 67, 71–4, 77, 88–92, 94–5, 99–104, 105, 109, 111, 113, 115, 123–4, 126, 143–8, 155, 159, 163, 165, 167–70, 175, 178, 180, 186, 188, 197–8, 200, 224
  blurring 54
  see also sex roles

self-esteem 41, 46, 50, 53, 55, 59, 78, 169, 225
sex roles 63, 67–8, 81, 84, 79, 84, 112–13, 117, 119, 204–8, 220, 222–3, 245, 246
sex-typing 67–8, 203, 207, 209
sexism 40, 65
sexual abuse 11–12, 156
sexuality 28, 35, 79, 87, 89–92, 109, 181, 192
Silberstein, L. R. 56–9, 117
similarity 33, 42, 62–3, 69, 86, 98, 119, 202–5, 208–12, 214, 219–21, 225
spillover 58, 92, 135, 224

stereotypes 55, 56, 82, 90, 112, 131, 155, 245–6
Stone school 44, 66
stress 3, 71–4, 76–7, 79–80, 86–7, 89, 92–3, 96, 98–9, 105, 110, 117, 123, 127–8, 134–5, 137–9, 143, 145–7, 153, 158, 172, 189, 196, 217–19, 221, 223, 225, 227, 230, 242
support 3, 16, 20, 24, 32–3, 36, 47, 50–1, 53, 56–8, 66, 69, 76–7, 93, 110–11, 113–14, 116, 125, 127, 131, 133, 135–7, 139, 144, 150, 155, 167, 175, 178, 180, 182, 187, 194–5, 218, 220, 222, 226–8, 234, 247
symbolism 4, 14, 17, 22, 23, 37, 91–2, 94–7, 99, 152–4, 156–9, 180–2, 201, 222, 232
Synod, General ix, 1, 27, 35, 226
see also Act of Synod

therapy 11–12, 14–15, 17, 20, 24–5, 27, 32, 67, 195, 198
traditional couples 6, 25, 52, 116, 120, 123, 125, 127, 130, 133, 135–7, 140, 142–3, 151, 203–10, 212, 219–21
transitional object 47, 89
triangulation 88, 97, 102–4, 114, 171
two-person careers 87, 99

unclean 13, 14, 16
undifferentiated 67–8, 199, 206–7, 223, 245

vicar's wife 20, 168, 178, 187, 222
see also clergy wife
vocation 10, 12, 16, 19, 21, 23–5, 30, 37, 41–2, 45–6, 49–50, 73–4, 76, 104, 116, 121–2, 132, 145, 152, 156–60, 161–2, 169, 179, 187, 194, 198–9, 216, 222, 224, 229, 236–41

Walrond–Skinner, S. 88
Winchester Report 92, 226, 228
women only ordained couples 6, 120–3, 125–8, 130, 132–8, 140, 142–4, 151, 203–5, 209–10, 212, 234